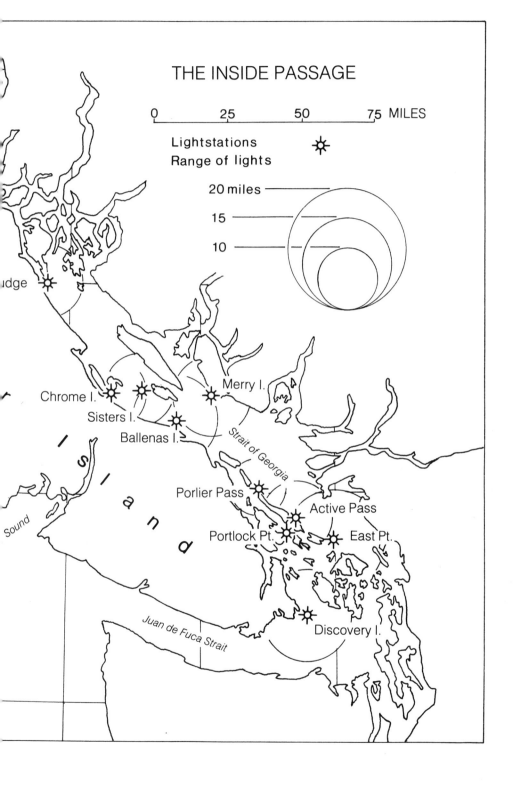

THE INSIDE PASSAGE

0   25   50   75 MILES

Lightstations
Range of lights

20 miles
15
10

ıdge

Chrome I.
Sisters I.
Ballenas I.

Merry I.

Strait of Georgia

I s l a n d

Sound

Porlier Pass

Active Pass

Portlock Pt.

East Pt.

Juan de Fuca Strait

Discovery I.

LIGHTS *of the* INSIDE PASSAGE

LIGHTS *of the* INSIDE PASSAGE

*A History of British Columbia's Lighthouses
and their Keepers*

Donald Graham

HARBOUR PUBLISHING CO. LTD.
1986

For all keepers of the light

Published by
Harbour Publishing Co. Ltd.
P.O. Box 219, Madeira Park, BC
Canada V0N 2H0

Cover design: Gaye Hammond
Cover paintings: Buzz Walker
Drawings: Donna Williams
Design: Gaye Hammond
Maps: Daniel Cartography
Editorial Assistance: Audrey McClellan

This publication was assisted by the Canada Council and the B.C. Heritage Trust.

CANADIAN CATALOGUING IN PUBLICATION DATA

Graham, Donald, 1947 –
   Lights of the inside passage

   Includes index.
   ISBN 0-920080-85-5

   1. Lighthouses—British Columbia—History. 2. Lighthouse
keepers—British columbia. 3. Pacific Coast (B.C.)—History.
I. Title.
VK1027.B7G73 1986   623.89'42'09711   C86-091501-8

Printed in Canada

Contents

Foreword

Lighthouse: the very word conjures up an image of solitary, sweeping power setting the mariner's infinite domain apart from the landlocked. Canada really begins at Langara Island and ends at Cape Spear, and whatever goes on across that mind-boggling expanse in between, no one shares as much in common as the keepers of those two lights. For all the political energy expended in the century between the National Policy and the Just Society, for all that sweat and hammering at the dented anvil of "national unity," they personify the elusive dream of forging a nation from one sea to the other. They could have traded places eighty years ago or last week with less dislocation than two-thirds of Canada's rootless people who pack up and move every ten years.

They also share a perception of their life and work far removed from the imaginations of some twenty million who talk on telephones, open their mail every day, have no inkling of how sweet a fresh pepper tastes after a month, who seldom thought of seals, whales, and wolves before Greenpeace, who waste more water than they drink. On the lights, nothing goes to waste. Even bent nails can be straightened and meals planned a month ahead to that day of delight when a helicopter comes hammering down through the drizzle with fresh food and a fat sack of mail. Reveling in their quarantine from smog-locked cities where the future seems always a car-payment away, lightkeepers still wonder, sometimes, what they might be missing.

The seventy-odd families who keep lights on the West Coast are heirs to one of the most effective and extensive networks of manned lighthouses left in the world: forty-three beacons which evolved piecemeal in the wake of shipwreck, brainchildren of an unsung architectural genius.

Canada took over three colonial lighthouses—Fisgard, Race Rocks, and Sandheads—when British Columbia joined Confederation in 1871. From this nucleus the Department of Marine and Fisheries (later the Department of Transport) established beacons in the approaches to the leading harbours, Victoria, Vancouver, and Nanaimo. Then, in belated, grudging response to an appalling sequence of wrecks along the dreaded West Coast of Vancouver Island (culminating in January 1906 with the wreck of the S.S. *Valencia*, which took three days to go down off Pachena Point with 117 passengers and crew), it made the "graveyard of the Pacific" proof against further catastrophe with nine manned lights and foghorns forming a corridor of light and sound from Sheringham Point in Juan de Fuca Strait to Triangle Island off Cape Scott.

The overseer of this revolutionary transformation, chief engineer of Marine and Fisheries and chairman of the Canadian Lighthouse Board, Colonel William Patrick Anderson was driven by his yearning to go down in history as one (if not the last) of the world's great lighthouse builders, at any cost. The people who took over and tended his far-flung concrete achievements paid hard.

For forty years Anderson's orders were executed, with varying degrees of enthusiasm, by a succession of marine agents out of Victoria: Captain James Gaudin, Captain George Robertson, Colonel A.W.R. Wilby, and Tom Morrison. Whatever their mindset or compassion, these officials co-authored a long, dark chapter in Canadian history, inflicting hardships few Canadians could even contemplate.

We never knew. Taking full advantage of their defenseless exile, Ottawa seldom missed an opportunity to repay lightkeepers' essential life-saving service by cutting wages and withholding decent pensions and benefits, guaranteeing life on the mudsill of society at a fraction the pittance paid "Indian and coolie day labour." One marooned keeper who had never, in twenty-five years' service, taken a holiday because he would have had to hire a replacement, prayed in an open letter to his fellow keepers that "the new order of things will mature before we die of old age."

The new order of things is at hand. Engineers in Transport Canada are committed to the hazardous course of automating lighthouses. To the extent they can convince their political masters that not a single life will be lost and that millions of dollars will be saved to pay some interest on the national debt, the lights will be abandoned.

This book, like its forerunner *Keepers of the Light*, will serve its purpose if it shows how both claims fly in the face of our forgotten history. "If men leave the lights," British Columbia's fishermen predict, "other men will die."

So many people, on and off the lights, helped to bring these "wicks" out of their isolated corner of Canada's consciousness that space rules out naming them all. Without my late friend and partner, Captain Hubert Lindsay Cadieux, who amassed a staggering collection of primary materials by and about lightkeepers, and Pen Brown, a fellow keeper who appointed himself unofficial archivist of the Victoria Coast Guard District, the project could hardly have been contemplated. Thanks are also due to Joan Scarf, files clerk at the Coast Guard office in Victoria; to Captain W.E. Exley, former superintendent of lights; to L.E. Slaght, the Victoria regional manager; to all the Coast Guard staff in Victoria and Prince Rupert; to Len McCann, curator of the Vancouver Maritime Museum; to Elaine Moore, curator of Prince Rupert's Museum of Northern British Columbia; and to Gordon W. Stead, former assistant deputy minister of Transport.

A whole generation of "lighthouse kids" brought the arid paper sources to life. Evelyn (Forsyth) Mackenzie is the *grande dame* of a rare and distinguished lot which includes Rose (Moran) MacKay, Rob Okell, Violet (Warren) Cummings, Devina (Allison) Baines, Tom Moran, Vic Aro, Archie Georgeson, and Roy Lally. Mindful of the conflict brewing between "professional" and "popular" history, which swirls quicker and closer to the issue of "truth" (though reality is seldom constituted for the convenience of historians) I have checked all interviews against documentary sources. Sometimes dates and places get mixed up, all right, but then neither meant much to people reared on islands where "time was just Nature's way of making sure everything didn't happen at once."

Veterans of the lighthouse tenders like Captain Norman MacKay and his mate, Roddy Smith, were invaluable when it came to salvaging the history of the northern lights after the mindless destruction of the Prince Rupert marine agency's files. Cecil "Nobby" Clark, historian of the B.C. Provincial Police, came up with the investigative file on the unsolved "lighthouse murder case," and corrected many errors of fact.

Jack Waddell helped track down his back issues of *The Organizer* and recalled his uphill struggle to bring lightkeepers out of the nineteenth century. John Skapski, a fisherman and poet who has been by these lights so often corrected some laughable navigational errors—but where I came from everyone moves on dry land in a straight line. Others offered crucial information and advice anonymously—so they must be thanked likewise.

Laurie Findlay was in it right from the start. As editor, critic, and typist she helped a few pages of notes grow into two books—a process accelerated by the Explorations Program of the Canada Council and by the B.C. Heritage Trust.

None of it would have happened without ten years on the lights with the likes of Jim and Jean Barr, Keith and Dorothy Nuttall, Mike and Carol Slater, Jean and Lina Beaudet, Gerry and Kathy Watson, and all my brothers and sisters strung out five hundred miles from Race Rocks to Green Island—especially Elaine, David, and Jonathan who, so it seems looking back, made a paradise of exile.

The Inside Passage

D readful as it was, the West Coast of Vancouver Island still remained British Columbia's safest shipping freeway well into the late 1890s. The alternative was the Inside Passage, that long corkscrew course setting the Island apart from the mainland. It was perilous enough in daylight, with tides pulsing and ripping through compressed channels. After sunset, or in fog, it was near madness to venture by echo and lead-line up the Strait of Georgia and into the maze of islands clogging Johnstone Strait. As one captain recalled, ''Any black dark nights they just had to tie up because there's no lights anywhere . . . you just had no hope. You couldn't see.''[1] Besides, shipping lanes intersected in the Passage. Vessels travelling back and forth from Vancouver and the Fraser to Nanaimo, Chemainus, and Victoria cut across the bows of others bound north and south. It was a busy intersection with no traffic lights.

In the mid 1880s the Department of Marine and Fisheries began setting up lights for traffic crossing the Straits. Once out of Victoria, captains steered past Fiddle Reef and around Trial Island, then headed for Discovery Island light at the entrance to Haro Strait. Three courses lay before them: Boundary Pass, marked by the East Point light on Saturna Island's southern tip; Active Pass, via Portlock Point and Active Pass lights; or Porlier Pass, separating Valdez and Galiano Islands. Within a decade, though, most traffic was heading north from Vancouver in a motley convoy through the Inside Passage towards the Klondike.

As late as 1898 Point Atkinson was still the furthest light north. In May 1904 the *Victoria Colonist* reported, ''An agitation has been started looking to induce the Dominion government to construct additional lighthouses on this coast.'' Polite petitions, and not-so-veiled political threats were pouring into the office of Colonel W.P. Anderson, chairman of the Canadian Lighthouse Board, and chief engineer of the Department of Marine and Fisheries. The lighthouse board sat in marathon sessions to keep pace with the paper. Echoing the sentiment of every Chamber of Commerce from Victoria to Port Alice, the *Vancouver News-Advertiser* declared, ''We have a strong claim on the Dominion government for such expenditure as this,'' since federal coffers were already swollen with levies from British Columbians ''in the shape of customs and excise dues, fishery licences and other items.'' The *Colonist* warned British Columbia's MPs to ''see to this matter before the present session . . . closed.''

Colonel Anderson weathered the siege, and his draftsmen worked overtime, cranking out plans. In a frenzy of construction they put up seven lights in ten years along the Island's eastern flank. When the construction crews left, three hundred miles of sheltered waterway were rendered safe, from the Ballenas Islands off Parksville, to Pine Island at the north end of Gordon Channel, near the top of Vancouver Island. Beacons on Ballenas Island and Sisters Rocks warned ships away from perilous rocks and foul ground. All the others, from Merry Island to Pine, gave crucial bearings for steering through the fast-running channels and passes. Ships went from one light and fog signal to the next, all the way north to the heaving Hecate Straits. There were still six hundred miles to go for the gold.

Active Pass

Every B.C. ferry on its run from Tsawwassen to Swartz Bay threads through the boiling tide of Active Pass between Mayne and Galiano Islands, slowing speed and blasting its whistle to warn unwary smaller craft around the bend of its approach. The sight of the tower and buildings of Active Pass light seldom fails to draw passengers out on deck, many for their first look at a "real" lighthouse.

Though its title certainly befits one of the busiest shipping routes crossing Georgia Strait, the Pass was actually named for the American steamer *Active*, one of the earliest steamships to pass through while engaged, with HMS *Plumper*, in surveying the international boundary in 1857. In the course of that survey the *Plumper*'s officers apprehended an American whiskey trader named Macaulay, who unknowingly played a key role in the expansion of the lighthouse network. After he was transferred to the *Active*, Macaulay flashed a large quantity of gold dust and nuggets, taken in trade from Indians up the Fraser River. When the *Active* berthed at San Francisco, Macaulay started talking and the Fraser gold rush was on.

Sailing ships had previously shunned Active Pass because of its strong rip tides and its narrow clearance of less than a third of a mile. In July 1860 the man-of-war *Termagant*, en route to Nanaimo to take on coal and to impress restive Indians with white supremacy, grazed Laura Point and carried away some trees with her foreyard. Twelve years later the bark *Zephyr*, bound for San Francisco with a hold full of sandstone, raked out her bottom on Georgina Shoals in a snow squall and went down with her captain and a deckhand. In 1898 the *B.C. Coast Pilot* warned that strong tides combined with slack winds to render the Pass "unsafe for sailing-vessels, unless indeed small coasters." For moderate-sized steamships "commanding a speed of not less than 8 knots, it is a useful pass," the *Pilot* allowed, "but it is advisable for large ships and those deeply laden to pass through at, or near slack water."

Still, the advantages of Active Pass more than compensated for its perils. It was forty miles in a straight line from Discovery Island, at the southern entrance to the Haro Straits, to the mouth of the Fraser River at Sand Heads via Active Pass—ten miles shorter than plying "the most dangerous and inconvenient part of the Haro Straits" between East Point on Saturna Island and Patos Island, across the boundary, "where the tides [were] strong and apt to send a vessel down Rosario Straits or over on the eastern shore." After 1885 the Active Pass light on Georgina Point, visible twelve miles on a clear night, with a fog bell tolling in thick weather, elevated Active Pass to the status of major shipping channel between Victoria and Vancouver.

When Marine Agent James Gaudin transferred Henry (Scotty) Georgeson, a former assistant on the Sand Heads lightship, to the new light at Active Pass, he established a lightkeeping dynasty. For the next five decades Georgesons served at Active Pass, East Point, Portlock Point, and Albert Head, and their name is intimately bound up with the early settlement of the Gulf.

Scotty Georgeson's odyssey began the day he was unjustly beaten by a school teacher when he was a teenager on the Shetland Islands. He ran away to sea, venturing into such far-flung corners of the empire as Africa, Australia, and New Zealand. On his last voyage he crossed the Pacific with a cargo of Chinese coolies bound for San Francisco. From there he jumped ship and made his way north to Victoria in the gold rush.

In 1858 he and a friend opened a makeshift hotel at Beaver Pass. Scotty quit that venture and came over to Galiano Island with his Indian bride from Lillooet. They pre-empted 146 acres adjacent to the bay which now bears his name, and built a house near Active Pass.

Five years later Scotty Georgeson secured the post of assistant keeper at Sand Heads, and then took over the Active Pass station in June 1885. He retired thirty-six years later in 1921, aged eighty-five, and lived the last four years of his life in a replica of the lighthouse, built by his son Peter on the Georgeson homestead nearby. Scotty led a rich life, garnering more than his share of adventure with which to regale the grandchildren straddling his lap. Any keeper of the time (and most today) would gladly have traded places with Scotty Georgeson, for Active Pass in the Gulf of Georgia was spared the worst ravages of vile weather and isolation. The Georgesons lived in a picture-perfect setting, and even had a postcard printed up with the caption "Our Lighthouse Home."

Scotty was appointed at a salary of $500, later increased by $50 for winding the fog bell. In mid-October 1893 a new steam-generated fog alarm was built and he moved quickly to secure the assistant's position for his son, raising the family's lightkeeping salary to $900. Gaudin had recommended this nepotism, reasoning, "If you have to employ a certificated Engineer at this time, there will be a general resignation at all the stations where there is a fog alarm in this province."[1]

Scotty Georgeson established a sterling reputation as "one of the best firemen on the coast," who could get steam up in a boiler faster than anyone else. In December 1913, however, the master of the *Princess Royal* charged that Georgeson's steam

Henry (Scotty) Georgeson, (left) with family,
(right) wearing the coveted Imperial Service Medal.

Active Pass Light circa 1880.

horn was quiet when he came through the Pass in thick weather at 3 A.M. on 19 December. "You will please advise me with reference to this matter as it is my intention to report it to the department and have an investigation," Captain George Robertson, Gaudin's successor as marine agent, threatened, "and if found correct it will mean serious trouble, as there are too many reports reaching me with reference to lightkeepers not attending to their duty." But these reports stemmed from the failings of machines, not men. Georgeson leafed back through his log and reported he "saw fog coming and went down to start engine at 2:30 A.M. but could not get engine to go. Fog set in at 2:40 A.M. Two of us working on engines, got No. 1 engine to go at 3 A.M. The engines coughed and 'stopped dead' three times over the next three hours."

Besides, it took time even for Scotty Georgeson to raise steam—a fact the captains seemed always to ignore. When the *Princess Adelaide* complained of heavy smoke and no horn in the Pass in September 1914, Georgeson pointed out that she did not signal until she was within two miles. For twenty years Scotty had relied upon Mayne and Galiano Islands as reference points for visibility. "Now if this guide is not satisfactory, we shall have to blow continually," he complained. "How is it that all the large steamers coming in & out in a dense fog do not sound their fog whistle within a mile of our station?"

Four years later, the *Princess Adelaide* waited too long. On the afternoon of 13 October 1918 Archie Georgeson, Scotty's grandson, was at the pipe vise in the fog alarm building, squirting cutting fluid and peeling threads off pipe for a neighbour while the alarm rattled tools on their racks. He checked the time. "Run out and see if you can hear the *Princess Adelaide* coming," Archie asked his friend. He rounded the corner of the building just as the *Adelaide* blew her whistle. "She's right here on the beach!" he screamed. Archie ran to the door and saw the black and white sweep of her hull "stuck up right in front of the lighthouse like a great big city," just seconds before the liner ran aground.

The Georgeson boys spent all day towing her life boats ashore, dragging them up on the beach, then launching and anchoring them again to save them from breaking up in the tide. "Of course, they naturally said that the foghorn wasn't going, but they were way off base on that because the foghorn was going about ten hours before he came in there," Archie stated. In fact, the captain had not even been on the bridge. His first officer calculated he had more than a minute to go before he called him up to steer through Active Pass, "but he was a minute and a half faster than he figured." The rocks sheared off the *Adelaide*'s propeller and crumpled her rudder like a tin can. Three tugs managed to pull her free.[2]

As he entered his eighties, Scotty left the more strenuous work of the fog alarm to Archie. "He was all eyes when he walked in and if he found a little speck of dirt or anything, you had to clean everything," Archie recalled. "Polish the brass and clean this up and clean that up and clean the windows, he ordered."

When Georgeson retired in March 1921, Arthur Gurney moved over from Ballenas. Gurney had been a constant irritant since he first went on the lights at Pine

CPR's Princess Adelaide *aground at Active Pass, 13 October, 1918.*

Island in 1907. He had schemed and attempted to manipulate marine agents for years, changing his politics chameleonlike, writing MPs incessant demands for higher pay and a preferential station, fencing over agents' heads with the minister. A heavy drinker, Gurney no sooner came into contact with neighbours at Ballenas than his flinty character sparked complaints. When he finally landed at Active Pass he was too old to enjoy his spoils: his children were grown and his wife Anna was in failing health. The Georgesons' twenty-six-year span of troublefree service at Active Pass was soon replaced by complaints from neighbours and (even worse) the Provincial Police.

In September 1932 Gurney's doctor certified that the lightkeeper suffered from insomnia "owing to domestic illness for the past three months. If this condition persists," the doctor wrote, "he will verge to neurasthenia & I advise that he immediately be allowed to leave for a month for the purpose of recuperating." Then in 1938 the Provincial Police sent Marine Agent Colonel A.W.R. Wilby a report "in no way favourable" to Gurney's conduct. The agent threatened to write Ottawa "if any other actions" on the keeper's part necessitated police investigation.[3]

By February 1944, after thirty-seven chaotic years on the lights, Gurney had had enough. He applied for superannuation. "My wife is a confirmed invalid," he explained, "and must be in a place in winter where she can go into a hospital." First, though, Gurney wanted to arrange for his son Tom to succeed him. His struggle laid bare the fact that patronage, officially illegal since 1919, was still alive and well in the lighthouse service. "He went to Pine Island a baby in Arms," Gurney wrote, "so he has most certainly done his service on Outside Lights." Giving Tom a spot on an easy light was the least the department could do to repay a man who had passed half his life in the light service, and who "never had a chance to give . . . [his] family the education they should have had."

William Stamford, the acting marine agent, favoured C.E. Carver from Nootka light to replace Gurney. In April, however, the local MP, R.W. Mayhew, warned him that, while he was resigned to accepting promotions based upon merit, he was "not prepared and...[would] not countenance the bringing of personnel from outside his district into the better positions in the Nanaimo Riding."[4] He insisted the appointment should go to Tom Gurney. Carver could have Active Pass, but only as a temporary appointment. He would have to make way for Gurney's son when Tom had completed his naval service.

This decision was a cruel blow to Carver, who was in failing health and desperately needed an "in station." Incensed at the injustice, George Smith, the retired son of Nootka's first keeper, and a veteran of Pine Island, Scarlett Point, and Nootka lights, wrote Colonel Wilby on Carver's behalf. It was a time-honoured covenant, if unspoken (and unwritten), that men "entering the service start on isolated stations and as vacancies occur, transfer to better stations according to their ability and seniority," Smith insisted, adding, "Personally, I would not like to see good stations become political homesteads; it would have a tendency to degenerate a civil servant into a toadying sycophant."[5]

Fortunately, the department ruled in favour of the Carvers, ending their eleven-year stint at Nootka. On their way down they called on Smith. Mrs. Carver declared, "Mr. Smith, I am so happy." And so might other keepers acknowledge their debt to Smith, for the conflict over the Active Pass succession in 1944 was the last gasp of the patronage which had ruled appointments and transfers for over sixty years.

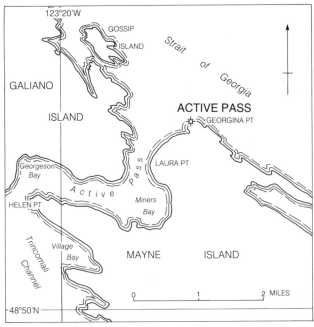

Discovery Island

The notion that women deserve equal pay for equal work would have been brushed aside as a colossal stupidity in the Victorian Age, when opinion held that universal suffrage would degrade the electoral process. Not a single woman was employed by government at Confederation. A year later, dismayed by the discovery that one had somehow slipped through the net and found work as a housekeeper, a royal commission concluded, "It is not proposed hereafter to employ female housekeepers." By the early 1880s, however, a few women clerks were at work on Parliament Hill. Their presence fostered profound misgivings. "They should be placed in rooms by themselves," another royal commission recommended, "under the supervision of a person of their own sex . . . and it would certainly be inadvisable to place them in small numbers throughout the Department." [1]

Practical reasons provided a cover for repressed sexual fears. Employment of women must be curtailed, it was argued, or they would surely take up positions intended for men who, after all, were "heads of families." Moreover, since women could not vote it was ludicrous to squander a position which might otherwise be held out as an incentive to "vote right." Patronage virtually guaranteed that women would never be hired. And the men who were hired needed no ability aside from passing the litmus test of political loyalty, as Richard Brinn had done when he was awarded the keepership of the new light on Discovery Island, five miles south of Victoria.

It was a real plum, Discovery, compared to the West Coast lights. Basking in the "rain shadow" which has made Victoria a mecca for the "newly wed and nearly dead," the island was a virtual suburban paradise compared to Cape Beale or even Point Atkinson. Discovery Island lies two miles northeast of Gonzales Point at the junction of Haro and Juan de Fuca Straits, astride the southern entrance to the Inside Passage. Thickly wooded and some three-quarters of a mile long, the island has a rocky shoreline with submerged boulders like slumbering whales extending some two cables off shore. Rudlin Bay, on the island's southeast side, is "filled with rocks," and the *B.C. Coast Pilot* warned that it "should not be used by any vessel."

Sea Bird Point, where the light was built in 1886, was named for the paddle steamer which arrived at Port Townsend in March 1858. On 7 September that year she caught fire, and her captain deliberately ran his ship aground on the Discovery Island shore. The island itself was named after Vancouver's famous flag ship by Captain Henry Kellet of HMS *Herald* during his 1846 survey of coastal waters.

Brinn's performance at Discovery spurred James Gaudin to vent his disdain for the pitfalls of patronage. On the night of 30 October 1892 the marine agent suffered a humiliating experience as a passenger aboard SS *Premier* when she passed Discovery in a dense fog, bound for Victoria between midnight and 1 A.M. There was no sound from the fog alarm. "It was only the careful navigation and good local knowledge of Captain Rudlin which [saved] many valuable lives and a fair steamer from destruction on the rocks near your station," he curtly informed Richard Brinn. Moreover, this was only the most recent of many complaints. He warned the keeper not to depend solely on his own judgment of visibility on foggy nights, and advised him to have the horn on whenever the lime kiln on San Juan Island was obscured. "That is your only safe course as your action in that manner would exonerate you in the event of an accident," Gaudin wrote. "I hope to have no further complaints about this work. The Department will not tolerate any dereliction of duty on this important subject."

Captain Gaudin seized upon the incident to attempt to convince Colonel Anderson in Ottawa that stations left in charge of "old men" like Brinn must have a paid engineer appointed when a steam fog alarm was installed. Captain Lewis and his officers on the *Sir James Douglas* had not considered Brinn "a fit person to entrust with the care of that station when the fog alarm was installed," Gaudin reminded Anderson, "and if I remember rightly you were not very much impressed with him

Discovery Island, 1900s.

during your visit four years ago.'' Since that time the alarm had given satisfaction—''thanks to. . .[Brinn's] daughter who. . . had the control.''

''I think you will agree with me that the appointment of lightkeepers solely by their political influence with the members is not always conducive to selecting the best men for efficient service,'' Gaudin pointed out, sheepishly adding, ''Not that I wish in any way to deprive members of their prerogative; but I think there should be some test by which the person appointed. . .[proves] suitable for the work performed.''[2] It took little skill to vote Tory (Liberals would say none whatever) and of all the keepers on the coast only Frederick Eastwood at Race Rocks and Carmanah's Phil Daykin were capable of machine work and making their own repairs. But there was one more coming. As she filled the breach during her father's dotage at Discovery Island, Mary Ann Croft was mastering the intricacies of the steam plant and the political machinery of the times.

Richard Brinn was on borrowed time in April 1899 when Harry H. Warden, a well-connected family friend in Victoria, wrote Captain John Irving, manager of Canadian Pacific Navigation, with ''what might be regarded as an unreasonable request. . . . Fully realizing your influence at the seat of the Provincial Government, I most earnestly wish that you would ascertain if it would not be possible for Mrs. Mary Croft to succeed her father. . . as keeper of Discovery Island Lighthouse,'' Warden asked. The woman was ''worse than widowed,'' since her husband was ''worthless in every sense of the word.'' He was in hospital and she was alone, responsible for raising her two daughters, aged eleven and twelve. ''It might not be prudent for the general public to know that the greater part of the responsibility of both light and fog whistle has fallen upon her for years—for her father is a feeble old man and it is a short time at best that he can live,'' Warden revealed. Without ''the pittance which the keeping of the lighthouse'' granted, Mary Ann Croft would be in dire straits indeed. Warden explained that she knew ''nothing about this,'' and hoped that Irving would ''not be offended by the asking of this favour.''

Irving immediately wrote the minister of Marine and Fisheries, Louis Davies, declaring, ''It would be doing an act of charity'' to let Mary Ann Croft ''continue in place when the inevitable time comes.'' However, Davies replied that a fully qualified engineer was required at a fog alarm station like Discovery.

The ''inevitable time'' came on 23 September 1901. Two days after her father's death, Mary Ann Croft advised Ralph Smith, her MP, that Discovery had a qualified assistant in Henry Cumner Watts, who had served with them for years. After sixteen years Discovery Island was ''just like an old home,'' she confided. ''I am entirely depending on the earnings of this station for a living for myself and family.''

While the MP pondered the unlikely request, James Gaudin hit Smith with a timely letter from the other direction. The agent had always held Mary Ann in his highest esteem, and reaffirmed her role in ''manning'' the station during Brinn's long illness. ''If it is possible to continue the operation of the station by Mrs. Croft and her Assistant, I am certain it will continue to be worked in a satisfactory manner to the shipping of the Province,'' he predicted. So, on 9 April 1902, Mary Ann

Croft made history, becoming the first female lightkeeper, and one of the first female public servants in Canada to work outside a subordinate clerical position.

And she did well, very well indeed, considering the steam plant at Discovery was virtually a twin to the monster at Point Atkinson which drove Walter Erwin beyond the limit of his endurance. Croft chopped kindling, packed and shoveled coal, hauled water, overhauled and maintained the plant, and shared the twenty-four-hour fog watches with Watts. When the plant was converted to gasoline, then to diesel, she winched fifty-gallon fuel drums ashore, rolled and wrestled them into the storage shed, and pumped up the day tanks by hand. She cleaned the lens, trimmed wicks, painted the tower and dwellings, fed, clothed, and educated her daughters for the next thirty years.

For the paternalistic Gaudin, Mary Ann Croft's career was something of a noble experiment. Minnie Patterson had already justified the high esteem he held for lighthouse women, yet he knew that, having shattered precedent, Discovery's new keeper faced a hard struggle uphill. He couched all his annual inspection reports in the most glowing terms. In 1908, her sixth year in charge at Discovery, Gaudin wrote Deputy Minister Gourdeau that Croft had "kept the station in a highly creditable and efficient condition." Since she only earned $900 (out of which she paid Watts) while other fog alarm stations with assistants paid $1200, Gaudin recommended her salary be increased "on the grounds of extra work in the case of the new lamp, the increased cost of living and labour." Ralph Smith concurred and on 25 March 1911 she finally received equal pay for equal work.

Captain Robertson, much more a stickler than Gaudin before him, was also swayed by the "lady lightkeeper's" expertise. "This station has been maintained satisfactorily during the past 12 years by Mrs. A. Croft, a widow of middle age, most active and enthusiastic in her duties," he informed the commissioner of lights after an inspection in January 1914. Such enthusiasm was certainly a rare commodity during Robertson's tenure, and he recommended a further wage hike, arguing that Discovery had the same fog plant as Egg and Pine Islands and should be reclassified accordingly.

By the spring of 1914 the rigours of keeping Discovery Island light were wearing her down. Mary Ann applied for six months' leave for "benefit of health"—her first such break in twelve years. Robertson granted the leave, providing, of course, that she pay a substitute during the whole time. Instead, she stayed and hired a second assistant temporarily. When Robertson applied to MacPhail, commissioner of lights in Ottawa, to upgrade Discovery's classification and pay, MacPhail seized upon the presence of two assistants as an excuse to turn his agent down. "If the keeper were a man," he declared, "it would not seem at all necessary to have two assistants."[3]

Mary Ann turned fifty-four in 1919 and began to lay plans for her retirement. She wrote Dr. S.F. Tolmie, her MP, that March to remind him of his "promise. . . to look into the the matter of. . .[her] request for a pension. . . . In nine years," she revealed, "I have had only three weeks holiday . . .

This is the case shortly put, as I do not believe in long and tedious stories. I think that after 23 years' service in such employment as the Lighthouse Branch, a person is due for some rest and something to make that rest free from worry for whatever few years that may be left.

I could make an appeal a mile long about the desolate situation of the Lighthouse Keeper in bad and stormy weather, but you know the coast, and you know the circumstances as well as I can tell you, if indeed not a good deal better.

I hope you will be able to convince those warmly housed gentlemen at Ottawa that when 23 years are taken out of a woman's life in a lighthouse, she is about due for a recognized and guaranteed rest.

After inquiring among his "warmly housed" colleagues, Tolmie was appalled to learn she could expect no pension at all, since the superannuation privileges for lightkeepers had been withdrawn during the CPR's cash crisis in 1882. The MP then proposed that she be awarded two years' pay, the equivalent of "one month's holiday for each year" Mary Ann had "been in the employ of the Government." The request was rebuffed. The Civil Service Commission would grant six months' pay on retirement—no more.

So Mary Ann Croft found herself in the same painful dilemma as her fellow keepers: retirement was a luxury they could ill afford. Her position became all the more hopeless after the 1924 Superannuation Act because she failed to see its ominous repercussions in time. In order to receive full benefits, all keepers would have to pay in retroactive contributions for the years they worked before the act came into effect. In Mary Ann Croft's case, she "owed" the government a staggering $550.

Unlike many other keepers who employed family members for assistants, Mary Ann had paid nearly half her salary to Watts all those years, yet the superannuation contributions were reckoned on the basis of her total earnings, amounting to approximately three-quarters of a year's pay. That was deterrent enough in itself. Besides, she still had her health, so elected not to pay in. By 1928, however, her health was failing and she reluctantly decided to make the retroactive payments. To her horror, Mary Ann discovered that she was a victim of fine print—the act allowed no such option after 1924.

In 1932, having run Discovery Island's light and horns for thirty years, she learned that the best she could hope for was a pension of $43 a month. "I am the senior lightkeeper in British Columbia, and the only woman in charge of a station," she desperately informed D.B. Plunkett, her MP, "I ought to get sixty-five dollars to live on, do you not think so?"[4]

Next she contacted J.H. King, minister of Health, who held out a crumb of hope by promising to explain her situation to his cabinet colleague, P.J.A. Cardin, minister of Marine and Fisheries. "Mrs. Croft has been a faithful servant," he insisted, "and I think you will find that your Departmental records are clear in regard to her service.'' But Cardin was busy cutting wages on the lights and was in no mood to boost pensions. On 31 August 1932, forty-six years after she arrived, Mary Ann Croft left Discovery Island for Victoria. The sixty-seven-year-old walked up the quay toward an uncertain future, with a cheque for six months' pay, and a pension of forty-three dollars a month. She rented a room in the Marine Chalet, where she could watch Discovery light from her window. Henry Cumner Watts, the man who assisted her all that time, left a year later. As her employee, rather than the department's, he had no pension at all. Watts died in Victoria in 1957, aged ninety-six.

In October 1934 Mary Ann Croft stood between J.W. Fordham Johnson, B.C.'s Lieutenant Governor, and Premier Pattullo in the glittering parlour at Government House. ''Most of us at various times have occasion to travel by night along the British Columbia coast,'' Johnson said, as reporters scribbled away, ''and as darkness falls our thoughts instinctively turn to those lonely and faithful servants who perform the highly responsible duties of keeping efficiently lighted those beacons which are needed for the safe navigation of ships and the safety of the travelling public.'' Then he presented the Imperial Service Medal to the first woman lightkeeper in Canada.

Discovery Island in the 1980's.

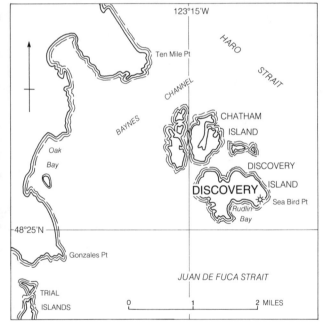

East Point

Lighthouses often went up over the hulks of wrecks, just as the East Point light on Saturna Island marked the final destination of the *John Rosenfeld*. She was a huge new barque of 2268 tons, built at Bath, Maine, in 1884. After taking on the largest shipment of coal ever to leave Nanaimo, she wallowed out of the harbour in February 1886, under tow by the tug *Tacoma*. Bound for San Francisco, they zigzagged along the international line through Boundary Pass between Patos and Saturna Islands. When *Tacoma*'s captain was misled by a fine mist and veered too close to the Canadian side, the *Rosenfeld*, with her deep twenty-six-foot draft, scraped hard aground near Boiling Reef. The tug *Alexander* tried in vain to pull her off at high tide, and the *Rosenfeld*'s owners faced the hard choice of selling her for salvage after sending a crew aboard to strip sails, rigging, and fittings. The *Beaver* removed some of the cargo.

While salvagers hotly debated whether the *Rosenfeld* should be refloated or wrecked where she stood, Saturna Islanders wasted no time plundering her cargo and sending it up their chimneys. One enterprising squatter even took apart the deck cabin and reassembled it ashore. Meanwhile, the Department of Marine acquired land from Warburton Pike, a local settler, and engaged ''a whiteman and a chinaman at $8.00 and $1.00 per day'' to clear the site for a new light. The U.S. government began constructing a light on Patos Island, three miles due east across the Pass. Together the two beacons would bracket the main shipping channel for all deep sea vessels bound to and from Vancouver.

The completed structure at East Point featured the now-familiar roof-mounted beacon. The white light flashed every thirty seconds, 140 feet above the splintered remains of the *John Rosenfeld*. A man named, appropriately, John Wick moved up to the new station from Victoria in 1888 and served for a year. Henry Georgeson's brother James replaced him.

A brush fire nearly consumed the new station in June 1889. James Georgeson was absent, but his "halfbreed" nephew George had come over from Active Pass for a visit and fought the flames single-handedly. H.G. Lewis, the acting marine agent, recommended that George be compensated "for his services in saving the buildings," and the department awarded him a cheque for $30.

Nowadays, with the Gulf Islands overrun by weekenders, it seems strange to conceive of them in their wild and isolated state. James's eldest son Peter, the first white child born on the island, heard firsthand accounts of tribal wars when the waters between Tumbo Island and Saturna ran red, and bones and skulls littered the beaches. James's daughter Joan remembered Skookum Tom, an old Indian friend, making an unlikely boast about white men's scalps adorning his belt. "I wasn't the least bit upset as I didn't know what a scalp was!" she recalled. "He was then civilized and quite nice to talk to."

She also recalled one stormy night when a neighbour, John Schultz, came pounding at the door, obviously bushed and boasting, "I've shot Jack the Ripper." James made him welcome and set out in the morning to find the unlucky victim's body on nearby Tumbo Island. He advised Schultz to give himself up to the authorities.

Twice a year James rowed or sailed across the Gulf to New Westminster for supplies. At the time, rice cost two cents a pound and fifty pounds of flour fetched a dollar, but fish, shellfish, and game were always free for the taking. James's children brought in extra money selling fish for twenty-five cents apiece. Georgeson also worked a homestead on Mayne Island and divided his time between farming and lightkeeping, leaving his daughter in charge of the station. He had been appointed at an annual salary of $480, which worked out to less than half the wage paid to the "Chinaman" who had cleared the station, so anything extra in the way of food or income was welcome. In October 1900, however, someone brought his frequent absence to Gaudin's attention. The agent cautioned the keeper that he "must on no account leave . . . [the] station without leave." In 1907 Gaudin recommended "that no station in charge of a white keeper should receive less than $500.00 per annum"—$225 less than the lowest going rate for "Indian day labourers."[1]

Like his brother Henry over at Active Pass, James was spared most of the harsher trials of his fellow keepers, but even though it was much more sheltered than outlying and exposed lights, East Point bore the full brunt of a northerly gale in February 1893. "The sprays were thrown over the house and damaged the cisternful of water. This is the first time since the establishment of this station that has happened," Georgeson noted. The boat ways were also ripped up and carried away in the pounding surf.

One of the greatest drawbacks in that idyllic place was water shortages. As they begin to pay for it by the bottle, North Americans have only just begun to appreciate fresh, unpolluted water as a precious commodity. It has always been hoarded like champagne on the lights. "It was a big place, nine rooms, and I had to keep them clean," Peter Georgeson's wife remembered of East Point station, "and we only had

James Georgeson at East Point.

a few gallons of water to use. We had rainwater and we had to wash the clothes and wash the kids and wash the floors and wash the dog all in that, and then put it back on the garden.''

James Georgeson suffered a stroke in 1909 and his son Peter virtually ran the station for a decade before his father retired. By 1920, with postwar inflation running rampant, James wrote to Deputy Minister Hawken, asking for an increase in pay. Since there was no fog horn at East Point he was not required to have an assistant, yet his vapour light certainly entailed a night watch. ''He is required to keep his son Peter as assistant,'' Hawken related to Wilby, ''preventing the young man from earning money elsewhere.'' As far as Ottawa was concerned, however, there was ''little probability of increasing the salary.''[2]

When James did retire, Wilby kept Peter's service in mind and wrote Ottawa declaring, "I am of the opinion that our Light Service is best maintained by the sons of men who have given the faithful service of practically all their lives to the Department." So true—yet inheritance of this sort smelled suspiciously like patronage. Even so, Wilby suggested the post "be advertised in the usual manner," then awarded to Peter Georgeson. "The knowledge and training of such sons can hardly be equalled for this work," he argued, "and also they have a tie which binds them to their work such as no stranger could possibly have." In the world of lightkeeping, nepotism sometimes seemed desirable and defensible. Peter succeeded his father. At the time of his own retirement over thirty years later, Peter Georgeson would point out with pride that his father, uncle, brother, son, nephew, and two grand-nephews were all lightkeepers.

In February 1935 R. W. McMurray, president of the West Coast Steamship Service, joined the list of pilots and officers who had "been agitating. . . for a long time" for a fog signal at East Point. There was already a horn on Patos Island, but McMurray pointed out, "This horn naturally does not denote to the mariner when he is abeam of East Point, and as you are aware, there is a very dangerous reef extending in a northerly direction 1¼ miles from East Point." The reef, scoured by strong tidal currents, confirmed East Point as "the most dangerous point on the route between Vancouver and Victoria," particularly in fog. Some vessels lost whole days tossing at anchor, waiting to fix their position off Saturna Island before venturing into Boundary Pass.

Moreover, there was continuous two-way traffic flowing past the point. Southbound vessels steering directly for Patos Island were "never sure when to enter the pass," McMurray pointed out. For this reason, the *Charles Crump* had recently run aground on Patos Island. McMurrary's request for a fog signal was endorsed by the B.C. Pilots, the B.C. Towboats Association, the Canadian Merchants' Service Guild, and "every master and officer" in the West Coast Service.

Wilby forwarded McMurray's letter to Ottawa, confirming that other vessels besides the *Charles Crump* had run aground, and many more had endured costly delays. The department delivered an experimental acetylene-powered fog gun in September 1937, housing it in a small shack some five-hundred feet from the tower. The gun fired every forty seconds but had the same limitation as the old fog bells: since the signal had no duration, officers had to keep an ear cocked for it. The gun frequently misfired, too, even in its first month of service. In November Peter Georgeson changed flints and cleaned the friction wheel three times in one thirty-six-hour period. McMurray wrote Wilby again that month to advise that all his officers had failed to obtain definite bearings on the gun. In a recent snowstorm, when the Patos Island horn was blasting away loud and clear, no one could hear the gun at East Point. "All our masters are, therefore, of the opinion that this signal should be changed to a horn signal when convenient," he concluded. In 1939 the fog gun was replaced with diaphone horns.

Peter Georgeson transferred to Albert Head that year, leaving a station that had been "in the family" for fifty-two years. Andrew Ritchie moved up from Race Rocks and stayed at East Point until his retirement in 1960. In 1947 an electric light replaced the outmoded kerosene lamp with its vapour tube, but the Ritchies continued to live in the drafty 1888 dwelling which had been condemned ten years before. The conditions of the dwelling, and the difficulties in obtaining supplies paled in comparison with the lack of adequate communication. As a qualified radio operator, Ritchie was appalled by the inadequacy of his transmitter with its fifty-mile range.

One night the Ritchies heard about a barge breaking loose from its tow up the Fraser River. Spreading their charts out on the kitchen table, they reckoned that tides and currents would draw the derelict into Tumbo Channel by sunrise. Sure enough, at dawn they saw the barge drifting toward the reef. There was no response from Victoria so their message was relayed via Friday Harbour. A tug was dispatched and saved the barge. The grateful owners commended the keeper for his "quick thinking and accurate navigation." Ritchie replied that they could keep their praise; what he really needed was proper radio equipment. A new transmitter arrived soon after, just in time to save a crewman from the *Neptune II.*

Like any other lightkeeper, Kathleen Ritchie instinctively kept an eye on the water. One November morning she watched an American trawler pass by her kitchen window, homeward bound from Alaska. As she reflected upon how happy the crew must feel to be headed home for Christmas, the vessel burst into flames and disappeared in a wall of smoke. She ran for the radio. "Emergency! Any one who can hear me!" she shouted. A listener in Campbell River responded, then broke off for Victoria marine radio. Kathleen gave the boat's position. Victoria appealed to all shipping for aid, then called in the U.S. Coast Guard. All the while Kathleen watched a crewman driven toward the stern by the wall of fire. He leaned over backward, deciding whether to burn or drown. Suddenly the coast guard cutter roared up astern and plucked him off as the *Neptune II* went under in a burst of steam and smoke.

In September 1960 the Ritchies retired and a wire went to the Quinneys at Pulteney Point light, giving them four days to pack up their four children, a horse, a cow, a dog, a cat, a twenty-one-foot cruiser, and three skiffs, for the move to East Point. The night before the *Simon Fraser* picked them up, Quinney and his ten-year-old son slaughtered, skinned, and butchered a two-year-old bull by lamplight.

As the Quinneys soon discovered, though East Point was nestled in the Gulf it was never immune to the ravages of rough weather. In the autumn of 1962 Typhoon Freda howled up the Gulf from the Pacific. Her 100-knot winds ripped out all communication between Saturna and the mainland, except for the transmitter at East Point. For three days and nights the seas rose forty feet up the rocks, enveloped the house in spray, washed through the windows to flood the livingroom, and ran down the eavestroughs into the freshwater cistern.

East Point Light.

In 1967, much to the chagrin of Saturna Islanders and the relief of East Point's keepers, the weather-beaten house and tower were torn down and replaced by a modern dwelling and skeleton tower. The *Victoria Colonist* nostalgically decried the "dissolution" of East Point in the name of progress. "By the time you read this there will be nothing left," it lamented. "However . . . the ghosts of memory will prevail as it has touched the lives of many people. Each room has held some tender moment of reminiscence."

East Point Lightstation, 1981.
Jim Ryan photo.

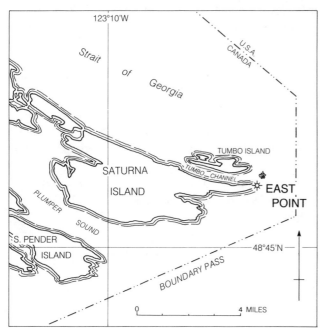

Chrome Island

C hrome Island stands just off the southeast tip of Denman Island, at the eastern entrance to Baynes Sound. For centuries the place held great significance for aboriginal people. Yellow Rock, as Chrome was known before 1940, is a veritable gallery of Stone Age petroglyphs, boasting the widest variety of rock carvings yet discovered on the West Coast. Artisans in the mists of pre-history chiselled whales, fish, animals, celestial bodies, contorted faces, and ''grotesque supernatural creatures bearing some resemblance to human beings'' into the rock face. The site is also unique in art pre-history, for the total carved surface demonstrates either the evolution of an art form over time, or the striking variations in one style upon two separate rock faces. Wilson Duff of UBC's Anthropology Department shared the awe that the inscrutable carvings have inspired in all the lightkeepers who have inherited Yellow Rock. ''The very mystery unfetters the imagination,'' he claimed, ''and you think of solitary shamans imbued with visions of their spirit helpers . . . of secret societies, or cannibal spirits, perhaps even of sacrifices.''

Whatever their origin and meaning, many of Yellow Rock's engravings were unceremoniously sacrificed to a few sticks of dynamite in the summer of 1890, when A. Brittancourt acted on orders from a Department of Marine and Fisheries imbued with the desire to establish another lighthouse up the Inside Passage. Since May 1888 coal companies at nearby Union Bay had badgered Ottawa through D.W. Gordon, their local MP, for a light at the entrance to Baynes Sound. Yellow Rock light went into operation on New Year's Day 1891, with Tom Piercy appointed as keeper. The original beacon, mounted on the roof of his dwelling, was a red lantern exhibiting a fixed white light.

The Piercys had ten children with them on the Rock, an area of less than two acres. One afternoon eight-year-old Harvey Piercy found an intriguing piece of metal, half buried in the dirt, and began pounding it with a rock. The blasting cap exploded with a deafening roar and flash, tearing off his thumb and mangling his other fingers. Lightkeepers were not supposed to leave their stations without written permission, so Tom bound up his son's torn hand as best he could, launched the station boat, and rowed him over to Denman Island as bilge water turned pink in the bottom. Holding the boat against the rocks, he gave his son directions to the nearest doctor—six miles away—and rowed home. Harvey beat his way through the bush to Dr. Beadwell's home, and was taken by horse and carriage to Cumberland Hospital.

The Piercys had left Chrome by 15 December 1900, when the steamer *Alpha* rode at anchor off Royal Roads, making ready for her last voyage. Bound for the Orient with 630 tons of salted dog salmon, 320 tons of bunker coal, and 32 tons of coking coal, she also carried her new owner, a Calgary speculator named Sam Barber, who planned to sell her for scrap at the end of the trip. Right now, though, her captain and first engineer argued heatedly on deck. Try as he might, the engineer could not convince Captain Yorke that *Alpha* was grossly overloaded. He quit in disgust, climbed over the side, and rowed ashore with his mate. Yorke soon engaged two less cautious replacements and weighed anchor.

By late afternoon the *Quadra* spied distress signals flying from *Alpha*'s yards. Drawing alongside, Captain Walbran was told, through Yorke's bull horn, that a bearing had burned out but the ship seemed in no immediate danger. These delays cost all her daylight, and *Alpha* limped along in the dark through blinding snow squalls. Strong tailwinds and a heavy sea soon compensated for the damaged bearing. By nightfall the doomed freighter was making near normal speed. Even though the Japanese lookout twice shouted down that there was a steady light dead ahead, the stubborn Yorke (who had no experience navigating the West Coast) bellowed out a string of mindless orders and kept the *Alpha* on a collision course for Chrome Island. The ship crashed into the rocks shortly after midnight, rebounded, struck them again, and held.

As heavy seas washed over her deck, Quartermaster Anderson plunged over the side with a rope around his waist. Scrambling up the rocks, he pulled a cable over and made it fast to a rock pinnacle. Twenty-six crewmen hauled themselves ashore and huddled together, badly bruised and torn by the barnacled rocks. Captain Yorke, Sam Barber, and five seamen shinnied up the mainmast, scaled the rigging, and spurned all the entreaties shouted up at them to use the proven escape route. Swells finally snapped the mast and swept them to their doom. William McDonagh, Piercy's successor, bandaged, fed, and sheltered the survivors until they were taken to Victoria.

Next day *Alpha*'s hull broke up and sank, spilling out her cargo. Local residents combed their beaches for the goods. They buried dog salmon to fertilize gardens. A local Indian stumbled upon an intact case of Geneva rum and was later found dead by the rock. The bodies began washing ashore a few days later at Lacon's Beach.

Theodore Nelson lashed them together and tied them to his skiff's stern. While towing them to the wharf, his boat capsized and two local boys, James Swan and John McMillan, pulled them ashore. James's father, Robert Swan, was the local coffin maker. He hammered three coffins together on instructions from Vancouver. Two of the dead, Sam Barber and Third Engineer Murray, were shipped off to Vancouver. The third was a man named McKay, a stowaway, who lay unclaimed until he was finally buried behind the church on Denman Island, where a large fir tree still marks his grave.

Over the years salvage crews and divers have picked *Alpha*'s bones clean. In 1957 a salvage barge hoisted up hundreds of tons of rusting scrap. In the summer of 1972 three divers came across one of her anchors jutting out of the sand. A tug brought the 1½-ton relic to Denman Island where it stands down at the ferry landing—a grim monument to five seamen who paid the ultimate price for their captain's folly.

When McDonagh resigned in August 1901, Deputy Minister Gourdeau complained that the keeper's $500 salary seemed ''somewhat high.'' He told Gaudin to find someone willing to work for less. The agent reported it would be an impossible feat ''owing to the current rate of wage earners in the Province . . . and if any one was found to accept it, there would be continual supplication for an increase.'' Chrome's soil was very fertile, though, and its keeper might hawk surplus produce over at the colliery's pitheads. As well, ''a live man could easily add to his income by fishing for dog-fish to make oil which would find a ready market at the Coal Mines.''[1]

John Doney, who came to Chrome in 1905, was more concerned about his children's welfare than the wages. He installed his three school-age sons on a parcel of land over on Denman Island where they could attend school. He and his wife stayed behind on the station. In February 1913 he asked J.D. Hazen, the minister, for permission to row over ''three times a week and see that the boys are all right.'' He would make the trip in daylight, he said, ''so as it will not interfere with my lighthouse duties.''

A week later Gordon Halkett landed at Chrome for an inspection and found only Mrs. Doney and her fourteen-year-old son there. This was the third time he had arrived to find Doney absent without leave. Robertson wrote the commissioner of lights to remind him that ''considerable trouble'' had resulted from lightkeepers leaving their stations. One of the first measures he had taken when he succeeded Gaudin had been to issue an edict to keepers, ''warning them that they would have to obtain written permission from . . . [his] office each and every time they left their stations except on government business''—even to fetch supplies in broad daylight.[2] Doney chose resignation over an indefinite sentence at Chrome, and moved over to his homestead on Denman in November 1914.

In the meantime, the department had been installing aids to navigation around Chrome. In 1905 two day markers were erected in separate towers, twenty-eight and eighteen feet tall, and 290 feet apart. Viewed in line from seaward, they gave a bearing for the centre of the channel, where the water ran seven fathoms deep.

Powerful new diaphones, the ultimate compressed air fog horn invented by J.P. Northey, a Toronto machinist, replaced the hand horn in 1903. In October 1920 W.H. Whitely wrote Colonel Wilby on behalf of British Columbia pilots, asking for a new light at Chrome because the existing fixed white light ''might be taken for a light in a farm house, or a vessel at anchor.'' Further appeals came in from the Canadian Merchant Service Guild, and the president of Canadian Collieries at Dunsmuir, who explained that four or five offshore ships called at Union Bay for coal every week. Doubtless this tonnage would be ''greatly increased'' due to an impending oil shortage on the Pacific coast. Since they were ''at all times up against competition of Puget Sound Coaling Stations,'' Dunsmuir's insisted upon ''the very best aids to navigation.''

Wilby could not have chosen a worse month than March 1922 to build a new tower. As a result of ''*heavy* winds . . . and at times rain and snow squalls . . . it took two men to handle one wheelbarrow,'' his foreman reported. Even so, the new tower—a steel skeleton supporting a wooden cupola—was completed by the end of March, and the steady light was replaced by a revolving type flashing every six seconds.

Allan Couldery arrived in August 1922. In the winter of 1926 he was chastised for burning too much heating oil in his dwelling. He asked for special consideration since they towed logs and bucked them for fuel to save coal. His explanation gives some insight into living conditions at Chrome. The bedrooms were always cold and damp in winter. Rain seeped through the walls. Even ''clothes and books in cupboard mildewed,'' and Couldery had to heat the house at night since he never retired before midnight, and often much later, in case of fog or snow. The kitchen was a low rough shed running the length of the west side of the house; freezing in winter, it was ''like an inferno'' if they cooked with the woodstove in summer.

Next summer a friend from Vancouver informed Couldery that the department was legally bound to supply its lightkeepers with a ''suitable dwelling.'' Conceding, ''I have not seen the Act myself,'' Allan nonetheless reported that theirs was ''not a 'suitable dwelling' for *any* decent human being, even for a lightkeeper.'' He went on, ''The foundation (?) is infested with all kinds of beetles, wood mites, wood lice etc. & these crawl in hundreds every day but chiefly at night, all over the house. They drop into the food cooking on the stove, into our beds, our hair, on to our dining table.'' To keep their uninvited meal-time guests at bay, he stood the table legs in tins of coal oil. ''Both Mrs. Couldery & I are up nearly all night killing these pests to try & keep them down for we have not been used to such conditions & cannot endure them crawling over us in the dark.''[3]

Couldery insisted that Wilby press Ottawa for a new dwelling, demanding either ''relief & some degree of comfort after [the] day's work,'' or a transfer. Someone had offered them a house over in Bowser, on Vancouver Island, but they could not bear to live apart. ''A tent won't stand up in the gales we have here,'' he explained. Much to the Coulderys' relief and the bugs' dismay, a new dwelling was built in 1929.

Their relief was short-lived. Mrs. Couldery had been sick all that year. She lay helpless in bed for three weeks before her husband finally carried her aboard the *Charmer* to take her away to St. Paul's Hospital in Vancouver. In June she wrote Wilby to say that she was in hospital "for a good rest," and was "not allowed to move at all." Her doctor had prescribed vast quantities of fresh milk and cream. "How I am going to get milk and cream at Yellow Rock I know not," she despaired, and begged the agent for a move to a shore station. Wilby replied that there was no opening at present, "although the matter . . . [was] being kept fully in mind."[4] Couldery had not even informed the agent of his wife's condition. "The reason I did not let you know is that I don't want to be a nuisance to *anyone*," he explained.

At 12 P.M., 11 February 1930 Wilby received a message from Halkett aboard the *Estevan*:

MRS. COULDERY DIED THIS MORNING AT YELLOW ISLAND ARRANGE PROCEED THERE PICK UP BODY . . . NECESSARY FOR SHIP'S CARPENTER MAKE SOME SORT OF BOX.

On the morning of 22 December 1932 the worst gale in Couldery's ten-year vigil at Chrome hit the station. "I was unable to go up the tower to put out the light as sheets of sea spume washed over the rocks deluging the place & making it unsafe to struggle against it," the fearful keeper wrote that morning. All day he watched helplessly as the waves came hurtling at him. They hoisted up the boat house and bore it away. "I am therefore marooned," he explained, "& must depend on the first boat passing me to take this letter to the Post Office."

In August 1933 Couldery's second wife went to Nanaimo to give birth. There were complications. He applied for leave to be at her side, but the department refused to pay a substitute. The keeper complained bitterly that he had only taken one holiday in the decade he had served at Chrome. "It does not give one much of a holiday feeling"—not when a lightkeeper had to pay his relief and was still responsible for the light, he complained. "Surely Ottawa wishes to be honourable with its employees or am I wrong to expect common honesty from the Department at Ottawa?"[5]

Then he left. The doctor had sent for him, "as the case was . . . serious." The anxious father engaged a relief keeper for three weeks. Wilby tracked down the renegade keeper in Nanaimo and demanded to know why he had absconded without leave. Couldery retorted that his wife came first; he would never neglect her when she needed him, even if Ottawa had "so little respect for its employees (who do their work faithfully and competently)" that it would "not even try to grant them their rights, or the holiday at the time it is requested. . . . I am sorry," he sarcastically apologized, "that the Department's servants in Ottawa are so 'isolated' that they receive three weeks annual leave without pay."[6]

Like Mary Ann Croft, Couldery had to eke out a living on $49.34 a month when he retired, since he refused to contribute back earnings to the superannuation fund. When he died in 1954, the department granted his widow a pension of $19.95 a month.

Eugene Moden's experience in January 1944 belied Ottawa's claim that Chrome was not an isolated station. One afternoon he crossed over to Bowser to claim some registered mail and buy fresh meat. An hour later he came down to his boat to find the sea "risen and rough." Moden pushed off anyway. His boat capsized two hundred feet offshore. "I had to swim and spent some time to tow and drag the boat ashore and do salvaging what I could." He tied up the boat at Bowser and trudged five miles, soaking wet, to Deep Bay, hoping to catch passage with a fisherman. No one would venture out until 10 P.M. The light was out until its exhausted keeper climbed ashore and went to the tower.

A mechanic named Hanson came to do some work at Chrome in December 1945. He stayed with the Modens and their three dogs, and left with fleas. He stormed into Stamford's office to report the "disreputable" conditions he had endured. The agent ordered the Modens to get rid of the dogs "and vermin" and clean up their act. If the station showed no "considerable improvement" soon, he threatened to write Ottawa.

This was a crushing blow to Evelyn Moden. "I can't get along with my husband out here very well, and those dogs mean a lot to me, they are my only companions," she replied. She could not bear to turn them out of the house. If Hanson bore them a grudge, fine, but why take it out on poor dumb animals? "Yes, you could write to Ottawa and so could I," she coolly threatened, "direct to Mr. Edwards [a senior department official] who bought one of my puppies some time ago."

Chrome Island Light 1963.

"And another thing," she added. "I do Moden's job here too, when he goes out on the shore and quite often he dont come back in time to light up I attend to the lights myself. So please dont be hard on the dogs, Mr. Stamford, as they are the only things I got here for my company." It was one of those things that had compelled agents right from Gaudin's day to roll their eyeballs toward the ceiling, shake their heads, mutter about the eccentricities of their keepers, crumple the paper, and aim for their wastebasket.

The Modens certainly had their quirks. He styled himself "Gen'l" A. Moden. "Say, Tom," he wrote T.E. Morrison, acting marine agent in the 1950s, "I am fed up with cranking these damn F.M. engines every 15 minutes," and asked for new ones. When Morrison pointed out he was using stove oil instead of gasoline, Moden replied, "I hope you feel O.K. after bawling me out," and listed a whole raft of other mechanical problems, hoping there would "be no piling ships up around here."

The "General" was stranded over at Bowser again in February 1950. He had gone over in the station boat for groceries, dropped anchor, and rowed ashore in his crude plywood skiff. When he returned, "big rollers and rough sea met . . . [him] at shore." He tried to paddle out to the boat but, he reported, "big rollers drove me back and filled dingy up with water and then they hoisted me up and dumped [me] into the sea rocks busted dingy bottom and broke one oar . . . and half of my groceries gone God knows where." It was a wild gale, and no one dared take the keeper out to his boat or over to Chrome until morning. His wife was in Vancouver so the beacon was out all that night.

The "General's" last dispatch dated 13 January 1951 revealed a man at the end of his physical and mental tether. Evelyn had deserted, depriving him of an assistant and even canine company. His loneliness expanded like a malignant growth:

OFF THE RECORD
Dear Sir
    Illness says the lighthousekeeper—Yes-sir sailormen and lightkeepers—get ill sometimes, but not having the time for it, that other people have and there being no doctors at sea and lighthouses, just seaguls, they soon pick up. Ashore, if a man's ill he goes to a horsespittle and has a nice nurse to wait on him, at sea or at the lighthouses the mate or men in office they come down or phone down and tell him that there is nothing the matter with him and ask him if he ain't ashamed of himself to be sick. Ye-ah, that's [the] way it goes. Yeah sir mighty promising, looks like that I ever get heat in the house and fresh water all fixed up this year. Wife says: no heat in the house, no water to drink I won't stay here, and went where she gets everything for the money I sent her for the last five months. I have had a housekeeper for a month, she would not stay on a account of walls being wet and bed room cold I myself sleep in sleeping bag try all these things sometimes.
                    So long.[7]

Chrome Island Lightstation 1981. Jim Ryan photo.

Since helicopters and inflatable boats became a part of lighthouse life in the 1960s, Chrome has ranked high as a preferred station. Though cramped, it offers a fair measure of isolation, yet holds out the one great consolation for keepers who have given their best on more isolated stations: the opportunity of boating children to school, weather permitting.

All summer long, boats flying red and white pennants advertise novice divers below, gliding over and around the *Alpha*'s dismembered carcass. Anthropologists and tourists alike are still drawn to Chrome to stand by the helicopter pad and marvel at the surviving petroglyphs. But the keeper's days may be numbered. In spite of the hundreds of lives saved by Chrome Island's keepers since the *Alpha* went to wreck (with more than fifty incidents of assistance to mariners in 1984 and 1985 alone), the minister of Transport issued a directive to abandon and automate the station in April 1985. There will be no effect upon search and rescue services, the department claims, since the role is not specified in lightkeepers' job descriptions.

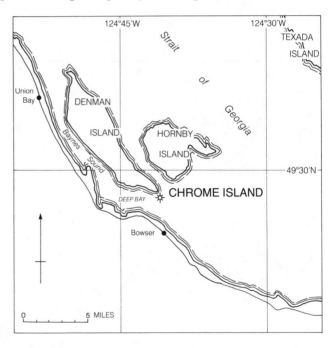

Portlock Point

In July 1890 Captain George Rudlin of the steamer *Islander*, engaged in ferrying passengers between Vancouver and Victoria through Active Pass, asked his friend James Gaudin to establish a manned light at Portlock Point on Prevost Island in the Gulf. The Point was dangerous to approach on account of some low-lying rocks to the southeast. Gaudin wrote William Smith, deputy minister of Marine and Fisheries, recommending that a stake light similar to one recently erected at Brockton Point on the Stanley Park shore should suffice to show the way from Swanson Channel to Trincomali Channel at the southern approach to Active Pass. It would also assist lumber freighters bound for the loading docks at Crofton, Ladysmith, and Chemainus.

Thickly wooded, three miles long, and 1¼ miles wide, Prevost straddles Swanson Channel. The north shore is an unbroken line of cliffs; the south is indented by several small bays and creeks. The island was the private hunting preserve of the Prevost Island Club, which had stocked it—at considerable expense—for the pleasure of its exclusive membership. When Gaudin investigated upgrading the stake light to a permanent manned light in August 1894, the Club members were ''jealous of the intrusion of strangers on their preserve.'' These were no politically naive Indians from the boondocks who would stand idly by while a portion of their reserve was surrendered—they even had the nerve to insist that their Club, rather than the Liberal party, should choose the lightkeeper from their own ranks! When they learned about the salary, however, the huntsmen seemed quite content to let an ''intruder'' take on the job.

Construction was completed in 1896. The new wooden tower stood fifty feet high, elevated seventy-two feet above high water. The fixed white light displayed a red sector over nearby Enterprise Reef. A small kitchen leaned up against the tower, and a boat house and fog-bell tower stood a quarter mile away on the shore. Richardson, Portlock's first keeper, had standing orders to wind the spring-loaded bell and make sure it rang every fifteen seconds in thick weather. Richardson resigned in 1905. A man named Gillespie ran the station until April 1911. Then George Andrew Watson took charge.

Watson was one of the first passengers carried west on the CPR in the autumn of 1885, a veteran of the tense troop of Ontario clerks and farm boys who marched with Middleton all the way from Qu'appelle to Batoche to snuff out Riel's short-lived Metis nation. It was a grand imperial venture, that campaign against the "savages" in the Northwest, and must have made a deep impression upon a young man. Yet when Watson recalled it a decade after coming to Prevost Island, it seemed he regretted fighting on the wrong side. For George Watson came to be a spokesman for his own downtrodden minority: those who suffered the oppressive conditions of life and labour on the West Coast lights. Like Riel, he was branded insane for his troubles.

"Continual supplications" for a living wage had resulted in a slight increase in salaries in 1911, the year Robertson succeeded Gaudin as marine agent. Gillespie got the increase that year, but Watson was hired at the previous wage. The new agent insisted that he "give satisfaction" for four years before he could expect Gillespie's rate. Moreover, Watson was told to provide his own fuel, and his hungry stove consumed eight cords of wood each winter.[1]

When he learned from his brother back in New Brunswick that the eastern cost-of-living was only half that of the West Coast, George wrote Francis Shepherd. The lightkeeper's logic impressed the Nanaimo MP, and he asked the department to grant his constituent an immediate pay raise. Captain Robertson conceded that an increase might well be in order since Portlock, like East Point, had a vapour light which must be watched all night long. All the same, Halkett had recently censured Watson "owing to the untidyness of the station," and the agent ruled out increasing Watson's wage until he showed he deserved it.

Halkett went back to Portlock Point in a hurry on Halloween night 1913, after the Provincial Police wired Victoria that its keeper had "gone insane." "On my arrival," he reported, "I found the lightkeeper very weak and his wife told me the night before he had been very violent and threatened her life." Still, Watson seemed rational enough to be left there. Halkett placed a temporary man in charge for a few days to ensure operation of the light. "Watson's mania," the superintendent confided, "is his small salary which he states is not enough to allow the service of an assistant and is wearing him out by forcing him to work more than he's bodily able to do."[2] Such was the straitjacket in which lightkeepers found themselves.

By July 1914 Watson was rational enough to write the minister. He rehashed the cost-of-living comparison and revealed how he could expect no raise until he had put in four years. Meantime, how could he keep his wife and two children ''on a salary that wouldn't any more than keep one at the prices. . .[they had] to pay'' at Portlock Point? For good measure, he included a detailed description of his duties.

> Now my light is a Diamond incandescent petroleum vapour burner, 25 m/m the same as in Active Pass that they class six and is paid over twice as much as I am they say [because] there is a steam operated fog [alarm] there now I have a fog bell to attend a quarter of a mile from my light and when it is in operation I have to travel that every three hours to wind the clockworks to keep it running and that travel is over a bluff of rocks and no shelter from storm and wind in bad weather.

Watson also had to watch his vapour light from dusk to dawn between those hikes. ''Now I think I am writing to a man of honour and justice and I hope to be treated on the square,'' he concluded. George appended a detailed account of their income and outgo so the minister could plainly see for himself, in Watson's words, ''just what I got for sixteen hours a day three hundred and sixty-five days a year and see if you could keep yourself and your family on that.'' Though he was a ''white'' keeper, entitled to $500 under the 1907 formula, Watson was earning only $460 a year after three years and three months' service.[3]

Watson had clearly misjudged John Douglas Hazen's sense of justice and honour, for the minister merely referred his appeal back down the ranks to Robertson. Appalled by Watson's strategy, the agent rebuked him scathingly for ''gross insubordination,'' threatening that he would be ''summarily dealt with'' if he ever dared write Ottawa again. He pronounced the keeper's portrayal of low wages and long hours to be ''far from the facts,'' and suggested, ''If you are not satisfied with your position, please send in your resignation as there are a number of people only too pleased to accept it.''[4]

To the commissioner of lights in Ottawa, Robertson explained that Watson was ''demented'' over his salary—an uncompromising dissident, though ''harmless except on this one particular point.'' The agent recommended that a doctor examine him ''as to his mental condition.''[5] Nevertheless, Watson's one-man agitation had some effect: in November 1914 Portlock Point was reclassified upward and his salary rose by ninety dollars a year.

In February 1916 steamboats reported hearing no fog bell pealing over at Portlock Point. Robertson sent some mechanics to Prevost Island. They reported back that the governor spindle was bent and one of the gear wheels sprung, ''which could only happen through a careless accident, or be done deliberately.'' Convinced that Watson had vengefully sabotaged the bell since he received no pay for winding it, Robertson demanded an immediate explanation. Watson replied that on 9 March he had been too sick to work. He had gone without shoes for some time and had broken his toe on the rocks. After five days of steady snow, he hired a boy to come over to shovel the trail to the bell; then he ''tied [his] foot up with rags and a piece of

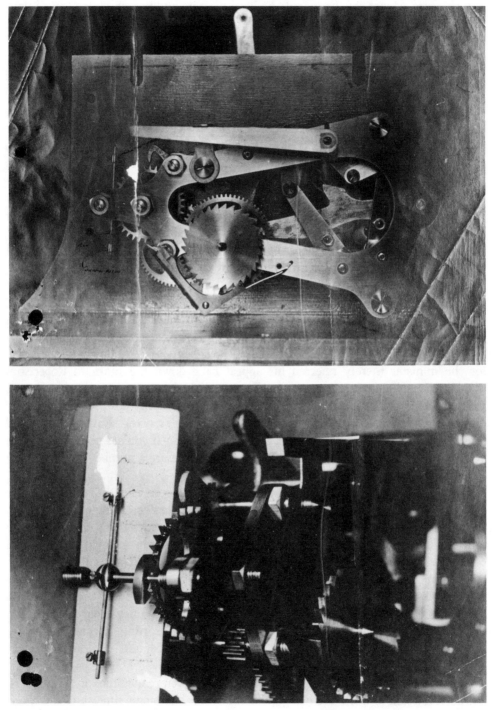

Watson's nemesis: the clockwork fog bell.

deerskin and hobbled over to the bell.'' The machinery was jammed and he paid the lad all the cash he had—eighteen dollars—to pump the hand horn instead. As for the charge of sabotage, Watson retorted that his letters about repairs rated as much attention in Victoria as ''a dog barking on the street.'' ''Now I don't consider myself a dog,'' he declared, ''and I think I will get a hearing and a square deal if I apply to the proper place.'' He demanded an official inspection and court of enquiry to lay the charges to rest, but this request was denied.[6]

In 1915 the Watsons lost their eldest son in ''the sands or mud of Northern France.'' George reckoned this was sufficient sacrifice without the department's checking off five dollars a month from his wages for the Patriotic Fund. ''Now I have served my country in the north west and stud as a target for the Savages,'' he reminded Robertson, and warned in his curious blend of Huck Finn and Geoffrey Chaucer, ''If i am to bee troden under foot . . . in this country i have my old rifel yet and i am not to old to fight for liberty.''

Poor diet, damp conditions, and too many sleepless nights soon reduced the Watsons to semi-invalids. As early as 1 July 1914 they had turned all their life savings over to a local doctor and still found no relief from recurring bouts of arthritis, pneumonia, strep throat, and gastric attacks. Yet George continued to give sterling service, turning out of his sheets though feverish to plod barefoot through rain and snow over the well-worn path to the bell tower. In July 1916 the Harrison liner SS *Barrister* ran up on the rocks in a heavy fog. The Vancouver pilot was at her helm and claimed that Watson's detested fog bell had been silent, but a subsequent inquiry attributed the cause to yet another mechanical failure. Watson, on watch as usual, was cleared.

The Watsons' health deteriorated steadily for a year until May 1917, when George was crippled by shortness of breath and excruciating chest pains. He reported, ''Although i dident give up and lay down i tried to work the sickness off[f] and tended my light with the help of my Wife until she fell sick on the 12th of June 1917 then we were both sick and on the 14th of june 1917 i was down and i tied A knot in the flag as you had instructed me and turned the flag up side down and hoisted it half mast.''

Watson nursed his wife and went about his duties another four days and nights, reduced to going on all fours over the rocks to his bell at a snail's pace, muttering curses at the CPR steamers passing by with their passengers waving gaily back. Finally he gave up and crawled into bed. He and his wife tried to console one another and waited. The light sputtered out. On 16 June a Cowichan Indian came ashore with fish for sale. As he stood in their bedroom doorway, Watson begged him to fetch the doctor from Port Washington on Pender Island, and to get word off to Victoria.

Two days later Robertson sent F. Cullison, one of his assistants, over to check the Indian's report. Watson would not leave. Cullison relit the vapour light, then sailed over to Port Washington for the night. In the meantime one of the Watsons'

"...i have my old rifel yet and i am not to old to fight for liberty..." The George Watsons of Portlock Point, 1916.

neighbours came calling. Alarmed at his friends' condition, he fetched Cullison back. The assistant again pleaded with Watson to come away to hospital. The keeper refused to budge. The shame of poverty overrode the hammering agony in his chest. They could neither afford a doctor nor pay a substitute. In his pain and rage Watson became hysterical; when Cullison retreated he was "beating the bed with a cane and acting like a lunatic."[7]

Next day Cullison brought John Georgeson, Scotty's grandson, over from Active Pass. This time, he said, "the keeper's sick wife got out of bed and begged us not to come in and refused us admittance." Georgeson stayed behind to comfort them as best he could. Unable even to write now (certainly a debilitating condition for him), Watson dictated a letter for Robertson, begging the agent "in the name of humanity" to come there immediately and see him.[8]

Instead, Robertson sent Gordon Halkett to have his turn at Watson. The superintendent of lights brought Dr. Frazer over from Port Washington. These two met with no more success than Cullison before them. After a cursory examination Frazer prescribed two weeks in hospital followed by a month's convalescence. But "Mr. Watson was much worried and excited owing to the fact that he had no money to pay a substitute during the time he was ill," the harried Halkett reported, imploring Robertson to hire one, as had "been done at other times."[9]

Finally one of Watson's neighbours on Mayne Island took matters into his own hands. T. Mayne chartered a launch to ferry the stricken lightkeeper to Vancouver, met the boat on the wharf, and helped carry Watson's stretcher to a waiting ambulance. Doctors at St. Paul's Hospital put him on the critical list. Mayne wrote Robertson that he had committed Watson to hospital, "considering that this action was one which common humanity dictated." He explained, however, that he was a casual friend, "not so situated financially . . . to bear his expenses, during his illness and convalescence." Mayne further pointed out that Watson's condition was "due to him faithfully carrying out his duties," and asked for "special consideration" on his friend's behalf.[10]

Robertson thanked Mayne for his concern, then suggested that he had somehow been misled in thinking that Watson had been "neglected." Watson, he emphasized, had succumbed to a "severe attack of influenza with bronchial catarrh and marked cardiac weakness, which does not tend to show that it was due to the elements.'' Leave of absence was always available if he provided and paid for a substitute. Lightkeepers were paid a salary, Robertson lectured Mayne, and ''as long as their services are satisfactory with good behaviour, they are retained, but the Government does not provide superannuation or any other expenses.'' For his part, the agent had already applied to Ottawa for sick pay during Watson's absence, in view of his satisfactory service. ''Government,'' he stated, ''treats their employees in the same way as any Commercial Firm.''[11]

Not so, according to S. Percival, a Port Washington storekeeper who rowed over to Portlock with the Watsons' mail and was surprised when no one came down to meet him. He walked up to the house and found Watson's wife in despair over their finances and George's health. Percival had been carrying them on credit for three months. ''It would certainly be a great hardship if Mr. Watson's salary is not paid in full during his illness, or if he has to pay a substitute in full during that time,'' he indignantly wrote the agent. ''A private employer treating one of his regular and old employees in such a manner would be considered very mean and unreasonable.''[12]

Watson was back on Prevost Island in fair form in mid July. With a shaky hand he penned a venomous note to Robertson, demanding ''to know if the mariners are not supposed to stop and see what is wrong when the flag is at half mast at a light station. If there is no protection for A light keeper i dont see why he Should expose him self to all Sorts of Weather to Protect the Mariners now i am going to find out before i stop this time if there aint sum rule that aint all one sided.''

He was starting all over again with the agent, though this time there would be no polish, no fawning, not when he was eighty more dollars in debt to the doctor, ''besides the nurse for. . .[his] Wife and her medison.'' His last store bill totalled $140.20, his last quarterly cheque $174.37, leaving them just $34.00 to stretch over the next three months. Moreover, the department was still deducting five dollars a month for the Patriotic Fund. ''I have starved now long enough and went without close for the Public if they cant give me A living and cloths i dont Want to Work twenty hours A day for them,'' he threatened. ''Now i think charity will begin at home with me this time.''[13]

July 1918 was one of the driest summers on record along the coast. A brush fire broke out on Prevost Island and Watson (hopefully with some ''close'' on) chased the flames single-handedly for four days and nights. No sooner had he smothered them with wet sacks than they would flare up somewhere behind him and race through the tinder-dry grass. At one point the fire threatened to gain the upper hand and he considered evacuating the island since there was no pump or hose on the station.

That fall the captain of Watson's nemesis, the CPR's *Princess Adelaide*, charged the keeper with negligence again, claiming the fog bell was mute when he passed Portlock at 3:30 A.M. on 7 October. The lightkeeper's log confirmed it had been ringing, save for a period of twenty minutes when there was another mechanical failure. At any rate, Watson informed Robertson that the captain should easily have

Watson's detested fog bell with Portlock Point Light in distance.

picked up the sound of the nearby Helen Point fog bell. Unfounded charges of incompetence, heaped upon all the other abuses he had suffered, shattered what little patience and decorum he had left. How dare they flog him with blame! ''Their tail is too Salty to swallow without fresh water,'' he retorted. Robertson should tell that captain ''he had too much old tom in his sack . . . he is always lost in the fog for he cant navagate A Boat in the fog and if he shit the Bed it would bee some ones fault and not his so tell him for me to clean his ears and stay at his Post and run in sounding distance of the bell at Portlock Point and he will hear it-if-it-is-in shape to bee run and if not he will hear the Hand Horn.''[14]

Some time in the summer of 1919 Watson picked up a copy of the Montreal *Family Herald and Weekly Star*, and read an article full of incomprehensible patter about how the Dominion's lighthouse keepers led an easy life. The Department of Marine and Fisheries apparently provided all necessities of life but food and clothing! This was too much for Watson and there was no containing his smoldering contempt. He had tried everything by now—letters to his MP, the agents, the minister. There was only this one last taboo to be broken, and George let fly with a searing thousand-word indictment of the federal government, the closest thing ever to a lightkeepers' manifesto, addressed to the *Star*'s editor. He began by illustrating the gap between his wage (which he reckoned at a dollar a day for sixteen-hour days) and the current price of everything from canned milk to butter and bacon. While other men across the land lay ''tucked up in their blankets where they are warm sleeping sound,'' he and his fellows sat awake on watch. ''I am not the only one on the Pacific Coast that can tell you that the lightkeeper has to clean and paint the lighthouse and any other buildings that may be at his station. . . . It is just a slave pen,'' he declared, offering to produce, as proof, Robertson's circular letter that forbade a keeper's leaving his station without written permission.

Having laid bare these general conditions, he described his own experience during that grim spring and summer of 1917, before his neighbours finally committed him to hospital, telling how CPR steamers passed the station twice a day, ignoring his distress signals. ''I crawled to the light on my hands and knees all that time,'' he went on, ''and lit the light until all the oil in the vapour tank was gone and then I had to let the light go out.'' Then there were the medical bills, still unpaid. Unbearable as it was, Watson's lot was just part of a greater corruption. How, he asked, could the government blame hard times on the War, yet sell army boots to the British government for $4.40 a pair when the same pair cost him more than twice as much? He gave dates; named names: Robertson, Cullison, Halkett, Hazen; and offered to supply reams of letters, pay stubs, and other documents to support his expose. He had worked all the regular channels with one result: ''These Honourable gentlemen that I have mentioned in this letter calls me a fool and says I am crazy,'' he wrote.

> Citizens of Canada, I think now that I was a fool to work here sixteen hours a day to protect lives and property for less than one dollar for eight hours service. . . now citizens of Canada I suppose I will be condemned as a Russian Bolshiviki by the Government [and] as an Agitator as is the word amongst the long stockin English but I am a true born Canadian and my Father was a true born Canadian my Grandfather was born in Scotland and served under General Wellington at Waterloo and I was in the Service in the Northwest against Riel the only one boy that I had lays in the blood stained sands of France whilst I am a slave under British lord isam or Military Isam I cant say which[.] is our Country ruled by British Lords[?] I would say our honourable Governor general gets a salary of one hundred thousand a year and he is a British lord about fifteen hundred a week to live on while I get fifty eight dollars a month to support my self and family on. It is time [for] every working man to think who makes the high cost of living and not blaim the farmer who we all look to for our bread and meat. The British Lord dont produce anything but foul wind and he cares nothing for Canada but the hundred thousand that he gets he dont care what child has no sugar so long as he has wine on his table a fine car to ride in and a fine lunch at the Club.

It was as if the red flag of revolution rather than a knotted, upsidedown ensign was snapping in the breeze from Portlock Point. Now was the time, Watson proclaimed, to shoulder arms against ''the men that sits in Ottawa and gambles on the necessaries of life as they are doing at this very time and telling you that it is War time that is making all the unrest.'' It all came down to this: ''Is there any one man that will see his child starve when those men has plenty in their larder? No, they will say we must have bread for our children too. There citizens is where the unrest starts whether it ends with bread or blood shed.''

> Signed G.A. Watson
> An abused lightkeeper
> Neither naked nor clothed,
> bare footed nor shod
> And there seems to be no
> help for the Widows Son.

In a postscript Watson implored the *Star*'s editor, ''[Print] the above . . . and see if it will help me or hang me [for] I cant live on that salary any longer and if it dont help me it will show some other poor fellow that might be mislead. . . .''[15]

It must have been a tremendous release for George Watson to unburden himself, to spill out the lightkeepers' insufferable plight in such a great dam-bursting purge of florid oratory, even if it seemed certain to cost him his job. All he had to look forward to now was the next issue of the *Weekly Star*. Incredibly, it seemed at first that Watson's manifesto might have some effect. The deputy minister wrote Victoria, demanding to know if the keeper's outrageous claims had any foundation. A.J. Dallain, the acting agent, explained that he received the same treatment as other lightkeepers of the same class. ''I am taking advantage of this occurrence to respectfully report that in British Columbia the salary attached . . . is not sufficient to support a lightkeeper and family,'' he declared. It was especially insufficient in Watson's case, where the keeper could not take on outside work and had no arable land to supplement his diet. ''I am of the opinion $70.00 a month salary is about the lowest for which a family so situated can obtain the necessaries of life in British Columbia,'' Dallain stated. In spite of his sympathies, however, no increase was granted.[16]

In June 1920 the Union Jack was again flying upsidedown at Portlock Point. Halkett landed and found Watson in bed, laid low by another ''severe attack of inflammation of the lungs and possibly a slight attack of pneumonia.'' And once more Watson stubbornly refused to budge unless he was carried out against his will, fencing with his cane. Halkett returned with a doctor from Saltspring Island. She acceded to Watson's wishes but advised that he be hospitalized if his condition deteriorated any further. The wheezing Watson informed them that he had been too broke to buy meat or vegetables for some time. After a furtive search through the larder, Halkett was stunned to find nothing but ''flour, coffee, milk and butter in the house.'' The superintendent left a labourer behind to ensure reliable operation of the light and bell.[17]

Wilby, the new agent, sent Halkett's report on to Ottawa as proof that Watson had ''only a very bare living''; if he had ''to pay a doctor or hospital bills, he must practically do without even the bare living.'' The keeper had recently placed his daughter in hospital. As a result of the added expense he was ''practically unable to buy sufficient food to keep his house going.'' Wilby reminded Ottawa of Dallain's recent plea to boost lightkeepers' wages to $70 a month after the *Weekly Star* featured Watson's bombshell manifesto. Now he recommended an increase to $100 a month.

Watson entered Lady Minto Gulf Islands Hospital (named for the Governor General's wife!) at Ganges on Saltspring Island on 21 June. A week later Dr. Sutherland allowed him to go home. His ''pneumonia had resolved,'' but Watson was ''very worried about financial matters,'' saying he could not ''afford sufficient food at present prices & could not pay for Hospital treatment.''

With Robertson gone, Watson started all over again on Wilby. ''Dear sur,'' he wrote, ''as I have been at this station for nine and one half years and have never yet received A living sallary and trusting that you are a man With A human heart and that you will inter seade in my behalf to see in the name of humanity that I receive A living Wages for the time I have to labour and stay here in exile as it may be called I am asking you to consider this just the Same as if you was in my Place and had A Wife and child to feed and cloth on that Pay.''[18]

Watson reckoned firewood cost $400 a year—money which might otherwise pay off his mounting burden of debt. Since his entreaties had so far come to nothing, he sent his well-thumbed bills and pay stubs to a Victoria lawyer. Lindley Crease wrote Wilby asking the department to pay for the keeper's fuel, adding, ''Neither this firm or any other client is financially interested in the result of this application.'' Though his letters to Ottawa prove he knew otherwise, Wilby replied that Watson's present salary should be sufficient. ''In the matter of fuel,'' he related, ''payment for this supply was cut off by the Department some few years ago.''[19]

The new marine agent did want to pay Watson's medical bills at least, but Hawken declared, ''The department does not see its way clear to recommend payment inasmuch as Lightkeeper Watson's case is not different from that of other Civil Servants who fall ill.'' If the department caved in and came to the aid of one man, it would have to help them all. There was only one recourse left: charity.

Wilby contacted the Red Cross in Vancouver. ''He has had considerable sickness in the family and is pretty hard up against it,'' the agent wrote. ''Whilst I would not wish to make a practice of asking the Red Cross Society to defray the whole of such expenses, yet in this case I am of the opinion were they to do so it would be a great benefit and I therefore recommend it.''[20]

Watson had not heard back from Wilby before 3 October and he took up his pen again to relate, with characteristic spleen, how he had spent $500 of his own money ''to try to live through the hard crisses of the War and other men has been having a good time Whilst'' his family had suffered. There were men working, ''or pretending to work,'' for government for three times his wages. ''So now Please regester this Kick to the Minister of Marine,'' he asked.

Three weeks later Wilby informed Watson that he had set up a ''scheme instituted by the Red Cross Society for the benefit and betterment of the living of lightkeepers on the B.C. Coast.'' The Red Cross would pay Watson's medical bills. Watson asked the agent to thank the society for helping him when he was in distress. ''State to them that I feel myself indebted to them and if ever I can repay them for their good samaritan heart, I will not forget that they paid the host at the inn.''

The Red Cross would also undertake a survey of lighthouses in British Columbia. ''The object of this survey was in no way to criticize lighthouse conditions,'' the society emphasized, '' but merely to ascertain what were the possibilities of suffering and distress arising that it would be clearly Red Cross work to alleviate.''[21]

Charity is often merely the postponement of misery, but Watson's ten-year crusade finally paid off in a modest salary increase to $70 a month in December 1920. The department even landed a new stove. George was overcome with gratitude. ''You might think I am to ignarent to acknoledg a kindness shone to me but I was Teached different When I was young and the deavle is not always as black as he is painted,'' he told Wilby, ''and I think you will find it so in my case you Will find if I am treated right I will do all in my power to treat you the same I suppose you Know When you are not treated right and I think that I Know When I am not treated right and I give you credit for what you have dun in my favour and I wish you every sucess in your respective office and that you may prosper there in and have all the happiness the World can afford you and your family.'' Watson noted that his increase was ''not large,'' but with back pay it would let them ''live hand to mouth.''

As for Halkett, Watson especially wanted to thank the superintendent, saying, ''[I remember] favours that he dun for me and famely When I was sick and When he found us With very little to eate in the Station but I hope to be Able sum day to repay him but I hope it Wont bee under the Same scercamstances as I was in at the time he was the good semaritan.'' In 1921, after another year's satisfactory service, Watson received a $30 raise in his annual salary.

In January 1921 a gale roared up the Gulf. For an hour and a half ''it was hard to tell Weather the station Would bee left standing or not.'' Shingles and siding went ''riping of the Kitchen shed and flying over the hill into the Water.'' Watson scurried out to check the damage and was struck by flying shingles. He hurriedly dodged back inside ''and trust to fate whilst the Storm raged the missus had the child ready so as to fly at the first brake in the tower.''

As Watson approached seventy, he had some cause for satisfaction. His thirteen-year struggle had won meagre and piecemeal increases in pay, and a new stove, and had established the precedent of allowing indigent lightkeepers recourse to charity. But too many bread-and-butter meals washed down with coffee and tinned milk had taken their toll. In September 1924 he spotted a leaking fifty-gallon oil drum in the storage shed. Watson tilted it on its rim to manoeuvre it into position to be tapped first, but he lost his footing and the five-hundred-pound drum fell on him, rupturing him on both sides. He was in constant agony, with his intestines squeezed between abdominal muscles, yet he wanted desperately to stay on one more year until the compulsory retirement age of seventy.

Wilby sent out application forms for superannuation. Since Watson had been working thirteen years before the 1924 act came into effect, he would have to pay in 5 percent of his back wages for all that time, and check off the same percentage from his current wages. Watson erupted in sheer red rage. ''That is a fine thing to do give the service of three hundred and sixty five days and three hundred and sixty-five nights in the year and then go hungry to give your pay to keepe a nest of stool pigons in Ottawa,'' he blasted.

> Not me. It is getting to close to being A Slave and that is one thing that I will never bee. They can make me give hot led but not the bread out of the mouth of my War orphant the old Scar is to deepe in my old heart for that and I dont Consider A light Keeper is in that class of service [to make contributions] for he is deprived of all pleasures and enjoyment he dont have a Sabith day let alone A public hollow day and those other service men has all these and their nights to. A light Keeper is A convict compared to these men and he is Always at Work at night When they are at rest now if those men Chose to give their labour and their pay to the Stool pigons I have nothing to say about it but I will not give one cent nor one hours labour to them I have paid taxes and revenues in Canada for forty seven years and now I have to pay three taxes on everything I pay and still the drones want the bread out of my mouth.

''Dont think that I lay any blame on you,'' he reassured Wilby, ''you had nothing to do With the [Superannuation] Act. . . . I suppose I will get bread for myself and war orphent and Wife after I am out of here just the same I trust in god and I never went hungry onley in this station.''[22]

The flag of distress was up within a month. This time a CPR steamer reported it and Halkett rowed over to Prevost Island. Watson lay in bed in a pool of agony, beyond hope. Without medical attention his crushed abdomen had suppurated ''until he. . .[was] now unfit to carry on his duties.'' Halkett left a man to attend the light and gave Watson a month's notice.

Wilby endorsed Halkett's recommendation. He wrote Watson that his case was now before the department in Ottawa, and thanked him ''for the loyal services'' he had given ''as Lightkeeper at Portlock Point.'' In November 1924 he received a gratuity of $188.33 and an annual annuity of $262.69—less than a third of his previous year's wages.[23]

If the Victoria agency expected relief from Watson's caustic diatribes, his replacement, J.N. Waugh, soon shattered their delusion. Indeed, from Waugh's tone, if not his grammar, it almost seemed that Watson had never quit the place. In June 1930 he complained, ''Sanitary arrangements at this station are appalling and a disgrace to any Civilized Government.'' The outhouse perched over a precipice and ''the night soil,. . .exposed to all the winds of Heaven,. . .[formed] a perfect breeding ground for flies during the Spring and Summer.'' When the wind blew offshore it was "a very pleasant advertisement to passing vessels." Ships hardly needed a fog bell to detect Portlock Point. There were no bathing facilities either. Two years later Halkett must have had a feeling of deja-vu when he came to Prevost Island. The station was in "good condition," but Waugh was "in poor health having asthma badly but . . . still capable of carrying on his duties."

In 1932, at the height of the Depression, the department reclassified Portlock Point as a "close in" station without a fog alarm, and cut wages. Waugh would be paid a mere $85 a month—less than Watson had been earning a decade before! Christmas week 1933 he begged the decision be reconsidered. Though lacking his predecessor's shrill tone, Waugh couched his appeal in identical terms: his work demanded a twenty-four-hour watch with never enough to pay a substitute or take a holiday. All other civil servants, "including those with salaries of many thousands a year," could take leave without hiring a substitute. Besides, he argued, Prevost Island *was* isolated, cut off by "two miles of storm swept water" from civilization. "It would therefore appear," Waugh concluded, "that the Department in making this decision is discriminating against the lowest paid subordinates. This seems very unjust. The trifling amount saved by this niggardly economy will be more than counterbalanced by loss in efficiency and will, in the long run, [be] subversive to morale."[24]

Three years later a doctor examined Waugh on the station and pronounced him "totally incapacitated for the performance of . . . [his] duties." Wilby refused to extend his sick leave and demanded he resign.

Sickness had always been poverty's constant companion at Portlock Point. Harry Georgeson was so sick in January 1942 that his wife May informed the agent, "He is very weak & cannot stand up & cannot eat." May and her two daughters, for their part, had been suffering mumps for a month. "Now don't worry about the station or us," she closed, "lots of people are in worse predicaments than we are today." This was a welcome attitude indeed, and Wilby expressed his appreciation of such spirit which, if "exercised by all and sundry," would make "a much better world."

In July 1941 A.H. Perry, district engineer for the Department of Pensions and Public Health, came away from Prevost Island with a water sample. Back in the lab, bacteriologists squinted through their microscopes, found it "highly contaminated," and recommended the water be boiled to kill off the high count of fecal coliform bacteria. Watson, Waugh, and Georgeson had been drinking their own sewage. Use of the well was discontinued and a system of gutters, drains, and cistern replaced it.[25]

If George Watson had lived long enough to climb out of a float plane with the *Vancouver Sun* reporters who visited his old home in March 1960, he would, for once, have been at a loss for words. "The life the Reddys lead on Prevost is as close to Nirvana, that Buddhist state of perfect beatitude, as most of us will ever come," the journalists exalted. Though Portlock's keepers still hovered near the poverty line—"as poor as any saffron-robed monk" on $3400 a year—Jack Reddy confessed his greatest mistake in life was that he "didn't come to the lighthouse 20 years ago." Obviously he knew little or nothing about the keepers and the conditions they

Portlock Point Light circa 1930.

had endured two decades earlier—men, women, and children who were sick shadows of the ''lusty, well adjusted, happy people'' who had inherited the place.

Thanks to radio, correspondence school, and regular visits from doctors on Saltspring Island, the Reddys, ''touch wood,...[hadn't] had to raise a distress flag.'' The article, ''Idyll of B.C. Coast Life,'' set the tone for countless more to come, as float planes and helicopters added the lights to reporters' beats, supplying convenient copy for slow news weeks, and granting wholesale poetic license in the bargain. What did it matter, anyway, if Jack Reddy could ''hardly afford a holiday'' when there were ''no buses to catch. No seasonal layoffs. No plaguing insecurity. No money in the bank, but no unpaid bills either''? Who, locked into a dead-end job and the suffocating boredom of suburbia, would not trade nine-to-five and their second car for Portlock Point, ''where every window of the Reddys' rent-free, four bedroom, red-roofed white-siding department of transport house admits what is among the finest weather and the most exciting scenery in the world''? Besides, as Thelma Reddy pointed out, ''There is no juvenile delinquency on this island.'' After all those hours of individual attention, with school work spread out on the kitchen table, her thirteen-year-old Michael stood far ahead of his peers academically, ''a sensible and capable boy, not bold or silly.''

Though they had no children to shield from the perils of delinquency, James and Marian Heanski were certainly pleased to replace the Reddys, trading Fiddle Reef's claustrophobia for Portlock Point. Nor could they call themselves convicts after Watson's fashion: they had their own power boat and often ran over to Saltspring Island, picked up their car, and caught the ferry home to Victoria for the day. After one such holiday on 1 March 1964, James kissed his wife good-bye and set out for the station.

Two days later, the keeper made his rounds after supper and noticed the beacon was out over on Enterprise Reef. He passed the information along with his scheduled weather report at 7:45 P.M., to be broadcast with the next notice to shipping. It was the last anyone heard from James Heanski. As the RCMP later reconstructed his final hour, the keeper lit a kerosene lamp, set it on an end table, and settled into his favourite stuffed chair with a book, looking up out the window at the light between pages.

Half an hour later Mrs. Bernard Stallybrass was watching the sun set over Prevost from her home on Galiano Island when she saw a lurid red-orange column of flame leap up from the roof of Heanski's home. She telephoned the local fire warden, and Victoria Coast Guard radio contacted the tender *Sir James Douglas* anchored in Montague Harbour.

While the *Douglas* made full speed for Prevost Island, Virginia Shirley at Port Washington, two miles away, was shaken by ''a terrific explosion.'' Thinking it was an earthquake, she ran outside, then watched in horror as a huge fireball splashed high over Prevost Island.

The B.C. ferries *Queen of Victoria* and *Queen of the Islands* interrupted their scheduled runs to send off shore parties while passengers lined the rails, aghast at the fiery spectacle ashore. The Coast Guard tender arrived and put a crew ashore with a portable pump. By this time Heanski's house was a raging inferno, and it soon forced the seamen into full retreat. The *Douglas*'s sister ship *Camsell* brought reinforcements with more pumps. By midnight the fire was under control. All that remained was the chimney, rising from a heap of steaming embers.

Heanski had disappeared. RCMP Corporal K.R. Aquilon organized a fruitless search of the island. He telephoned Marian Heanski that night and learned that James had set off for Portlock Sunday afternoon. A guard was posted by the ash heap, and next morning Heanski's charred trunk was found lying face down in the cellar, covered with smoking timbers. Under the corpse were the remains of his easy chair and a few fragments of carpets and floorboards. To the left of their grisly find, searchers unearthed the metal fragments of the coal-oil lamp.

So ended James Heanski's life, and with it the manned lightstation on Portlock Point, though the tower and fog bell survived unscathed. In 1969 the department installed an experimental wind generator to power a Xenon tube light, and placed Portlock Point on the lengthening list of unmanned lights.

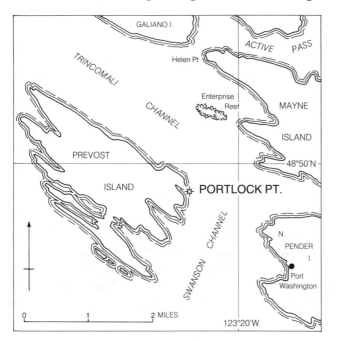

The Sisters

In August 1932 Colonel Wilby reminded his deputy minister in Ottawa, "It has always been our endeavour to keep a lightkeeper no longer than is absolutely necessary at Sisters Station." Since the light had gone into operation in 1898, seventeen keepers had come and gone, taking few pleasant memories of their stay away with them. Reiterating the policy three years later, G.E.L. Robertson, director of pilotage on the West Coast, referred the commissioner of lights to Sisters' position. It would take some hunting even with a lens to find that "speck on the chart. . . . In fact, Sisters Island has only a little bit of a walk around the rock," Robertson pointed out, "and it is a very hard place to get on and off in winter weather and a good place to leave a man on as short a time as possible."

If the commissioner had taken the trouble to unroll the chart across his desk, he would have found Sisters Island marked as two small black rocks only seventeen feet above high water, two miles southwest of Lasqueti Island off Parksville. In 1897 Gaudin had warned Anderson to expect more "urgent appeals for aids. . . owing to the increase of shipping to the North being caused by [the] rush to Alaska for gold. . . . This point," he counselled, referring to Sisters, "is the first that should be lit," and a small beacon, similar to those already operating at Bare Point and Berens Island, was installed that May. The light's range would be short, broken by surrounding points of land—two miles to the northwest and six miles southward. There was "not a shadow of danger to the east or west of it," the agent wrote, recalling an earlier inspection of the site, "and no outlying dangers on the shore of Lasqueti." A bell would suffice for a fog warning. It would be necessary, however, to provide room for a family and a means of storing potable water "in such a manner that it. . . [would] not spoil through the spray which no doubt. . . [would] be pretty well carried over the roof in high winds."

Gaudin visited Ronald McNiell, Sisters' first keeper, in March 1899. McNiell glumly reported "a long and tedious winter" since he had "not seen or spoken to any person since his installment in December." McNiell resigned in August. Next came a man named Higgins and his common-law Indian wife. In March 1900 Higgins reported she had left him because of the clamour of the fog bell every thirty seconds, which cracked plaster throughout the interior. Higgins followed his wife in February 1901, and Alfred Jeffries left in his turn in October 1902, "due to his wife's illness." Sisters, five years old, was already a revolving door.

Gaudin had high hopes for Benjamin Blanchard, a qualified machinist and expert boat handler, a man who could "perform repairs to the building without asking extra payment for every little bit he" executed.[1] Blanchard stuck it out for two years with his wife and daughter—something of a record at Sisters. During that time, rain fell in the house long after the weather cleared outside, since the contractor had failed to use galvanized shingle nails. Blanchard resigned in June 1904. His daughter had seriously injured her arm, and the salary was far too low.

W.C. Ferneyhough came in June and went in November. The department dismissed his complaints about Sisters' sodden conditions as "altogether exaggerated and misleading." If he had only followed the example of previous keepers "who took the precaution to place a pail under the drip to prevent any inconvenience," he would have had no grounds for complaint.[2]

Meanwhile, Ben Blanchard had heard somewhere that lightkeepers' salaries were about to go up by 24 percent. He came back to Sisters after Ferneyhough. The increase stemmed from Colonel Anderson's decision to build a fog alarm on the Rocks, and construction commenced in October 1907. Still, it was a long wait—almost too long. In March Gaudin received a desperate letter from Sisters by way of a fish packer. Blanchard was "on the verge of starvation." He implored the agent to send out the *Quadra* with provisions from Nanaimo.[3] When the diaphones went into operation, Blanchard's salary rose from $500 to $800, out of which he was required to pay an assistant. Mrs. Blanchard filled the bill and they achieved a measure of financial relief, but by May 1910 the keeper had decided to resign "to obtain educational advantages for his young family."

With waves constantly washing up and over the rocks, launching a boat and hauling it back up its ways was always a perilous venture. Walter Buss went out to

Early photo of Sisters Light.

pick up mail and to see a dentist on 19 November 1912 and was unable to land on his return. A fish boat was wrecked on one of the rocks around 7 P.M. that night and the crew cowered in the dark, screaming for help as the tide rose and heavy southeast swells tried to wash them off. By 8:30 P.M. on the twentieth, thinking their ''time was coming any minute,'' they waded across to the station after the wind suddenly changed direction. No one was home. ''Everybody in Nanaimo tell[s] me I have no business paying for the boat the way it was lost,'' the infuriated skipper informed the minister of Marine and Fisheries. ''If Mr. Buss had been there with the lighthouse boat there was no possible chance at all for us to lose our boat.''

Buss was immune to any reprimands. He had written asking for an increase in pay that August. When Robertson flatly turned him down, he decided, ''I cannot see my way clear to take on the duties of lightkeeper another year,'' and sent in his resignation to take effect 28 September. He had only remained at Sisters awaiting a cheque, now a year overdue, for expenses incurred putting up two technicians for a week in November 1911. ''I am not by any means running a charity boarding house for the Flotsam and Jetsam of the lighthouse and Marine service,'' he tersely reminded Robertson. ''Now to my mind I think it is casting reflections on the Marine and Fisheries Staff to have its employees beating the keepers out of board bills.''[4]

Robertson tried to make the keepers' toehold on Sisters somewhat more bearable—and infinitely safer—by proposing a mail service to the rock in March 1912. It would cost $72 a year. The commissioner of lights in Ottawa scotched his plan. After all, Sisters lay in the inside channel. Since ''so many other points throughout the Dominion'' were ''more unfavourably situated, . . . if the Sisters were supplied with a mail service, an inconvenient precedent might be established.''[5]

As the topography virtually ruled out raising children, the department always had great trouble enticing married men out to Sisters. Allan Couldery was anxiously awaiting an appointment in July 1918 when Robertson dispatched Gordon Halkett to Vancouver to offer him Sisters light. One glance at Halkett's photograph of the station was enough. ''Reluctantly, very reluctantly,'' Couldery was ''compelled to decline the Keepership of the Sisters Light Station.''

The department relied heavily upon bachelors, but men soon grew despondent alone out on that rock—with predictable results. Halkett reported in March 1915 that the station was ''kept in a disgraceful condition,'' and Robertson warned the keeper to give his ''pig sty . . . a thorough house cleaning,'' as he planned ''to be around in the vicinity . . . shortly.''

In June 1924 earwigs came ashore. Within a month of securing a beach head, they completely overran the station. ''Towards evening they come out and spread all over,'' Charles Clark reported. ''My wife's nerves are in such a shape I am afraid I shall have to send her away from the station.'' The Clarks had a two-year-old child, and the boy was defenceless against these ''most repulsive creatures,'' confined as he was to the dwelling and walkway around it.

The insects multiplied by the thousands, keeping pace with Clark's attempts to kill

Sisters.

them. At sunset they poured out from under the shingles and up through the floors, a teeming bronze mass which cracked and splattered underfoot. Night after sleepless night, the Clarks lay in bed with the child between them, listening to the insects plop from the ceiling and cupboards. Summer was a sweltering siege. "We have to keep all doors and windows tightly closed so you can imagine what it means living in a house during hot days without fresh air," Clark told the agent. "[I am] sending my wife and child down the first opportunity... & I would not think of bringing them back again to this station."[6] Dallain, the acting agent, sent out coal oil, disinfectant, and a mixture of flour and plaster of Paris, "a deadly bait" which had proved "effective for pests of this kind at other stations." Clark seems to have won the battle against his tormenters, but it was a pyrrhic victory. He resigned.

Joseph Pettingell doubtless astonished Wilby with a letter from Sisters in January 1925, expressing how "greatful" he and his wife were for their appointment, and promising to give his "undivided attention" to duties at the station. His first duty was to draw drinking water from the engine room reservoir and tote it up to the house in pails, for the water was well down in the cistern when the Pettingells first came ashore. Gratitude dwindled further by May 1926. When the *Berens* brought supplies that month, Pettingell put his wife aboard the tender, to be taken to hospital. "What is the sickness I am unable to say," he wrote Wilby, "but it has been coming for quite a few days, yesterday & last night, at times, her tongue clove and she could not move it." In October the keeper reported that they were all covered "with a terrible itching rash that spread over... [their] bodies with some rapidity." Every balm and ointment from their medicine chest had been smeared on with no effect. "With my wife it still comes on towards night, same with my oldest girl," Pettingell said, "with the younger one she is still covered from her feet up." Wilby recommended the Pettingells be transferred to Cape Mudge the following May, since they had been at Sisters "for some time [two years] and the environment. . .[was] beginning to affect their health."

There was always the awareness of living just beyond the sea's reach, a sensation quite literally brought home to Jonathon Fleming during Christmas week 1932, when a "terrific So. East gale" made him wonder if Sisters Rocks might be restored any minute to their pre-1898 condition. "The following is a list of damage done by the storm," the keeper wrote in a still-shaky hand:

> Boathouse wrecked and most of it washed away with equipment and personal effects. Boatways washed away and boat damaged. Owing to weight of oil drums the oil house was saved but was shifted on the foundation and sides and floor damaged. Outside walk of engine house badly damaged, and drain pipes leading to water supply tanks broken and washed away. Toilet, sidewalks and platforms all wrecked and washed away. Pipe guard rail round dwelling twisted out of shape and broken. During the storm I could not get away from the dwelling as heavy seas were breaking over platforms.

"As the rowboat is out of commission," Fleming concluded, "I will have to signal for Mr. Williams to come over from False Bay and get this letter for mailing."

If there is anything more terrifying than being all alone and under assault by seas capable of twisting two-inch metal pipe like pretzels, Charles Lundgren experienced

Sisters boat house demolished by storm.

it in August 1944. He had replaced S. Greenall, who had fled Sisters after only one week that summer. At one in the morning Lundgren awoke to a distant rumbling somewhere far below his bed. The dwelling began to "shake violent," shuddering on its foundation. All the windows smashed. Lundgren fled outside in his nightshirt, covered with plaster. The light was out and he climbed the tower to find a pane had fallen down and shattered the vapour tube. "I putt in plase Aladdin lamps then 4:50 A.M. an other shock struck the house but not so violent," Lundgren reported, "i whent outside and it was 15 craks in the foundation and the plaster from the siding fell down onto the floor." Six panes in the tower and "som of the lens wher cracked."

He had brought an assistant and fifteen dogs with him, turning the dwelling at Sisters into a reeking kennel, hopping with fleas. Victoria turned a blind eye to such conditions, knowing full well by now how difficult it was to lure people out to Sisters and keep them there. Art and Elsie Tolpitt took over in February 1945 and walked into a revolting situation. "Often wish you could see us both in our mad scramble to get straightened out," Elsie wrote W.L. Stamford, the agent.

> Oh Boy! What fun we're having along with the dirt, fleas & old relics of furniture. The smell is vanishing by degrees, thanks to the simple things in life such as soap, fresh air & darned good elbow grease. While at Cape Beale & Cape Mudge I developed a spare tire around the middle, but I've lost it already with perpetual motion ten hrs. a day, but now I see my knees are like sand paper, but so long as we get this place sweet and clean I don't mind. We can't even handle a thing but what our hands are covered in filth & grime; Never in my life have I seen such a contaminated mess that those two partners made this place. I'd like to string them up especially the dog owner; Every Floor was stained from his dogs.

Elsie looked forward to having Halkett come over, sometime in June, to witness the transformation they had wrought. First, though, she and Art promised to take their "Life Buoy Soap and walk off the rocks and really go to town on [them]selves . . . . But with it all," she confessed, "I must admit I'm very happy & contented & really like the life of a light keeper's wife . . . ."

In March 1947 Elsie was seriously ill and the department granted the Tolpitts three weeks' leave. Art resigned and Lundgren, the detested dog owner, came back—just in time for one of the coldest winters ever on the West Coast. Water froze in the pumps, rupturing pipes. Lundgren warned, "If this violent cold dont stopp the Coal Box will be empty." He was shovelling two hundred pounds a day yet Sisters Rock was "a iceberg . . . a decepart place to be in." Moreover, Lundgren was now almost incapable of packing more coal. "You have neglected to send hoist wire that i ordert 8 monts ago," he reminded Morrison. "Hoist wire rotten and brocke and the Raol [roll?] fell a topp of mi injured mi legs and left hand i have been crippled for a mont—Just for the neglegkt of the Department to send safe equipment."[7]

R.B. Roberts lost the station boat to a high tide and a fierce gale from the northwest in November 1959. ''The storm struck with such violence & so suddenly that I barely had time to secure a line to . . . [the boat] before it was swept over along with the part of the landing to which it was lashed,'' Roberts recalled. ''Storm damage to all parts of the station, the dwelling excepted, is a regular occurance.''

Half a century of such assault and battery had left the dwelling in a ramshackle condition. The department considered moving the station over to Lasqueti Island, with power supplied by submarine cable. Instead, a concrete structure combining engine room, tower, and living quarters, went up on the original site in 1967. Sisters was converted to a ''crib'' station, like Sand Heads, with keepers landed by helicopter for two-week stints. Even at that, two weeks at the Sisters can seem too long.

Above: Sisters 1981. Jim Ryan photo. Below: Phillip and Edmund Cox.

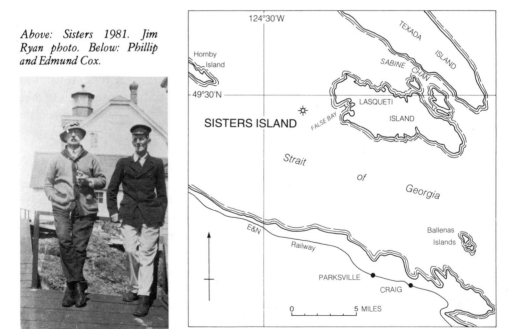

Cape Mudge

Quadra and Sonora Islands form a cracked wedge, prying Vancouver Island apart from the mainland, and channelling the Strait of Georgia into the maze of capillaries in Discovery Pass and Johnstone Strait beyond. Tides don't run there; they race through the narrow channels in an ominous, pulsating surge up to twelve knots, sweeping everything afloat along with them. From the polished stone beach at Cape Mudge one can watch power boats head full throttle into the anarchy of the current, engines growling in protest as it drives them helplessly backward. "This part of Gulf of Georgia forms a sort of playground for the waters," Captain Mayne warned in 1860, "in which they frolic utterly regardless of tidal rules." They relax for a scant ten minutes every six hours when the tide turns.

Casualties of this tidal playground, such as the Victoria freighter *Standard* in 1890, usually joined the catalogue of mystery wrecks, going down in minutes with all hands. Through fog or squalls their crews rode a roller coaster, blindfolded, to their doom. The alternating current masticated hulls and cargos, regurgitated them as flotsam back down the strait, then sucked it all up the narrows again. Such was the fate of the steamer *Estelle*, bound north from Nanaimo to supply a lumber camp in 1892. Four years later Bob Hall, postmaster and storekeeper at the Indian village at Quathiaski Cove, was swept into oblivion. The eighty-six-foot *Petrel* of the Coastal Towing company, en route to Alert Bay in 1952, disappeared so fast that her crew never even had time to send a distress call.

Captain Dionisio Galiano first named the southern cape of Quadra Island Punta de Magallanes, but in July 1792 Vancouver rechristened it in honour of Zachary Mudge, his first lieutenant on the *Victory*. At Quathiaski Cove, Vancouver encountered a large settlement of Indians "who uniformly conducted themselves with the greatest civility and respect." The department responded quickly to the needs of Klondike traffic, and erected a lighthouse on the Cape in 1898. John Davidson, a fiercely independent Scotsman, took over the station that year. What with regular mail delivery to Quathiaski Cove, and neighbours and friends within walking distance, Cape Mudge was a far cry from its isolated island counterparts. There was even a steady supply of outside visitors. When the fog spilled into the narrows, vessels bound north and south in that high season of gold fever let down their anchors to wait for the right tide, and local residents rowed out to the moored ships to trade news and gossip over the rails, while Davidson's hand horn bawled away in the background. As a result, the Davidsons led comparatively ''normal'' lives, free from the rigours of isolation which took such a heavy toll in health and sanity. John did suffer from failing eyesight, however, and applied for leave to see an optometrist in September 1909. He had not taken a holiday for eleven years and thought the department might provide and pay a relief. They refused.[1]

In spite of weak eyes, Davidson was still able to perform the usual lightkeeper heroics. The steamship *Cottage City* had had nine years' service on the east coast before she passed through Panama in 1899 and began freighting passengers up to the gold fields. On 26 January 1911 the 230-foot vessel cleared Seattle bound for Alaska. She was soon swallowed up in blinding snow squalls. At 2 P.M. Captain Jensen steered into the mouth of Discovery Pass, expecting to take a bearing from Cape Mudge almost any minute. Fifteen minutes later the steamer collided with a rock reef two miles south of the light.

Davidson was crouching outside, pumping his horn. He knew there was no way anyone could make shore in a direct line, not with a heavy sea sluicing through the

Cape Mudge in Davidson's era.

channel. He scuttled down the beach waving a white flag, and directed the lifeboats to put in around the point in a sheltered bay west of the light. The first boat came ashore with "all the lady passenger. . . they were 14 ladys and one child about 4 year and the snow was so depth they had to walk on the beach but i thought i would never get them to the house," he reported.

> They were all very cold and i gave them all a little hote rum and they were soon all right and then the men was comen all the time so the too cooks came and we got them to work and about 9 PM the Captain came so after he had some thing to eat the too bed rooms was cleared and the ladys put to bed so what the bed did not hold had to get on the floor they were men laying in the light room in all shapes and they were some sleeping in the lantern but down stairs was full right up so by the time they had all breakfast in the morning the steamer came in sight and by 11 A.M. they were all going but if you would see the house with dirt and wet and Mrs. Davidson was very sick and could do very little I had to keep the fires going all night they were all wayes call for coal and i told them the government was to poor to supply coal at Cape Mudge Station . . .
>
> Sir i dont no if you can read this or know but my nerve is not Right settle yet and I have a *bad* cold.[2]

Coming five years after the *Valencia* trauma, and Minnie Patterson's rescue of the *Coloma*'s crew at Cape Beale, Davidson's exploit boosted Marine and Fisheries' prestige considerably. Henry Thompson, commander of the Marine Service, forwarded a fifty-dollar cheque for the keeper, which Gaudin passed along with the homily: "It is a pleasing incident in connection with this Department that they do not overlook any act of kindness or heroism of their service, worthily rendered in your case."

The Davidsons had many more letters of gratitude too—from the *Cottage City*'s passengers and crew. John insisted he would always treasure Gaudin's most, though, "in Remmbrance of our Dear old Superintendent and Agent," adding, "Sir I only did my Duty but i dont want know more wreck while I am hear."

Gaudin heartily agreed. On 14 February he called Colonel Gourdeau's attention "to the urgent necessity of replacing the mechanical horn with new diaphones." Twenty-one "Masters and Pilots of American Steamships plying these waters" had signed a petition in November, pointing out the inadequacy of Cape Mudge's hand horn. They insisted Ottawa replace it without delay with "a first class automatic signal." After Gaudin retired, Victoria shipmasters continued to badger Robertson, claiming the racing tides ruled out "making good their course up the Strait for any distance" without a reliable fog horn. All petitions went unheeded until 10 January 1912 when the manager of the CPR Coast Service wrote Captain Robertson demanding to know when the shipping of the coast might "obtain the benefit and safeguard of this fog alarm." Colonel Anderson gave his approval within the week.

Halkett landed at Cape Mudge that June and began surveying a plan for the fog alarm building. The only safe and effective site lay directly in line with the light, so they would have to raise the tower six feet. "Owing to him proving such a satisfactory Light-keeper for nearly 20 years," Halkett recommended Davidson be retained to man the new fog plant. "Now Sir i want a favour from you," Davidson told Robertson, "i want to worken on them buildes you know i dont get much of salary and Mrs Davidson was six weeks in the hospital last winter so that put me behind." He boasted that he could turn his hand "to any think," and had done so, putting up other buildings over two decades although, he added, "i never got know pay for all my worken."[3]

No sooner was the diaphone installed and the new concrete tower poured than the captain of the *Princess Beatrice* charged that he could not hear it when he slipped by the Cape in heavy fog on 3 August. Davidson explained that the timer was faulty, yet he could plainly see over to the island all night. "If the fog was dence i would have hand horn goen," he wrote. Although the captain had never complained before, he had a poor record, and Davidson suggested that "it would be a good job for the Government to get a pillar of fir[e] to go before the Captain on that boat and then she would not go on the rocks so often."[4]

The testy Davidson brooked no interference from Victoria and complained bitterly whenever crews were sent out. "I dont want know man to fixe the Lamp if you send what i want i will soone fix it," he declared in August 1911. "And i never send for anything i dont require." When supplies failed to arrive, he scornfully accused clerks of filing his requisitions in the "waist" basket, and lectured Gaudin that lightkeepers should never be expected to do their duties without supplies. After opening Robertson's August 1911 circular letter that warned all keepers against leaving their stations without written approval, Davidson scoffed, "I am 13 year hear and i never had a holy day for the Department and if you call that a white man country i have another name for it."[5]

From his vantage point on the Cape, John and Annie Davidson watched a twenty-year procession go by and witnessed a revolution in waterborne commerce. "I mind the day when ye kem roond the Cape," he told John Antle, an Anglican missionary. "Y'r sail was up but it was no pullin' and yet ye gaed along at a guid rate. I was fair surprised till someone tell't me about the contraption called the gasoline engine, and then I kenn'd about ye."[6]

Even if Davidson gave Gaudin and Robertson a break from the raving tone of so many desperate, marooned men and women, the attitude of the "hero of the *Cottage City*" underwent a profound change in the post-diaphone years. The keeper was fifty-one when the plant was built in 1912. Like Walter Erwin at Point Atkinson he had no inkling it would more than quadruple his work load. In addition to bucking and splitting driftwood for fuel, both Davidsons now shared a twenty-four-hour watch since the Scot could ill-afford an assistant.

Five years later he wrote H.S. Clements in Ottawa (one wonders if the new MP had any time for other work than dealing with impoverished lightkeepers), demanding a raise in pay. "The work is too much for one man," he said, "and own to the increase in liven there is nothing in it." When he learned that Tom Grafton at Point Atkinson, and Harold Okell at Trial Island made $300 a year more for running an identical fog alarm plant, it was the last straw. On 18 September 1917 he forwarded his resignation—"to take place as soon as you can get a boat hear." He had no regrets, saying, "[I have] always tried till do my Duty i have give 14 years of the best of my life to the Dept. and in that time i never was on board a government boat or never had a holy day from them.'"[7]

Robertson asked Davidson to reconsider. In any event it would take at least six weeks to find a replacement. Davidson peevishly pointed out in six weeks he would be moving in the winter rain. The work, he repeated, was just too much for one man. The wages beggared them. He should at least get an increase to hire an assistant. "They must think in Ottawa that Lightkeeper lives on air," he snorted.

The Davidsons spent one last winter at Cape Mudge. In April John appealed, in vain, for a two-week leave of absence: "We are boath sick and our eyes is getting so bad we can hardly see anything."[8] All that summer they went about their work, the blind leading the blind, until the night of 12 October when he sent a garbled message: " . . . thick fog nothing to do but i am leafing hear to night the Agent at Victoria is only makie a fool of the Keeper at Cape Mudge." Deputy Minister Hawken granted them $500 a year as a pension "for faithful service during 20 years." Every year after, Davidson wrote from Vancouver, thanking the department for this "God send," adding his "kindes Remmber and all good wishes to all old Friends in the Marine Dept."

Herbert W. Smith came from the Nootka light to replace Davidson. He also inherited his salary and immediately wrote Colonel Wilby asking for a raise. "I would not trouble you," he wrote, "but the High cost of living which has apparently not reached its limit Drives me to it." He had his son for an assistant but the boy had found more "lucrative employment." Smith's arthritic wife perished in the Spanish flu epidemic of 1919 and now he was alone at the station. The department still paid $300 less at Cape Mudge, since it had less fog than Point Atkinson, even though Wilby explained to Ottawa that duration of fog was at best a poor index for salaries since a night watch must still be kept. In April Wilby offered Smith a promotion to Cape Beale at a higher salary.

But the keeper wanted to stay. That May Wilby granted him three weeks' leave without pay. Herb had "a friend coming out from England," and had "promised to meet her on arrival as the object of the visit is matrimony." He and his boy had been "batching" since his wife's death, he confided, "so I think you will understand a Housekeeper and the refreshing influence of a Woman would be appreciated."

Unfortunately, Smith had little time left at Cape Mudge to enjoy the influence, refreshing or otherwise, of his mail-order bride. In April 1927 he was forced to "relinquish" his position due to ill health. He had been suffering recurring fits of dizzyness (possibly from mercury poisoning) for some time. He spent the winter bedridden, laid low by "a bad attack of flu and a touch of pneumonia." On two occasions, he related, his "Mind went completely blank for ½ an hour." His doctor advised Smith he was "at the end of. . .[his] active career," listing high blood pressure, failing kidneys and bladder, "and Heart not beating good." Smith was sixty.

The light had been fitful and erratic all that winter and spring, with its vapour tubes continually choking up with carbon and sputtering out. "I have frequently to rush up to get a New Tube in to keep the light in operation," he explained. Smith dreaded the very real possibility of falling down the iron steps in one of his black-outs, yet he was sorry to leave. "I like the work and like the station," he wrote Wilby. Moreover, the keeper had made no provision for his old age, aside from an annuity fund, and deemed it "a personal favour" if the department could help him out in this matter.⁹

Joe Pettingell moved his family up to Cape Mudge from Sisters Rocks on 1 December 1927. Right from the start Cape Mudge had been a coveted station, offering ready access to school and all the other trappings of civilization, but if Pettingell had been attracted for that reason, he soon changed his mind. In July 1931 he wrote Gordon Halkett a remarkable letter, asking to move back into isolation. "We appreciate being alone more than we do by being in a community where temptation not only has caused us much unpleasantness & is certainly doing my family much harm," he confessed. "In fact right from the beginning of coming to this station, bad luck, unpleasant words and outside temptation seems to have followed us." Pettingell hoped that Halkett could read his "reason for wanting a personal interview" between the lines.

However tantalizing it may be to wonder what lurid temptations were revealed later in the privacy of Halkett's office, Pettingell's letter illustrates the dilemma of long-term isolation. Those who thrive away from the real world sometimes pay a heavy price, losing the knack of give and take which governs all social relationships. As these skills atrophy, they become social cripples, unable to function fully beyond their personal shores. Lightkeepers today know well what Pettingell meant, even if his letter raised a few eyebrows in Victoria fifty years ago. As high as a holiday or trip to town might figure in lightkeepers' priorities, the attraction soon pales when they find they have been missing the worst, along with the best, that society has to offer, and they usually end up craving the peace and monotony of isolation much more than they had wanted to escape it.

The Pettingells apparently survived their withdrawal from isolation unscathed, and in the end, it seems, were delivered from "temptation." Since he could not afford an assistant, Joe's older daughter Dorothy began helping him in 1931, and continued until 1943. In the autumn of 1941 Pettingell tumbled down the tower steps and ruptured a vein in his leg. A doctor in Campbell River diagnosed phlebitis and amputated his great toe. Upon their return the Pettingells found a relief keeper named Berry had been engaged and had been provided with a paid assistant. "I can not help resenting this injustice," Mrs. Pettingell wrote the marine agent,

Above: Joseph Pettingel at Cape Mudge. Below: Cape Mudge 1981. Jim Ryan photo.

"knowing as I do the terrible long hours my husband has put in at this station." Why, she demanded, had they not been willing to pay an assistant before? "I cannot help it, but I think my husband has never had a square deal."[10]

As soon as Pettingell had been released from hospital, the agent came calling. He suggested that the keeper resign and settle for whatever superannuation he had coming. Incensed, Pettingell wrote a letter to Victoria, pointing out that he had been injured at work. Surely he deserved his full superannuation if he quit, but he proposed, instead, that he be transferred to work in the yard in Victoria. It was a futile appeal. The Pettingells left Cape Mudge in 1943.

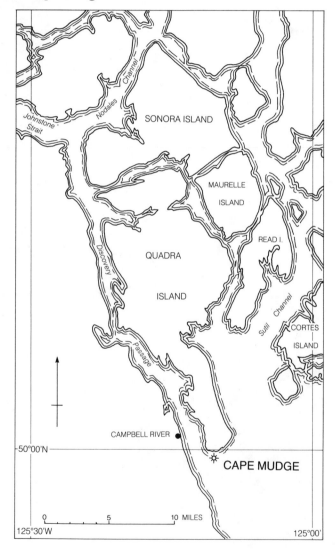

In the spring of 1794 Lieutenant Eliza, in command of the Spanish survey vessels *San Carlos* and *Saturnina*, stood at the rails of his ship, amazed by the size of a pod of whales surfacing near a group of islands about two miles offshore from present-day Parksville. Eliza immediately dubbed them the Ballenas Islands. British Admiralty charts mistakenly labelled the group "ballinac," perhaps misreading earlier maps, but the error was corrected by the Geographic Board of Canada in 1905.

The group consists of two larger and a number of smaller islets. The northernmost towers 250 feet above high water, providing precarious footing for a few trees, and terminates in a sharp, bare nipple of rock. The southern island is wooded. From seaward they appear as a single piece of land, but are separated by a channel "less than a cable wide" at its eastern entrance. In 1898 the *British Columbia Coast Pilot* warned that no safe passage lay between the two islands, "steep and bold on all sides . . . conspicuous after passing westward of Nanaimo."

In September 1898 Captain Smythe took the *Egeria* out on yet another survey of navigation routes, concentrating this trip upon the increasingly crowded Inside Passage. Affirming that "the number of vessels passing these points is continually on the increase," he advised Gaudin to put a manned light and fog alarm on Ballenas as soon as possible. Gaudin immediately endorsed the recommendation, and, upon securing Colonel Anderson's approval, sent out a survey crew from Victoria in May 1900.

The whole agency was in a flap that spring and summer. Minto, the Governor General, was on his way from Ottawa. There was nothing like gold braid and all the grandiloquent trappings of aristocracy to excite Victorians in the Victorian Age, and the Department of Marine and Fisheries laid grandiose plans for a viceregal cruise on the *Quadra* up to the Yukon. James Gaudin had no time to spare for any personal inspection of Ballenas. Instead he directed his foreman, George Frost, to approach William Brown, a resident on the island, who, Gaudin believed, ''was pointed out the position'' for the light.

As a result, the tower at Ballenas went up in the wrong place, atop a high knoll in the centre of the south island.[1] It was a wooden rectangular design, ''surmounted by a square lantern painted red,'' and exhibiting a fixed white light seventy-five feet above sea level, visible for eleven miles. The fog alarm stood almost a quarter mile away near the shore.

The island was originally the personal property of Charles Drummond. Drummond had drowned rowing home from Nanaimo one night, but in his will he had bequeathed Ballenas to his Indian wife Maggie. Maggie, in turn, married Wilhelm Betait, a German immigrant who later anglicized his name to Brown, and William Brown was appointed first keeper of the misplaced light. Soon after taking charge, Brown sent off to Germany for his nephew Wilhelm Betait to come and assist him.

In May 1905 James Gaudin landed at Bamfield in the course of an inspection of the West Coast lights, and walked up to the cable station. A radio operator handed him a bizarre message just copied from Ballenas: ''SEND LADY RELIGIOUS DETECTIVE AFTER DAVE McROBERTS SETTLER ON LASQUETI ISLAND HE IS IN VICTORIA NOW I HAVE LEFT THE STATION SEND A MAN.'' From the Nanaimo City Police, Gaudin learned that the lightkeeper was ''now in the city lock up quite insane and irresponsible for his actions.'' The agent cabled a friend in Nanaimo to arrange for a temporary replacement, and broke off his tour ''to investigate the trouble.''[2] Upon landing at Ballenas Gaudin found a relief, John Allen, in charge, and learned from Maggie that she had committed her husband to the lunatic asylum at New Westminster, ''he being hopelessly insane and violent.'' She promised to continue to man the light until Brown's nephew arrived.

Apparently there was still some hope for the deranged keeper—Brown was back on Ballenas that June. On 21 April 1906, however, Captain Foote of SS *City of Nanaimo* telegraphed: ''LIGHTKEEPER BALLINAS WANTS YOU SEND IMMEDIATE RELIEF, APPARENTLY INSANE.'' Gaudin called in the B.C. Provincial Police who frog-marched Brown back to his rubber room at New Westminster. He never came out again, and Gaudin succeeded in appointing Wilhelm Betait in his place.[3]

No sooner had the crazed keeper been shut away than Gaudin was forced to confront his oversight of six years before. In its mistaken location, Ballenas light was worse than none at all since it stood in the centre of the island and gave no bearing for either shore line nor the channel. The CPR, Grand Trunk Pacific, Union Steamship Company, and Greer Coyle Towboat Company all began working the now-familiar levers, going over the agent's head to force Gaudin to move the light.

In June 1906 they won. The deputy minister wired Victoria, ordering Gaudin to make the move. ''Get best advice possible and locate as seems best taking everything

Engine room, Ballenas Island Lightstation.

into consideration and duly weighing reasons for which light was placed on highest point of the island,'' he ordered. Gaudin was hardly anxious to dredge up the reason for *that* fiasco, especially since Gourdeau ordered that the new structure was to be ''permanent and no mistake should be made as to location.''

In the course of his consultation with ships' captains, the agent learned that the fog alarm building, which stood near the shore on the northwest tip of the island, could often be seen when the light was obscured. By now most traffic bound north or south had grown accustomed to using the outside channel—the inside channel was suitable only in fair weather. Ships setting out from Nanaimo would pick up the light and horn as they reached and rounded the Snake Island bell buoy. ''If they were going North by turning and steering for the light, they are outside all dangers,'' he concluded. In June the Nanaimo pilots underwrote the new site and Gaudin had materials ''on the ground,'' waiting for the go-ahead from Anderson.

Before deciding finally on the new location of the tower, Gaudin put up a dwelling for Betait next to the fog alarm. Betait had continued to live with Maggie Brown, but by the spring of 1910 their relationship had soured. His brother, ''a qualified engineer,'' had emigrated and shared their cramped quarters. Gaudin learned that Maggie consorted ''with her Indian relatives and . . . [was] an unfit person to have charge of the light.'' Moreover, as long as they lived with her on the southwest island, the Betaits had to row a mile over to the fog alarm—and a long hazardous mile it could be through winter gales. In February Maggie ''turned them out of the house.''

In January 1912 the wooden tower on the South Island was pulled apart, taken across piece by piece, and resurrected on North Ballenas. Two years later the fixed white light was replaced by an occulting version with a flash each twenty seconds.

Arthur Broughton Gurney came down from Pine Island to replace Betait in the fall of 1912, bringing his wife and three children, and a reputation for shiftlessness

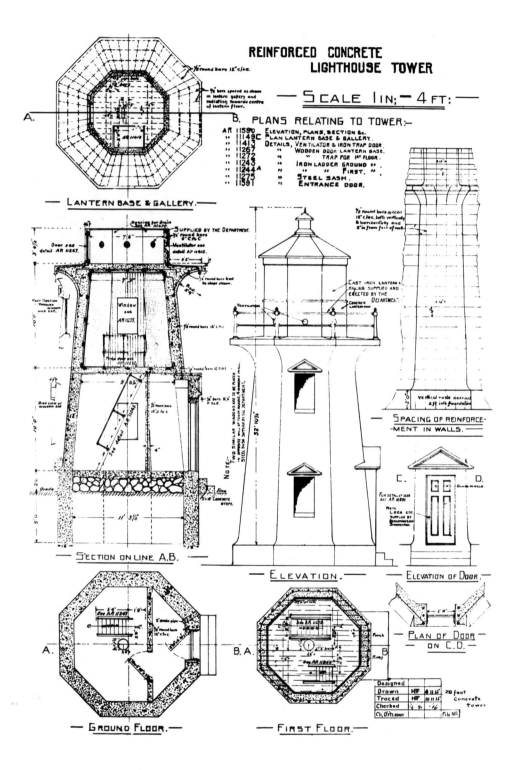

Building second station, Ballenas Island.

and hard drinking. During his five-year stint at Pine, Gurney had incessantly pestered Gaudin, and Robertson after him, for higher pay and a less isolated station. Ballenas seemed to fulfill the latter need for a time.

In a ploy to augment his income, Gurney wrote his MP, H.S. Clements, that December, proposing to dispense with the required male assistant. Incensed by Gurney's embarrassing though characteristic breach of discipline, Robertson reiterated his standing policy: "All lighthouses, large and small, in British Columbia that have fog alarms in connection, have always had an assistant which the Lightkeepers have to pay themselves." To do otherwise "would disorganize the service." The sheer labour involved in running a horn for three days, or "even as long as a week at one continuous stretch," was more than one man could bear. If the horn shut down because its keeper "was having a needed rest," the agent argued, "I think you will agree [it] would not cover us if there were any lives lost. . . ." Besides, all keepers had to "go a considerable number of miles by water for mail and supplies," and if a man left his wife and children alone, "some serious accident" might result.

Public safety always overrode salaries, though Robertson asked Clements to help increase allowances for hiring assistants. "Besides the lonely life they lead and the strict attention they have to give to their duties," the agent explained, "they are in no way compensated for the services rendered." Yet Gurney had willingly taken a cut in pay to bring his family closer in. If he did not have to pay an assistant he would be pocketing more than he had earned at Pine Island, where an assistant was indispensable.

Brown may have been mad but at least he was quiet, like Betait after him. Gurney, by contrast, packed a bulging file with correspondence, much of it barely legible (perhaps owing to his habit of stretching his budget to order scotch whiskey by the case) and concerned, above all else, with money and moving. He wanted a carpenter sent over to build a water closet. "A lightkeeper capable of taking charge of the Ballenas Station should have enough intelligence and skill to erect a rough small dwelling of this kind," Robertson dryly replied. His station was slovenly—"in marked contrast to the majority of lightstations." Canvas slings and snotters were left to rot on the ground, and he seldom even wiped down his engines. Neighbours over at Craig's Crossing mailed Robertson vivid descriptions of the threats and scathing abuse they endured while Gurney was "away on a debauch."[4]

Altogether it was conduct which hardly endeared him to Robertson, whose own reputation, along with the department's, rode with his keepers. On the outbreak of war in August 1914, Gurney wrote asking for a supply of rifles and ammunition. "The only conclusion I can come to is that you are either suffering from reported visits to Nanaimo, or badly scared," Robertson fumed. "You will in future stay at your station and not be running around the country as you are doing." He threatened to report Gurney to Ottawa if he heard "of any more carryings-on at Nanaimo and other places," as he was "getting heartily sick of the reports reaching" him.[5]

He had a problem on his hands, no doubt about it, but, perhaps out of respect for Gurney's years of service, Robertson merely reproached him, even after both Nanaimo and Vancouver pilots complained in January 1915 that the light did "not receive the ordinary care it" required. The agent thus lay the cornerstone of a policy which allowed difficult, dispirited, even dangerous men to remain in charge of their

Ballenas.

lights while assistants came and went as if through a revolving door. Meanwhile, men who might have given their best to the calling kept looking for work.

The war held out a great opportunity for Gurney to boost his income and prove his patriotism. A wartime order-in-council allowed government employees to enlist, "with the consent of the head of the Department," and continue to receive full salaries during their service. By enlisting, Arthur Gurney could turn Ballenas over to his wife and draw army pay as well. A Boer War veteran, he must have known he was overripe for cannon fodder at thirty-nine. He signed up in 1915 and turned Ballenas over to Anna.

By August 1916 the keeper's slipshod maintenance was telling on the fog engine. Anna wrote Victoria asking for an "expert overhaul." "I have no option but to say . . . that this is a matter of pure carelessness," Robertson answered, promising to report any failure of the horns to Ottawa.

For two prosperous years the war passed Gurney by. During that time Robertson's gorge rose time and again as letters from residents around Ballenas continued to plop on his desk. John Vickers wrote from Craig's Crossing in March 1917, relating that, over the course of a four-day "debauch," Gurney had caused an ugly scene at a rooming house, accusing Vickers—in language "that would make a dog blush"—of stealing his whiskey, and threatening him in front of witnesses right at the dinner table. Later he turned "fighting whiskey crazy" when Vickers refused to row him home. "I don't see why I have to tote a whiskey crazed light house keeper at his beck and call," Vickers wrote, adding that he was reporting the incident to the Provincial Police.[6]

Another letter came from Arthur Cecil White, a super patriot from Mistaken Island, who had watched "a certain unspeakable, diseased, rotten-gutted Teutonic abortion named Wilhelm Betait" land at Ballenas. The German was apparently "persona gratisimma" with the Gurneys, but White insisted that his very presence threatened the "regermanization" of the Ballenas Isles. All lightkeepers now had orders to prevent Germans from landing at their stations, but Anna Gurney offered an acceptable explanation: she had lent him the station boat to fetch supplies. Nevertheless, Robertson ordered her "to take every precaution to save [the Department from] letters of this kind."

Gurney finally got into uniform in 1917 and served as an officer recruiting and transporting troops to England. Now that their finances were in better shape, the Gurneys began to seek a shore station with ready access to school. In Vancouver in January 1918 Gurney met a friend from the Quathiaski Cannery on Quadra Island and learned that John Davidson intended to resign his post at Cape Mudge. Anna immediately wrote Clements. "I have three children who have never been able to attend school," she complained, "and our salary is so small it does not meet running expenses, not to mention sending them ashore to school." She reviewed their eleven years' service and her husband's "war service." Even if the Davidsons were not leaving, they should, she declared. After all, they had no children and could easily exchange Cape Mudge for Ballenas.

This was the second time the Gurneys had detoured the department and taken their case directly to an MP. The irate agent informed Clements that he had taken the Gurneys off Pine Island in 1912 because "at that time they contended they would be able to have their children educated if they were given Ballenas station." With a commissioned officer's pay, as well as his wage, Gurney was "better off than the average lightkeeper," more than able to foot the bills for sending children away to school. For his part, Robertson was lobbying the provincial government to educate lighthouse children, even "if only through a correspondence course."

The Davidsons had joined the service in 1898 and, "during the best of their lives, they were only receiving a very small salary." Though they were childless, Robertson still wanted them at Cape Mudge. "In their old age they should be allowed, if they wish, to remain at this station which has been their home for twenty years," he insisted. Besides, if Cape Mudge were available there were many keepers who would have priority over the Gurneys for reasons of "long service, younger families, and a better record."[7]

In October, when the Davidsons resigned and Herbert Smith shipped down from Nootka to the coveted light, Gurney complained bitterly to Clements. "My wife wanted so much to get ashore. . .[and] I have also done my bit soldiering," he bragged. "I think I might have got consideration before a man who has not been in

Ballenas Island Lightstation 1981. Jim Ryan photo.

the Light service as long, nor yet has been a soldier.'' He wrote Robertson, two years later, to say that he had to send his children, now in their teens, to boarding school so he had less income than when he came on the lights fourteen years earlier. He pledged he would be ''deeply grateful'' for a shore station around Vancouver or Victoria at the same salary. It would also be a balm to Anna who felt ''this isolated life very much.'' At long last, in January 1921, word came confirming Gurney's transfer to Active Pass.

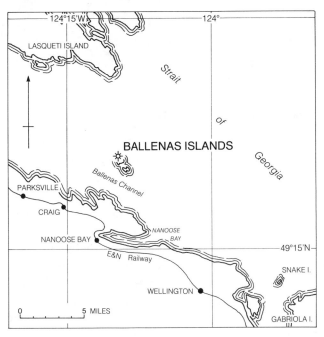

Gordon Odlum lighting up at Ballenas.

Porlier Pass

orlier Pass light can be considered a benchmark—the first built to cater exclusively to steamships. Up until the 1900s the riptide swirling between Galiano and Valdez Islands had rendered the pass unsafe for sailing vessels. As late as 1905 the *B.C. Coast Pilot* warned that the channel was "narrow and...rendered still more so by sunken rocks; the tidal streams run from 4 to 9 knots, and overfalls and whirling eddies are always in the northern entrance. CAUTION—In consequence of the numerous dangers existing in Porlier Pass, mariners are advised to avoid that passage." Even so, masters of the new steamships were already throwing the *Pilot*'s caution to the winds (which they could now ignore as well), and brazenly cut through the pass to save time en route to Ladysmith's coal chutes. Only those with long service or good memories recalled the fate of the *Del Norte*.

In October 1868 her captain brought her out of Nanaimo after refuelling and elected to take the shortcut. He steamed into the pass in a thick fog, then decided to turn back halfway through. But the pass proved too narrow to make the "U" turn, and the racing flood tide drove the 190-foot steamer upon Canoe Reef, shearing off her rudder and keel. For two weeks salvors tried to extricate and refloat the *Del Norte* until the ship disappeared after a violent gale on 11 November.

Late in 1901 J. Hunter, superintendent of the Esquimalt and Nanaimo Railway, joined the captain of the Vancouver-Ladysmith ferry and several "Pilots and masters of local steamers" to press for a range of lights on the north end of Galiano Island. James Gaudin sent their petition along to Colonel Gourdeau in Ottawa, explaining that vessels were flaunting the long-standing warning about Porlier Pass "in preference to making the long detour through Active Pass or going around Valdez and Saturna Islands." He proposed that "arrangements could be made for the economical exhibition of these lights" by engaging a local man to maintain them, as part-time work, at a wage somewhere between $10 and $25 a month.

Always impressed by economy, Gourdeau gave his agent the go-ahead to begin construction and to hire Peter Sit-who-latza, a local Indian, for $25 a month. It would have been an ideal arrangement, even saving the department the cost of a dwelling since Peter lived nearby on the reserve. But politicos, when they cut up their spoils, pay scant attention to cost. Ralph Smith "put his foot down on it" by nominating Sticks Allison for the job. "Of course, I dare not disobey these instructions," Gaudin replied, and grudgingly offered Allison the post for $30 a month, "as these lights . . . [did] not require arduous work in their operation."[1]

Gaudin had mixed feelings about Allison's appointment. On the one hand he had already offered the post to the Indian and dreaded the effect upon the band when Sticks relieved him: the Roman Catholic missionary had warned that the Indians "were not at all times reliable, also that the disappointment of being relieved by a white man after a short time of office, might create an ugly feeling to exist between the lightkeeper and the Indian after he has been relieved under these circumstances." Besides, no dwelling had been built, so Allison would have to seek shelter in a crude twelve-by-sixteen-foot lean-to shack left behind by the carpenters.

The new keeper was no stranger to rough living, however. As a nine-year-old, Francis Logan Allison had run away from his home in Greenock, Scotland, in 1875. He joined an uncle aboard a sailing ship and went ashore a few years later at Glace Bay, Nova Scotia, where he spliced cable in the local coal mines. He set off under sail again, around the Horn this time, and disembarked in British Columbia. He first found work as a farm labourer, then went down into Nanaimo's coal shafts until 1901, when he was lucky to crawl out alive after a mine explosion. While in hospital he befriended a little Italian boy, sharing fruit and candy with him. When the boy's parents demanded to know the source of this largesse, he answered, "The man with the sticks gave it to me," pointing to Allison on his crutches. The nickname stuck; Allison became known as "Sticks," and few people would ever know his real name. He was still using sticks to get around when he took over the new lightstation at Porlier Pass in November 1902, and was lame for life after he put them aside. But there he stayed, above ground with the sea at his doorstep, for the next forty years.

Sticks Allison wasted no time complaining about his spartan accommodation. The floor had been laid on bare ground and its boards soaked up water like a sponge. He asked Gaudin to have it raised two feet off the ground, and to build on an addition. "I think we should do everything to make the poor man comfortable," the agent wrote Colonel Anderson; "[he] lives there in solitude all the year round." There were other drawbacks. The new keeper also had to fetch water in pails for "quite a long distance," until Gaudin ordered a 400-gallon tank be installed to collect rainwater from the roof. Sticks also had two fixed lights to watch: one at Race Point and a second beacon on Virago Point, accessible only by boat. (When in line, the two beacons gave proper bearings for the northern entrance to Porlier Pass.)

The agent first inspected Porlier Pass in April 1903 and found all equipment, the towers, and their illuminating apparatus, in "very fair condition." As for the musty dwelling, Gaudin remarked, "[As is] customary with our experience of the absence of a woman at a station [it] is not as tidy as could be desired, but on the whole I consider Allison makes a very good lightkeeper.'' Fortunately, Sticks seemed to have ''sufficient tact'' to keep on friendly terms with the Indians.

In March 1906 Allison reported that his makeshift shack was taking on water again, and Gaudin backed his keeper's request for a new dwelling. ''I think the application for a new dwelling for this station is quite in order,'' he wrote Ottawa, ''and feel you would endorse it if you saw the place the man has to live in.'' Besides, Allison was in love with Mathilda Georgeson, Scotty's granddaughter from Active Pass. They married in 1907.

Allison, who knew as well as any mariner the dread of being lost in fog, soon won a legendary reputation aboard the steamers for his dedication. For a year before the department landed a hand horn at Porlier he would hobble down to the shore and stand just above the incoming waves, beating a five-gallon oil can with a stick in response to a steamer's whistle day or night. Later, when the hand horn arrived, he cranked it as soon as he heard a signal and kept pumping away, heedless of wind and weather, until the ''all clear'' came back through the mist. In return, the CPR issued him a lifetime pass to travel free on their fleet.

''The safety of the ships and sailors was instilled in us at a very early age,'' his daughter Devina (known, along with her sister Frances, as ''Miss Sticks'') recalled sixty years later, ''and we often [blew] the boats through the Pass. At the age of eight I was taught to tend the Race Point Light and it came to be my special charge. I would clean lamp glasses and polish the brass lamps. My dad always checked my lights when he came from lighting Virago Point Light. He told me it was to see if I had gotten the door locked properly. When one is brought up on a lighthouse, you learn responsibility and to care what happens to people, a feeling that never leaves you.''[2]

In spite of all that traffic out front and the Indian reserve behind them, the Allisons were far more isolated than their fellow keepers to the south. Nanaimo was a day's sail away, and when company came it was usually people stumbling ashore after trouble out in the pass. ''My dad often brought strangers home in the evening for a meal, and sometimes a bed for the night, if they were caught without food or blankets,'' Devina remembered. ''It seemed we always had folks in for meals especially in the evening. Sometimes they would stay and we would loan them a lantern to find their way home.'' During Allison's tenure, hundreds of unexpected guests from seaward came up to the new house, soaked and shivering after Sticks rescued them when their boats swamped off Race Point. He lent them clothing and gave them a meal while their own clothes hung steaming by the stove. ''My father was not a religious man, but he was a good man with a heart of gold,'' she recalled. ''He would give the shirt off his back if someone needed it. We girls were taught to pray and to love God and to trust him. When and if we were in town, he would send us to Sunday school.''

Devina and her sister Frances were typical lighthouse children, adept at substituting imagination for playmates. On floor-washing day, she remembered, "Daddy used to clear out all the kitchen chairs and everything and pile them on the veranda. My sister and I would line them all up with boxes, get our dolls out, and we'd sit there and watch the picture show. The picture show was the clouds." Seventy years later Devina claimed, "I can still see different things in the clouds that we used to see when we were kids." They had a special, secret place called "down on the grass" where they played. When airplanes made their first appearance among the broken lumps of cloud, the girls would tie a rock in the corner of a handkerchief and would "zoom it from one end of the spot to the other."

There were only two blemishes upon their otherwise idyllic existence: the die-hard animosity of some of the Indians infused with the "ugly feelings" which Gaudin had shrewdly anticipated, and the pay, always the pay. In spite of Allison's reserve of tact, some band members seemed bent upon revenge. After receiving complaints in August 1903, Gaudin counselled Sticks to tread carefully in his dealings with them as they were "treacherous," especially "those residing in the vicinity of the lighthouse who were under the impression when the lighthouse was being built that they would have been entrusted with the operation of the lights . . . and not without reason either."

As early as March 1904 Allison was writing Ralph Smith to thank him for his appointment, but also to ask for a raise to $45 a month. Because he had two towers to maintain, he had to "use . . . [his] boat twice a day in rain or snow to go to one of the towers." He had to cut and haul his cord wood a mile. "Mr. Smith," he wrote, "these things all add to my work and as there is no land goes with the lighthouse, I have to buy all my vegetables and pay freight on all my groceries from Nanaimo; Sir, it soon takes away my wages." Gaudin had been out three times and "found things to his satisfaction," and promised to recommend an increase.[3]

By August 1905 Allison's reserve of tact was depleting as fast as his savings. The Indian agent for Cowichan District forwarded a letter to Gaudin from some Indians complaining of verbal abuse. "I do not wish to condemn you unheard," Gaudin told Allison, but warned him, "This Department will not tolerate any of its officers to use offensive language to any persons, not even to Indians." In future, he instructed the keeper "to have nothing to say to them, good, bad or indifferent."

In March 1909 smallpox erupted on the reserve. Allison immediately wrote Victoria asking for disinfectant. Gaudin advised that disinfectant was a futile means of prevention and ordered him to take his family at once to hospital at Chemainus and "get vaccinated," which was "the best preventative." Upon his return Allison could not ignore his neighbours' suffering; he flouted Gaudin's orders and went onto the reserve to minister to them.

In July 1911 the Indian agent forwarded more complaints to Victoria, alleging that Allison had been "under the influence of liquor, etc." It was Robertson, now, who warned him that "such conduct, if true, will not be tolerated by the Department." Allison rebutted the charges. Though "of the opinion that where there is smoke, there is liable to be fire,'' the agent was willing to overlook the complaints. If they continued, however, he would have ''no option but to recommend . . . [Allison's] dismissal.''

They kept coming in, though, and by March 1915 Robertson's patience was clearly wearing thin. ''I have had more trouble from you than any other keeper,'' he told Allison. Unless the keeper mended his ways and was prepared ''to do what is right by the Government,'' the agent would recommend ''that the sooner the Department makes a change at Porlier Pass, the better.''

Allison was crushed. He had blithely walked into a situation poisoned by Ralph Smith's ''kindness,'' to which the Indians responded in kind. Even so, Allison attributed the slanders to a jealous neighbour, Andy Deacon, who wanted his job. Deacon, Allison charged, had threatened to stir up the cauldron of hatred if Allison refused to apply for a transfer. ''I can find you an Indian who lives here, he was offered money to come here & fight Me & also to pay his Fine if I Prosecuted him,'' he revealed. ''Another Indian was Entised & Promised Pay to Come & Shoot my dog.'' Charges of his abuse and mistreatment of Indian neighbours were

> imaginary ones, Cannot be Real. As I never have yet in My 14 Years Here on this Station Been anything But their Friend I have begged off indian agent to feed & Care for their Sick which I Had been doing I Have letters of thanks here in my Possession from Officers off the indian Dept. Appreciating my Kindness towards them. Capt. Robertson I never yet Entered an indian House unless it was to see & give aid to the Sick. My Carryings one as your informants tell you off are only I want his job I must get a lighthouse & their only way is without outside detection is use the Superstition of the indians & tell him anything about Frank he beleaves it Capt. I know my own friends here & I also Know my foes. Capt. Robertson I would Rather think you would Protect one of your Crew until you yourself Knew the man & his Character.[4]

The charge that Allison was mistreating the Indians was blatant slander. Every Christmas Eve Sticks cleared out the kitchen, tied two huge Christmas puddings up in pillow cases, and plunged them into copper kettles boiling on the stove. When he had lit up in the evening, the family rowed off for the reserve with two jugs of brown-sugar sauce steaming on the floor of the boat. He sent his daughters up to the houses and waited in the boat with a breadknife. The Indians came down in turn, carrying ''a plate for each one in the house, whether it be man or woman, and for each child, and a little bowl or jug,'' Frances remembered. ''They would bring their utensils down and Daddy would have his knife and he would carve off a slice of pudding for each one in the family, and pour some sauce in their container.'' The Indians, Devina affirmed, ''were our closest friends.''[5] After visiting the Indians, they pulled on up the bay to the ''Jap'' fishboats riding at anchor, and divvied out more pudding, pouring the last of the sauce into ornate ceramic bowls held over the side. ''Now no work, no fish Christmas Day,'' Allison exhorted the puzzled

Japanese. "That's Jesus' day. Everybody rest. Suppose you don't rest; then Jesus bring no more fish. You go out catch fish after Christmas-time—no fish!"

But what cut deepest was Robertson's opinion that Allison was the worst troublemaker in the agency—an odd assertion since Arthur Gurney had long ago earned that dubious distinction. Sticks was stunned and depressed by this wounding rebuke. "Capt. I never bothered you with any writing," he defended himself. "I never Visited the Office But once Since you took Charge." His neighbours all said "that Mr. Allison. . .[was] a Very decent & Obliging Chap," and he also had a raft of letters from people in distress he had saved. Still, it almost seemed as if Deacon's devious manoeuvring might have its intended effect.

Worse trials lay ahead for Sticks Allison. Mathilda died just before Christmas 1915. "Now, as I look back, I can see my dad become a broken man," Devina recalled. "He just lived to bring up his two little girls and although he was very strict, he was a good father and we loved him dearly."

Fortunately, Sticks's malaise had little effect on his performance. Early one December morning in 1917, a CPR barge snapped its tether in the pass. "We heard the whistle blow and my dad hopped out of bed, and, of course, I hopped right out after him and trotted outside," Devina recalled. "We could see these lights and the waves were really tremendous. . . . When she would go down in the tide-rip, there was just the top mast that would be showing, and then she would come up over the wave again."

Allison and the girls watched as the barge careened back and forth in the pass, railway cars jumping their tracks and teetering like dominoes above the water. For two hours the crew clung to the barge's rails and capstans, until their runaway ran aground on Lilyhill Point, next to Virago Point. Sticks rigged a breeches-buoy, made the line fast, and hauled the shaken seamen across, one at a time. The spectacle of box cars crumpled like accordions, with wheat and flour running out their seams to fill the barge and the bay, and sides of mutton and pork riding in the swell, drew scores of scavengers, whites and Indians alike. "It was just around Christmas time and it was quite a good cargo," according to Devina.

In the autumn of 1918 the Spanish flu hitchhiked over the Malahat and settled down amongst the Cowichan Indian band. Bound to the station by Robertson's standing orders, Allison waited in dread for their turn, his alarm mounting with the keening of survivors as the dead piled up like cordwood on the reserve. It came in January. The virus attacked the girls first, but Allison barely had time to nurse them before it debilitated him as well. "When my 2 girls got delerious & myself only able to get around, I wrote to Mr. McMurtrie Prop[rietor] of Hotel Abbotsford at Ladysmith, asking him to have the Dr. Sent out immediately as we were all sick," Allison reported. Fortunately, two doctors were dining together at the hotel when Allison's letter arrived, and McMurtrie took it in to them. Dr. Watson put down his napkin, went to the City Boat House, and hired a launch to go out to the light and fetch them in. He instructed the crew not to let the Allisons stand up but to carry them aboard. "I was 72 Hours in Hospital before I got to sleep," Allison informed

Robertson, "the fever was so high & only for the good & Careful treatment of the Dr. and Nurses we all Pulled through." They spent thirteen "delerious" days in hospital, during which time Allison had to pay a friend, Captain Beale, to relieve him back at the light.[6]

The keeper had barely enough cash left to settle up with Beale, and he reeled under a staggering burden of doctors' bills. Then a B.C. Police constable appeared at his bedside, holding out a bill for $22.50 from the three men who had carried them away. He agreed that the amount was "exorbitant," but told Allison he must pay nonetheless. Allison refused to sign. The police forwarded the bill to Robertson. Even the agent considered the amount "an imposition," and demanded to know why he had not been informed of Allison's condition.

"Capt. had it been Possible for me to write you re the condition of myself & Family I Certainly would have done so," Allison replied, "but I thought I could fight it out myself But I was Mistaken & was a Near Call for myself & oldest Child as My Temperature was on arrival 103 & my Family 102 *each*." Dr. Watson wrote the department to confirm the expense was "absolutely necessary": three men were needed to carry the stricken family to the boat. Allison returned the bill, explaining, "My Salary is Not Enough as no doubt you Know what it costs to live. I am now in debt & god knows how I am to keep out of more." Wartime inflation had already dragged him into the red with his grocer for the first time, and Sticks offered to submit past bills as proof. Flour, for example, had shot up from $5.75 to $13.00 a sack. "As my foods are mostly can foods," he continued, "it is getting impossible to get Proper Nourishing food, let alone Clothing & Shoes for Myself and Family. This, Capt., is my first Request to you Re my salary . . . ." Robertson wrote the boat owner denying that the department was "responsible in any way for . . . individual sicknesses," and instructed him to go collect from the keeper.[7]

Allison began clutching at straws. Under pressure from the Amalgamated Civil Servants of Canada, McIntosh, his MP, had extracted a promise from C.C. Ballantyne, minister of Marine, that lightkeepers would get an increase in pay. Allison wrote the minister, reminding him that Parliament had long ago approved the appropriation; civil servants were to have received their increase in April 1919—over a year ago. Where was it? "I am one of those lighthouse keepers and as yet I have received no increase," he revealed.

> My time here on this light is fully 24 hours per day, 365 days per year and responsibilities equal to any first class light from a seaman's point of view. There are no holidays except I engage help and pay for a man out of my own pocket and it is impressed upon him that I am still held responsible for his position and Gov't stores in his charge. There is no coal or firewood given free, I have to buy all my fuel for household purposes and with the high cost of living it is impossible for a man with a family to feed and cloth them on a small salary of $58.00 a month . . . and pay for medical attendance and fuel.

Allison reckoned that inflation had shrunk his pre-war $58.00 monthly pay to $27.50. Moreover, he had two lights to run, one offshore, and he desperately needed rain gear and rubber boots.[8] Yet even in the deepest trough of the post-war economic crisis, Devina and Frances ''were taught to share,'' and would ''do up a huge box of. . . toys'' for needy children in Vancouver at Christmas. ''His pay was very low and his hours very long, but somehow . . . [they] managed.''

Allison still had received no reply and no increase by August, when he somehow learned that Ballantyne was en route to Victoria. ''I expect Mr. McIntosh to discuss My Salary as well as others with Minister Ballantyne,'' he wrote Gordon Halkett, and called upon the superintendent of lights to shore up his claim. ''I trust, Mr. Halkett, you will *if asked* Re this *Station* & *Conditions* Help to Get me an increase off Salary as you Must Know the High Cost off Living Hits Me Hard at Present. . . .'' He was only paid three dollars a month for pumping the hand horn, punishing work ''worth at Least $3.00 Per Night & Especially in Cold wet weather.''[9]

It is an indication of Allison's naivete and isolation that he should think his salary ranked so high on Ballantyne's agenda. He heard next from Wilby, who explained that writing the minister was ''most irregular'' (in fact, in those bleak post-war years it was becoming a desperate and demeaning routine). Halkett asserted that it had always been his policy ''to advance the interests of lightkeepers at every opportunity.'' While promising to do his best, he pointed out that Porlier Pass had ''not been as well kept as regards neatness of the grounds etc. as what the average Government property should be.'' He called upon Allison to make improvements at once.

Allison's only solid hope for a raise lay in the possibility of introducing a mechanical fog horn. In February 1921 Colonel Wilby asked for a monthly tally of the number and types of vessels plying Porlier Pass. Allison counted 121 tugs with tows, 80 steamships, and 35 CPR transfers. ''I can truthfully Say that this is below the average number as there are many boats Pass in the Night & at times when I am in the Bush Sawing wood or for Mail,'' he reported, estimating a monthly average of 252. The number gave an idea of the keeper's workload: in foggy weather he must have been out pumping the hand horn an average of eight times a day, at all hours. Colonel Wilby forwarded the traffic summary to Ottawa, along with his opinion that though a mechanical horn would obviously improve navigation, it was not yet ''an actual necessity and with the proper amount of caution the existing aid should be sufficient''—thus dashing Allison's last hope for improved wages. Sticks was sick all through November 1921 and went into the hospital again, ''but could not stay there as [his] salary would not stand for Hospital & Dr. Bill.''[10] In spite of money problems, however, Allison remarried in March 1922. His second wife, Elizabeth Gear, was a war widow with a sixteen-year-old son, Edward.

The loss of the tug *Peggy McNeil* with all hands but one on the night of 23 September 1923 was a sobering reminder of the perils of Porlier Pass. She had left Vancouver with two scows in tow that afternoon. Devina remembered, ''It was quite a calm night, although it was a strong, strong tide, and Daddy and I watched her come down the inside shore there—this was around midnight—and then went to bed.'' The *Peggy*'s mate, W. Ingram, came up on watch at 11:45 P.M. and noticed that ''the sea was really boiling when the tug entered the riptide of the pass.'' They had no sooner passed Allison's light when the tug pitched wildly and a hawser snaked ominously over the handrail. Ingram raced to the galley for an ax, but the *Peggy McNeil* started to roll before he reached it. She turned clear over. To his horror, Ingram found himself underwater with the deck overhead. When he finally fought his way out to the surface, he saw the scows bearing down on him. He swam for one but was helpless in the grip of that mighty current. ''One large whirlpool dragged me under and I thought I would drown before reaching the surface again.'' The tide bore him within reach of a bell buoy and he grabbed hold. Catching his breath, Ingram struck out again for the scow, reached it, and pulled himself aboard. From his vantage point he could see his mates clinging to the other scow's line. He spent his last ounce of strength trying to pull the two together, shouting at them as the scows bucked and plunged wildly in the current. ''These men had been in the water for almost three-quarters of an hour and were losing their strength, for one by one they disappeared.'' A fishboat found Ingram drifting by on the scow next morning and took him to Nanaimo. He bought a ferry ticket to Vancouver and marched into the offices of the Pacific Tug & Barge Company, seawater squelching in his shoes, and declared to the incredulous clerks, ''[I am] all that is left of the *Peggy* and her crew!''[11]

Allison's steadfast dedication to mariners' safety combined with his mounting expenses to spur his determination to have a modern fog alarm plant installed at Porlier. Along with his monthly report for November 1927 he wrote, ''A great many [seamen] are complaining about the fog horn at this time of year.'' Not without cause, since Porlier was one of the few stations still relying upon the obsolete hand horn. The New Westminster owners of the launch *Bobby* listened for it in vain on the night of 2 December and came storming up to the station next day, ''very hostile,'' demanding to know why he had tried to drown them the night before. Their launch had struck a reef off Valdez Island around 6:30 P.M., and they blamed Allison, who reported the incident to Wilby.

We said did you here a steamboat blow 3 whistles to us & they said yes & did you hear us blow back to them—''Yes.'' They thought that was two boats blowing to one another. This steamboat was inside & each time she blew we blew & when she passed the house she blew she was allright, & in the gulf now & so we came in the house, untill another big whistle blew. These New Westminster men say they expected a siren whistle in a dangerous pass like this & didn't think they had to blow to us & were going to report us for not keeping the siren blowing continually. We showed them our hand horn & then you should have heard there talk.[12]

Aerial view of Porlier Pass tower, 1981. Jim Ryan photo.

There was no better indictment of the hand horn: it was an adequate aid to steamers who called for it, but useless to smaller vessels who had no horn of their own to sound the request.

By 1929 Allison sought escape from his downward spiral into debt in drink. First wartime inflation, then the Great Depression had torpedoed his financial security, and if he had hoped by remarrying to recapture the halcyon time with Mathilda before the war, the vision soon dissipated. Elizabeth Allison paid the price of his ruin.

She had fled his mush-mouthed rages three times before Christmas week 1929. On the night of 22 December Sticks brooded over another bottle of rum. Their quarrel, when it came, escalated far beyond insult. Allison seized a shotgun by the barrel and swung it in a vicious arc at her head. She jumped aside and the walnut stock shattered on the floor. With her son Edward fending him off, she managed to elude the rampaging Sticks until 2:45 A.M. when he finally passed out. Next day she called at the Ladysmith Provincial Police detachment to swear out a complaint. Though Allison had no recollection of the incident, he stated in court that, "since he married her, he tried to do everything to make her comfortable, and could not understand why she wanted to leave him." At one point the judge cleared the court "owing to Mr. Allison's filthy language." He granted Elizabeth a separation, and ordered Allison to pay her $40 a month maintenance.[13]

Elizabeth wrote Colonel Wilby in January to inform him she and Edward were now living on a Home Oil barge anchored near the station. She related that Allison had left the station without leave the day before, and was last seen with two cronies on their way into the Travelers Hotel Beer Parlour. "I am very sorry to leave my Light House home as I love it there," she lamented, "if only he could leave the drink alone."

Wilby sent a report to Deputy Minister Hawken in Ottawa, recommending Allison's dismissal. But then Halkett came forward to state that neither he nor any of the mechanics or seamen on the *Berens* "had any ground for suspicion that Allison was in any way a drinking man." Throughout his twenty-eight years' service there had "never . . . been one complaint as to the proper keeping up of his lights and foghorn." Why not at least hold out an opportunity for him to retire gracefully?

By way of explanation for his recent behaviour, Sticks sent in a bizarre letter charging that he had been slandered as an informer for his daring exploits on behalf of the Provincial Police. He claimed he had captured a murderer and two burglars who had broken into the store at Ladysmith, and tied them to chairs at the station. He was also the bane of local "Dope Peddlars," and had laid a great many other criminals by their heels although, he complained, "Even yet I am Called a Stool Pigeon to Strangers by *Residents* here."

Allison's days at Porlier were surely numbered, yet his long and celebrated service seemed to fly in the face of the notion that he was coming apart at the seams. A.W.

Niell, his MP, asked Wilby: "Could not justice be tempered with mercy, considering his long service and give him a chance to retire so that he could get superannuation allowance?" Then George Askew, an influential Victoria yachtsman, took up Sticks's case. He had called at Porlier in late January, as was his "custom on . . . yachting cruises," to check on the weather in the Gulf. He was outraged to learn of "Capt. Allison's" imminent dismissal. "In justice to our much beloved Lighthouse Keeper Captain Stick familiarly known to us, we feel like loosing a real friend, a trustworthy servant," he wrote. In spite of his "family problems," his first loyalty had always been to mariners. "I know he has always been on the job, always has his light and horn been working. Over twenty years of faithful service to Mariners. I assure your Department a voice of protest will be heard," Askew wrote, and warned Wilby to "stay his dismissal until" the department was "more fully informed." If not, he threatened, "Influence will be brought to your notice why so many of us demand his retention." The agent had better "give this matter . . . serious consideration."[14]

This was the stuff which moved men in office, men otherwise immune to the anguished supplications of isolated lightkeepers. On 12 February Hawken wrote from Ottawa, ordering Wilby to tell Allison the department was "disposed to overlook . . . [his] lapse of good conduct on the understanding that there . . . [would] be no cause for complaint in the future." This was poetic justice indeed. If the department seldom rewarded lightkeepers for their sacrifices, the seagoing public obviously did. Never before had a mariner come to the aid of a lightkeeper in such distress.

Allison thanked Wilby "with all . . . [his] Heart." As for Elizabeth, he wrote, "she is still my wife and I love her still." He wanted her back, but she was working full-time for Home Oil, pumping gas on the barge. Dejected and deserted, Sticks Allison began meandering beyond the bounds of rational behaviour. In his drunken reveries he cultivated the paranoid delusion that Elizabeth was consorting with other men, an opinion he committed to paper, mailed to puzzled neighbours, and blared in strident harangues from the rocks to passing boats. T.W.S. Parsons, acting superintendent of the Provincial Police, had quite a pile of Sticks's barely legible diatribes on his desk when he wrote Wilby, asking him to tell Allison "this practice must cease."

Sticks was in court again that August, this time as plaintiff, after sending the police a message: "ARREST EDWARD GEAR FOR MURDEROUS ASSAULT: ALSO ARREST MRS. F.T. ALLISON—MY WIFE—FOR THREATENING TO SHOOT ME AND DROWN HERSELF AT LIGHTHOUSE STEPS." On 11 August he had been on his way over to the Home Oil barge to deliver another diatribe about his wayward wife's "infidelity," when Edward intercepted him. The two circled each other out in the swirling pass, exchanging curses and blows with their oars. In court Allison's attorney moved to withdraw the charge and the judge held the keeper liable for costs. "From my observations on this investigation,"

Constable O.L. Hall reported, ''it was very clear to me that Mrs. F.T. Allison and her son, Edward Gear, command the respect of all citizens in that settlement.''[15]

By June 1932 Allison had become a full-fledged public nuisance. Constable Hall sent another report to the sub-inspector of the Victoria Police District. A Chemainus man had received a number of threatening and abusive letters from Porlier, and complained ''that when he. . .[went] by boat to the Allison Home Oil station for fuel—F.T. Allison from a high bluff. . .[shouted] for the full benefit of all in the settlement—accusing him of immorality with Mrs. Allison.'' He suggested the police talk to Wilby again. If a transfer could not be arranged, why not ''have Allison mentally examined''? Dr. Rogers at Chemainus had already offered to make the examination. ''If the Doctor certifies Allison insane, he could then be brought to Chemainus for the second Doctor's examination,'' Hall recommended.

The harried agent admitted Hall's statements were ''perfectly correct. . .so far as Allison's sanity. . .[was] concerned,'' but he had had no complaints about the upkeep of the station. Wilby ruled out a transfer, nor would he take any responsibility for ordering a mental examination, pointing out that the police had ''the perfect right to take this responsibility for themselves.''

Indeed, Allison continued to provide ample evidence that his obsession was no obstacle to his performance. In July 1934 he rescued C.D. Cotton, a Vancouver insurance broker whose party was swamped in the pass, and put them up ''while disabled'' for three days. Cotton wrote Wilby expressing his gratitude and admiration for Sticks Allison's heroics, and the agent wrote the keeper, ''All such letters pointing out the courtesy extended by employees have the very sincere appreciation of the Department, which all helps us to keep up the service of which we are all very proud.'' If Allison was mad, he was also indispensable.

Sticks turned seventy-five in 1941. He refused, however, to submit his birth certificate prior to retiring, even at the risk of foregoing his superannuation. He was holding out for the Imperial Service Medal—tangible proof that a much-maligned keeper had given superb performance for thirty-nine years at Porlier Pass. Wilby came to visit him at Chemainus before he left in the fall of 1941, and assured Sticks he would recommend him for the award. It had not arrived by January 1942 and Allison learned from McPhail, the minister, that it never would. It was a cruel blow and Sticks went after Wilby with the same cranky determination with which he had pursued his wife.

''He, I know, has not even Had any liking for me,'' he wrote McPhail. In all that time Allison was at Porlier, Wilby had never even visited the station. Sticks charged that the agent had ordered the lights moved from their original position (there is no record of the alteration), prompting a torrent of complaints from mariners. ''I am complaining & saying they are not in Position as formerly installed by a Mr. Anderson & Capt. Laudin [sic] 40 years ago just because I have tried to have above lights Rectified by that Agent I am Placed at Bottom of his List & he Refused to allow me the Long Service Medal, which I ought to be given for my Long Service.''[16]

The medal remained out of reach. Allison's last communication on file was addressed, in desperation, to McKenzie King, "Premier of Canada," complaining that Wilby "held it in his spitful way to refuse it . . . . Mr. McKenzie King, it is such servant as Mr. Wilby who are the ruination of the Liberal Party," Allison charged. "Mr. Wilby is a dommint & very a very ignorant person, when one knows him and is not liked by any [of] our lightkeeper nor any one of the seamen off the employ."[17] Sticks Allison died six years later, still without the medal he coveted—and deserved—so much. Devina and Frances both went back to Porlier Pass in turn, as wives of keepers who came long after Sticks Allison.

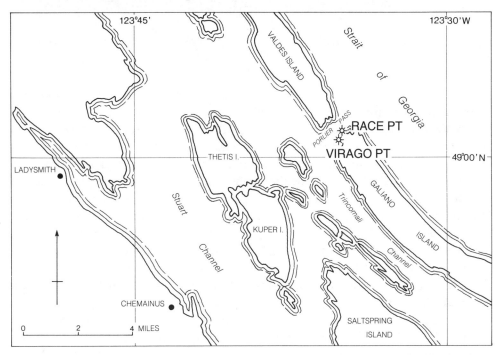

Merry Island

At the turn of the century, Welcome Pass and the Malaspina Straits beyond were becoming major arteries for seagoing commerce bound in and out of Vancouver. Situated off the Sechelt Peninsula, Merry Island occupied a strategic position separating the two waterways. The Vancouver Ship Masters Association pointed this out in 1901, in a petition—dispatched to Ottawa via Maxwell, their MP—"praying for the establishment of a lighthouse and fog alarm on Merry Island." Well aware of the steady and rising pulse of northern trade "owing to the advent of eastern Capital employed in the development of the fisheries, logging and mineral resources of our northern coast," Gaudin supported their petition. The anticipated shipping boom "looms up brightly for the near future and is quite assured," he affirmed, and every vessel would steer through Welcome Pass. A light and horn on Merry Island would surely be "an invaluable boon in dark nights and foggy weather."

When the profits of eastern capitalists were at stake, Ottawa could move with breakneck speed. The light went into service within a year—a fixed white beacon surmounting a square white dwelling fifty-seven feet above high water on Merry Island's southeast point. A dangerous rock lurked near the southern entrance of Welcome Pass, two cables off nearby Thormanby Island. There the channel sheered off steep and "bold" to a depth of eighteen fathoms. The mainland shore, the *B.C. Coast Pilot* advised, could "be approached to within half a cable."

Will Franklin took over the new light in November 1902. Will and Mary Ann Franklin were at Merry to stay, for they pre-empted the rest of the island under the Homestead Act, and began farming in a modest way, with flocks of sheep, ducks, and chickens. Franklin was issued a hand horn and was paid $360 a year. In March 1903 he implored R.G. McPherson, his MP, for a raise. Gaudin praised the "intelligent young man, who should be, according to the wages in this province, [paid] more than a dollar a day," while allowing that his duties were "not more arduous than those of other stations, the keepers of which enjoy the same salary." As a "white" keeper, Franklin qualified for the $500 minimum in 1907.

In fact, Will Franklin's duties were considerably more arduous than those of his peers. Owing to the swelling volume of traffic, he was continuously at his horn in the fog and pelting rain, while keepers of more isolated stations could often catnap on the couch or at the table and wait for their dogs—Pavlovian fog detectors trained to bark at the sound of the steamer's whistle—to wake them. (One had a parrot which screamed ''Fog's in!'')

Aside from steamers there was a steady parade of smaller traffic past Merry, ranging from tugs and fish packers to gasoline launches. On the evening of 4 March 1915 Leo Jessup left Vancouver with his wife, two children, and mother-in-law, bound for Nanaimo with all their belongings aboard his twenty-eight-foot fish boat. The eight-horsepower engine coughed and died near Bowen Island. They had no sail or oars aboard. At first there seemed no cause for alarm. Winds were light and they drifted along, hoping to attract another vessel for a tow. Then the wind changed abruptly, whipping the sea into white caps before a southeast gale. Jessup ran up a blanket and quilt for makeshift sails, and held the tiller all through the night. At noon next day Franklin watched them approach, ''well out in the fairway,'' through his binoculars. Jessup sat in the stern. The keeper half suspected something was amiss—only a madman or fool would be out mooching for salmon in that sea—''but no Signal or Sign did he give.'' Finally the boat ''began to get into Such a position off the Small island lying off the front of the house that . . . [he] Saw Something had to be done.'' The boat smashed into the rocks and began breaking up. Leo Jessup went after his children first, hoisting them up on the wave-washed rock. After his fourth attempt to wrestle his wife's mother away from the undertow, Jessup lost his grip and watched her disappear under the hull. Franklin launched his twelve-foot skiff into the gale, ''and after making the distance by inches found the Jessup Family had got ashore on Small island and the body of Mrs. I.J. Evans floating away which . . . [he] recovered. The boat was Smashed to pieces.''

Franklin brought the exhausted, grief-stricken family home. He kept them at Merry for nine days. ''We did everything we could for their comfort and recovery,'' he informed Robertson. ''Both Mr. and Mrs. Jessup were subject to heart trouble and had bad attacks the first few days here.'' Will rowed all the way over to Vancouver to fetch clothing and $72 in cash donations. The firm of Simpson and Balkwill offered the Jessups free passage home, and the B.C. Provincial Police donated $25. For his part, Will Franklin was $36 (nearly half a month's pay) out of pocket, and billed the department for the Jessups' ''board and care.'' Back in Ottawa the deputy minister noted that Franklin was now earning $480 a year. ''It would seem that the department has no responsibility in this matter,'' he ruled, ''and that the lightkeeper should look for remuneration to those who benefitted.''[1]

Aside from recording the commerce throbbing back and forth out front, Franklin's logs confirm that Merry was far more hospitable than most lights. He wrote about shearing sheep, slaughtering lambs, setting and selling turkey eggs—accounts which would have seemed like another world to the families living on the verge of starvation up the West Coast and on the northern lights. By 1918, however, he too was sinking into the quicksand of wartime inflation. "I have been trying to stave this off if possible until after the war," he wrote H.S. Clements in January 1918, "but by jove it's getting too much—with living gone up from 50 to 250%, I am appealing to you to use your influence for a raise in salary." Out of his annual salary of $570 Franklin supported his wife, her mother, and his mother as well. "So you see," he reasoned, "it keeps me guessing to make ends meet." All his supplies came COD from Vancouver because the government steamers brought him nothing, forcing him to pay "out of reason prices" on top of freight charges. "I think the lightkeepers should have been thought of before this," he opined, "as every other branch of the service has been given increases." For his part, Franklin wanted a raise of $250.[2]

Clements assured his constituent he would do all he could. In August Franklin received his quarterly paycheque—"The same old figure out of which I have to pay Five dollars to the Patriotic Fund," he wrote, "so that really I am getting that much less." It was "pretty tough" to make ends meet, he confessed: "In fact I am going in the hole. It makes me feel pretty sore—Suppose they think down in Ottawa that we can go hang."[3]

At Clements's behest, Captain Robertson wrote Franklin a week later, suggesting the keeper seek part-time work off the station. "While we appreciate what you are doing for the Patriotic Fund," the agent reminded Franklin, "a man's first duty is to his family," though he hoped the keeper could "keep it up. This matter rests with yourself," the agent concluded, "and no one can expect more of you than your best."

Franklin never gave less. In January 1919 he read Gordon Halkett's letter to the *Colonist*, written in defense of the department following charges of negligence in the wake of the infamous Sadler affair, when the Kains Island keeper and his wife went insane and their children nearly starved with no action from the authorities. Attempting by any means to diffuse the public uproar, Halkett and Robertson portrayed salaries on the lights as more than adequate—a fact seemingly borne out by the number of men the department could always find to take on the work. Besides, Halkett pointed out, the keepers drew extra pay for manning a hand horn.

To all the other keepers eking out a bare subsistence along the coast, the Sadler affair doubtless came as no surprise, but Halkett's statement about horn pay certainly astonished Will, and he was swift to pounce. "You state that extra remuneration is given Lightkeepers for operating Hand Fog Horns," he pointed out. "That's news to me—Here I have been operating the Fog Horn for fifteen years, but have never received anything extra for it—A little information please—I need the money."[4] Franklin dug out the instructions Gaudin had issued when he dropped the horn off at Merry in December 1903. "There is a great deal of Shipping passing here," the keeper reminded the superintendent of lights, "and my horn has been of good service during these years." In fact he had worn out the bellows of one horn after six years and had been forced to replace it!

There was no worming out of this one: on Robertson's orders Halkett had led with his chin in public to rebut Henry Sadler's expose in the press. Now Will Franklin might unravel the whole skein of lies about lightkeepers' "adequate remuneration." In March 1919 Franklin received a $95 cheque without any explanation. Obviously the department wanted the Kains Island episode to fade fast and forever from the public mind. For a while, even Will assumed this was a war bonus. Two other public servants he knew had received bonuses, but "evidently the Lightkeepers" were "further ignored."[5]

Indeed they were, but the shipping interests they served certainly commanded Ottawa's keen and constant attention. In May 1922 Andrew Goodlad, secretary of the Pacific Division of the Canadian Navigators' Federation, drew Wilby's attention to the mushrooming volume of passenger vessels, freighters, and towboats plying Welcome Pass. "The fog horn which is worked by hand is inadequate and . . . should be replaced by a more powerful horn operated by mechanical power," he warned. Wilby asked Franklin to count up the passing traffic, and for the month of May the keeper tallied 220 vessels: 90 passenger steamers, 127 tugs, and 3 freighters. These were only daylight observations, however. Depending upon when the fog was in and for how long, he would have been out with his horn at least seven times a day.

A radio station was established at Merry when the new diaphone horns were installed in 1924. The radio operator, Gerald Pike, kept in regular contact with Bull Harbour and Cape Lazo, reporting weather observations and exchanging logs of ship movements. Around 4 P.M. on 22 March 1927 Pike was on his way past the radio

Will Franklin at his post, Merry Island engine room.

shack with a can of gasoline to start up the engine and charge his batteries, when he heard a call come over the set. He went in the shack with the can in his hand and his pipe clenched in his teeth, and shut the door behind him. When he bent down to set the can on the floor, a spark fell in. ''I have personal experience with just such an explosion,'' James Cunningham, a B.C. Police constable, wrote in his report of Pike's death, ''and know what a cupful of gas in a can can do.''

Pike instinctively tried to save the building and equipment. Snatching up the flaming can, he ran outside, slamming the door. Then the human torch ran shrieking past Franklin's house and crashed headlong into an ivy bush. ''His trail can be followed across the engine room floor to the outer doors, and up the walk to Mr. Franklin's residence by burned bits of clothing and blood,'' Cunningham scribbled in his notebook. Franklin's mother-in-law doused Pike with a pail of cold water and helped him stagger into the house. Then she ran for the old hand horn and began pumping. Franklin, at work elsewhere on the island, came running. Seeing that Pike was beyond help, he filled pails and ran to fight the fire. ''Had he not great presence of mind and forethought, no doubt the whole of the lighthouse property would be in ruin today,'' Cunningham reported, ''and Mr. Franklin should be highly commended by his department.''[6]

The radio still worked. Franklin sent out an SOS, then hurried back to the house. While they waited, Pike, writhing in agony, gasped out his will as Franklin wrote, his parlour pungent with the sickly-sweet smell of roasted flesh. The tug *Leroy* sent in a skiff. Franklin and the crew placed Pike in the boat and set off down the coast, but the radio operator died shortly after arrival at hospital in Vancouver.

Traumatized, Will Franklin grew steadily more despondent and depressed. Mary Franklin wrote secretly to Wilby, asking for a month's leave to get him away from the island with its grisly reminders of Pike's horrible accident. ''It is essential that he has a change,'' she pointed out, ''and I myself shall not leave the island again until he has.'' First she asked for a month off; when that was turned down, for at least a week. ''No need to ask anything of Ottawa,'' she advised Wilby, ''down there they are too busy catching trains to go on their own holidays, so have no time to consider any for isolated Light-keepers.''[7]

Franklin finally took a week's leave—two years later in May 1931. It was no holiday. In March his mother-in-law had fallen down the back steps of the house. ''At the age of eighty, the shock has gone very hard with her, has been in bed ever since,'' he wrote Wilby. The B.C. Coast Mission sent a doctor over from Pender Harbour. He advised she should not be moved, and Will and Mary knew ''the time. . .[was] not far off.'' They did their best to make her comfortable until she died three weeks later.

The following February, after thirty years at Merry, Franklin advised he would be sixty-five come September. He wrote, ''[I] feel I would like to be free from the responsibilities whilst I still enjoy good health,'' and asked Wilby to proceed with his superannuation. The Franklins left the light but stayed on Merry to work their farm.

Merry Island Light with fog alarm building in foreground.

It was an easier transition than other keepers faced, without the sudden immersion into some frantic urban anthill with a pittance for a pension. But one last hurdle lay before them.

It is a fading memory today, after Medicare, how the medical profession plundered the lifetime savings of the old and indigent. Like other people paying income tax after 1919, the Franklins helped build and equip medical schools and hospitals, but their declining years were filled with dread as the prospect of thankless doctors' bills loomed up ahead. Countless other Canadians suffered their deterioration in silence rather than prove a burden to their offspring or, as in the Franklins' case, demean themselves by resorting to charity.

Mary Franklin died in 1941, and in May 1953 Will's second wife, Arley, wrote Marine Agent Tom Morrison that Will, now seventy-seven, had been flown by air ambulance to Vancouver where he was now confined to a nursing home. Medical expenses wolfed great chunks off his pension and gnawed away at their savings. Before the year was out, doctors had taken everything and demanded more. She refused to leave Will and return home, yet would have to bear her own expenses in the city until she herself was eligible for the old age pension. She asked Morrison "if there would be any chance of the Department being interested." She kept up the homestead on the island that summer as well as she could between trips to Vancouver, but the winter of 1954 would be her last. "I just can't manage bringing over the oil, wood, etc. any longer," she said, "besides I want to be nearer Will as long as I can and he misses me too." He wanted desperately to go back to Merry, she confided, "and one can't blame him, but he is becoming a greater care all the time, too bad we have to grow old, isn't it?"

"Doctors and medicine are a big drain nowadays," she complained bitterly. In fact, they had almost bled the Franklins white. All that remained now was Merry Island itself. It must go on the block, and if Morrison heard of anyone interested, Arley told him they "would consider any reasonable offer." In February 1954 the agent ordered the captain of the *Sir James Douglas* to take some of her furniture aboard and unload it at Vancouver so she could rent a small room. Later that year she sold Merry Island and watched heart-broken as its light slipped away in a boat's wake for the last time. "Do enjoy your retirement to the utmost," she advised Morrison in a farewell letter, "life is so short after all."[8]

Life was altogether too short for E.J. Leclerc, who took over at Merry Island light after the Franklins. He had been in poor health from the start, and on 17 December 1939 he wrote Wilby from Shaughnessy Hospital, thanking the agent for appointing his wife to relieve him. "This may be the last letter you will get from me," he despaired, "and if there is anything you can do to help my little family after I have gone from here, I will greatly appreciate it, and God knows they will need help for awhile."[9] It was indeed Leclerc's last letter. Wilby kept Helen Leclerc on at Merry, knowing that she was assisted by her two teenaged sons.

Reams have been written about the effect of the War Measures Act in World War II, particularly the shameful profiteering from the Japanese removal. Helen Leclerc was victimized by the same mindless hysteria about enemy aliens. Although her husband had been gravely wounded in the First World War, and Helen herself was born and raised at Quatsino, her parents were Germans.

In May 1940 David McKee, secretary of the Provincial Command of the Canadian Legion and British Empire Service Guild, received a letter from a man who signed himself an "Ex-Lightkeeper" (doubtless Will Franklin), "to the effect that there...[was] a German woman in charge of the Merry Island Lighthouse and Wireless Station." That August Mary Franklin appealed to Wilby "to have Mrs. Leclerc moved away. You know what is happening all over the British Empire regarding enemy aliens," she wrote. Why should Merry Island be an exception? In spite of the Franklins' neighbourliness, the Leclercs were "very arrogant." Helen was given to raving about "imaginary insults" to herself and her boys.

But the insults were no figment of the widow's imagination. One anonymous writer charged she was a "German Nazi" who entertained "all can of German friends" at the lighthouse. "How much longer are you going to employ that *German* woman at the Merry Island lighthouse?" Olive Hill, another island resident, demanded to know. Not only was Mrs. Leclerc an "enemy," she was neglecting the station. Boardwalks were falling to pieces "for want of a nail, but," she supposed, "the poor suffering tax payers would have to foot the bill." If Wilby would not act, he would soon "see what public opinion will do," she threatened.[10]

The agent hardly needed this wrangle added to his other problems. He adroitly referred the matter to the RCMP, explaining that he had "made the most careful investigation as to Mrs. Leclerc's status from which it would appear there...[was]

nothing to worry about.'' After all, she was a Canadian by birth, whose late husband had ''served his country in the last war.'' In reply to another of Will Franklin's letters, Wilby emphasized that the Leclercs were British subjects. Even so, he had already referred the matter to Ottawa and confided that he was calling for applications for the keepership. There was never a shortage of applicants waiting in the wings for Merry Island. George Smith, for example, craved a transfer from Pine Island. A steady diet of canned food had ''about ruined'' his stomach, he wrote in his application for Merry.

Wilby came over to the island a week later. The condition of the station gave the lie to Olive Hill's slanders. ''Both Mr. Stamford and I agreed there was little or nothing in them,'' he informed the chief of aids in Ottawa. Helen Leclerc had gone to hospital ''for what was apparently urgent medical attention.'' Wilby and Stamford called on Mrs. Hill ''and obtained an admission from her that there really. . .[was] no complaint as regards the supposed nationality of Mrs. Leclerc.'' Nevertheless, the keeper had already resigned on grounds of poor health. W.C. Copeland moved around from Carmanah in November to replace her, and George Potts from Estevan Point took Copeland's place in 1950. The Pottses' son Marc had contracted meningitis and suffered severe epileptic seizures. An ''in station'' like Merry Island made for easy access to hospital in Vancouver for treatment once a year.

In February 1953 George complained of ''a good dose of ulcers brought on partly by worry over Marc and partly from lack of sleep,'' as he had not ''had a four hour stretch since the beginning of December and in January. . .[he] had a stretch of days without getting. . .[his] clothes off.'' It had been a ''most dreadful'' winter, with one gale chasing another through the Pass at 70 to 100 knots. The Pottses worked full time just trying to heat their trembling house. Time had stood still at Merry since 1902. There was no electricity. George and Diana cut driftwood with a Swede saw, and hauled it for fuel. George paid a logger $3 an hour to come over and buck five cords of firewood one day. Then he and Diana toiled until 3 A.M. splitting it with maul and sledge, throwing it up past the tideline. Two hours later Potts went out to check the light ''and. . .was horror struck, the sea was almost lapping the engine room. . .and not one stick of. . .wood was left.''[11]

George yearned to be back up at Estevan Point since Merry commanded twice as much time and labour. There were aviation weather reports broadcast five times a day, which involved detailed descriptions of cloud configurations and ceilings, altimeter settings, and thermometer readings. Unlike keepers at Active Pass and Entrance Island, he was not given an assistant. At most other stations ''the other fellows. . .[had] a clear day to themselves and. . .[could] always catch a fish or two''; Potts seldom had time even to cross over to Halfmoon Bay for their mail.

I am on the go from daylight to 9 PM every day without a single break. I had one period this winter where I went 14 days without my clothes off and got only 10 hours sleep in that time. At the end of the period I used to sit outside in a chair to keep myself from falling to sleep. My wife gives me a hand as much as she can, but whereas with the other stations the wives can give the weather at 8 AM and allow the keeper to sleep in. Here that is not possible as Aviation weather entails a lot of detail and knowledge of sky conditions.[12]

Always a popular channel, Welcome Pass was now a virtual freeway. While painting the roof one day, Potts counted 680 vessels, and reckoned the usual traffic at ten boats an hour. With such a volume, tragedy was inevitable—a dreadful certainty which kept George fully dressed and awake night after night outside on his porch.

Potts was credited with rescuing the *Romac*'s crew off the rocks near Thormanby Island in August 1954, though he hastened to correct Wilby's impression, gleaned from press reports, that he was instrumental in the affair. "I didn't do anything extra from my regular duties," he explained. He had spotted an Air-Sea Rescue plane circling over Thormanby and radioed them to see if he could help. "Though it was rough," he admitted, "I have been out in a lot rougher weather." When he learned that two men were clinging to the rocks, two friends who had spent the weekend with the Pottses at Merry Island went after them while the keeper manned the radio.

Nothing unusual in that. "We have too much of this kind going on here," Potts warned, "a number of lives have been lost and boats sunk, since I have been here." He desperately needed an assistant. The thirty-six-hour stretches were getting to be a bit much, yet he "read in *McLean's* that an Eastern station has so much time on their hand that they have to have hobbies, and even that they have two assistants." Two weeks later he picked up a distress call from the American vessel *Neama*, which had struck a reef near Pender Harbour, passed the call on to Search-and-Rescue in Victoria, then contacted a nearby tug to pick them up.

Diana Potts looked out her kitchen window one night and saw a light over on the reef. "You won't believe this," she told George, "but there's a boat out there!" Potts ran to his skiff, launched it into the heavy sea, and steered clear around the island. Diana tied a rope around her waist, and threw the other end to him. George took the crew off one at a time as she hauled them ashore in the skiff.

Three crewmen of the motor vessel *Paige* also owed their lives to Potts's vigilance. Around midnight on 22 January 1955 the keeper heard voices shrieking over a heavy southeast gale. He ran out and saw the dull glow of a flashlight waving near the same islet from which Will Franklin had plucked the Jessups fifty years before. George dashed to the radio room and put out a distress call. Then he launched his twelve-foot skiff into the surf and headed for the feeble beacon. There was no moon, and with sleet and spray driving him backward, he smashed into a rock. The motor quit. He fought the whitecaps for fifteen minutes with his oars, and after several attempts managed to take the mariners aboard one by one, timing his runs to their overturned craft with the heaving swell. By this time his own boat was nearly swamped by waves pouring over its gunwales, but Potts steered his way back around the reef and home. The *Paige*'s crew, all suffering from shock and exposure, sat shivering in borrowed clothing in Potts's kitchen a few minutes later.

This time, the keeper's exploit made news. Reporters quoted Curry Wood, one of the men saved: "Mr. Potts performed a remarkable piece of seamanship. . .certainly at the risk of his own life from sure disaster."[13] In March 1957 the Lieutenant Governor held a ceremony in Potts's honour at Government House, and presented him with a framed certificate from the Royal Canadian Humane Association, certifying that "three men owe their lives to the presence of mind and heroic action, at the risk of his own life, displayed by Mr. Potts." The press photograph shows Potts, lanky and lantern-jawed, looking somewhat out of sorts in a freshly-pressed suit and tie donned for the occasion.

A year later George complained, "I haven't had my clothes off this month so far because of Vancouver smoke and fog." He was still picking up the pieces after a hurricane force gale sheared off their chimney, tore up the boardwalk, scaled shingles off the tower, hoisted the roof off the paint shed and splayed it flat. Suffering from exhaustion, Potts went to see a doctor in Vancouver in November 1958. While stopping short of attributing his patient's condition to "industrial injury or disease," Dr. Weaver signed a disability certificate, noting: "This man seems to be working quite hard—He should arrange to get more time off and not work too long hours."[14]

In response the department finally sent out an assistant, but Potts was appalled to learn that he would have to pay the man's unemployment insurance and compensation premiums. His "main kick" was the fact that the assistant had "no security for his family, no pension plan and no medical plan, and. . .[had] to exist on $225 per month"—less than half the wages for unskilled labourers in Vancouver who worked eight-hour days! Previously, Potts had confined his complaints largely to lack of sleep. Now he wrote George Hees, minister of Transport, in a manner reminiscent of Watson and the others forty years before, asking:

> How would you like to live under these conditions in 1960. Oil lamps, no electricity, no refrigeration, no radio, no TV, all our water has to be pumped by hand, and my wife having to wash in a tub with a washboard, and that's what we did for 2 years until I bought a lighting plant for $880 and pay $50 per month to keep it running. (We would not have stuck it but owing to my son being paralysed when he was 6 months, the doctors suggested this life for him, which I am glad to say has paid off). High paid stations with far less work get all this free. Some injustice.[15]

Hees received another letter about Merry Island from J.H.W. Willard, head of the science department at Prince of Wales Secondary School in Vancouver. Willard had visited Merry Island with his family, and came away full of praise about "the well-kept equipment and environs." He was also impressed by Potts's "know-how"

Merry Island 1981. Jim Ryan photo.

and the array of technical equipment. A.K. Laing, chief of aids, sent the letter to Colonel Keith Dixon, the marine agent in Victoria. "Commendations are so infrequent that I thought you might consider passing it on to the lightkeeper," he advised. Dixon balked, though. He considered Potts "one of the poorest keepers in the Agency," and branded him a "borderline psychopath." "It may be necessary to remove him within the next few years," he predicted, "and, consequently, I hesitate to pass on the letter."[16] George retired soon after. By his own reckoning, the "psychopath" from Merry Island had saved twenty lives.

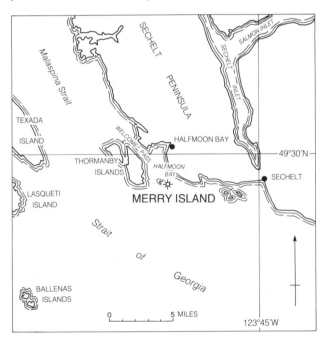

Scarlett Point

S carlett Point on Balaklava Island marks the north-western entrance to Christie Passage, one of the last stretches of sheltered water before northbound ships venture out past Pine Island into Queen Charlotte Sound. The Scarlett Point light station was completed in 1905, part of the construction spree sparked by the Klondike. The *BC Coast Pilot* added it to the list of lights that year: "White light, Fixed, 80 ft. high, vis. 14 miles. Character DT. White rectangular wood red roof, built 1905, visible from all points of approach by water." The fog signal was a primitive mechanical bell weighing half a ton. A weighted rope turned the gears which slammed a twenty-pound hammer into the bell steadily for three hours.

There were problems securing lightkeepers from the beginning. Samuel Anderson of Nanaimo declined the nomination of his MP, William Sloan, when he learned his salary would be less than a dollar a day, but Sloan succeeded in upping the wage to $450. A bachelor, Theodore Nelson, took charge in May 1906. The department granted him a "mail service allowance" of three dollars a month to have his letters brought twelve miles from Port Hardy. In May 1908 Nelson rowed out to a flaming fishing schooner, the *Clara C* of Tacoma, took off her crew, fed and sheltered them, and rowed them out to a passing steamer a few days later. On the minister's behalf, Gaudin thanked Nelson for his "humanity and assistance," promising to call the attention of the department to his "action in this matter." The department spurned Nelson's request for an increase in pay, however, and he resigned in September 1908.[1]

Gaudin took the unusual step of personally recommending William Hunt of Fort Rupert for Scarlett Point. Though Hunt had no political clout, Gaudin said he had known him "for some years," and knew "him to be a resourceful man who would be well adapted for a station like Scarlett Point." Gaudin had previously installed Hunt as temporary caretaker at nearby Pine Island light, and he had served briefly as Arthur Gurney's assistant there. In Gaudin's opinion Hunt was "much the more trustworthy of the two." Over the next three decades, Gurney and Hunt would give ample proof of Gaudin's contention.[2]

William Hunt with wife and sons on the boardwalk at Scarlett Point.

Hunt brought his Indian wife and two boys to Scarlett in 1908, and while there he sired seven more sons and a daughter. His correspondence reveals a dedicated and self-effacing man to whom many seafaring residents of that backwater corner of British Columbia gave their respect and owed their lives. In October 1910 Captain Robertson expressed his appreciation ''for the relief of persons alleged to have come to grief in Shusharty Bay.'' On 14 October 1911 the CPR's *Princess Beatrice* struck a nearby islet at full speed at 10:30 P.M. ''I had a Good Light on & they Dont Blame this station for it, she was Bound Down,'' Hunt reported.

Throughout the autumn of 1914 the Union Steamship Company and the Grand Trunk Pacific joined the CPR in pressing for diaphones to replace Scarlett Point's bell, and the department installed the plant in 1915 in a building east of the tower. Hunt's salary went up accordingly. His wife and older boys served as his assistants. In 1916 a Scandinavian ship ran aground off Scarlett Point, tearing a gaping hole in her bow and wrecking the lifeboat. William Hunt rowed alongside to take the crew off. ''I know all the rocks around here,'' the captain boasted, leaning over the side. ''And this,'' he said, pointing to the one jutting out from his bow, ''is one of them.''

The Spanish influenza cut a cruel swath up the coast in 1918, carrying off the very young and the old, leaving hundreds of grieving families in its wake. The Hunts lost a daughter-in-law and granddaughter over in Alert Bay. In November the virus landed at Scarlett. ''My wife and two sons have it and I think I can get them well again,'' he informed Robertson. ''I am using lime juice in warm water and sugar and it works O.K.''

When Theodore Nelson left the station the department withdrew the mail subsidy at Scarlett as an economy measure, so the Hunt boys, including twelve-year-old Vivian, took turns rowing to Port Hardy and back, always taking pains to collect mail and deliver it to neighbours scattered around the vicinity of Scarlett Point. The boys would also check the level in their father's tobacco pouch, knowing they were in for a good row—whatever the weather—when it ran low. William Hunt was a stern patriarch ''who did not believe in the frivolity of play.'' He once set his long beard on fire while lighting his pipe. ''I didn't dare laugh,'' Vivian recalled, ''there he was hitting himself to put the fire out.'' When the SS *Selkirk* struck a rock off Hurst Island in August 1929, Hunt's boys rescued the crew and rowed them to Port Hardy. According to Vivian (who still preferred oars to outboards in his eighties), ''It took me about five hours to make the 12 miles from Hardy Bay, except when the wind was blowing.''

On 22 February 1930 Hunt's oldest boy, Thomas Edward, set out to deliver mail and supplies to nearby settlers and never came back. His parents noticed the boat some time later, bobbing keel up four-hundred yards off the station. ''As far as I can make out, a comber must have struck the boat and turned her right over,'' Hunt wrote Wilby, ''he had his rubber hip boots on when he left here, he had them both off when we found his body next day.''[3]

Then the flu came back to Scarlett to torment the grieving Hunts. It was a virulent strain this time, immune even to William's lime juice concoction. He wrote Wilby out of an abyss of sadness that July: ''Just to let you know that my poor Wife Died yesterday at 3:30 P.M. . . . . . It is another Dirty Blow to me her body is only six feet from where I am writing this, my son was on his way to Hardy Bay to get the Docter to come here from Alert Bay, he was still in site when she Died.''[4]

Most men might be sent reeling after such swift and vicious rabbit punches of fate, but William Hunt rolled with them. He took twenty days' leave (without pay) in November 1931, leaving one of his sons in charge. The son had not been paid as a relief by 31 January. ''We both think it is a Long time to waite for money he has earned,'' Hunt wrote. The long-awaited cheque still had not come by mid-February. ''They have five little children of theirs to Look after,'' Hunt complained, and they needed the money desperately. ''The kids Christmas was spoilt through not getting the money.''[5] In October 1933 he requested another three weeks' leave to bury his eldest brother who had recently died in Fort Rupert. ''They told me that he wanted to see me befor he Died,'' he wrote Wilby, ''but I could not leave here as you were so strict about it.''[6]

William and his son Vivian spent over twenty hours in the fog plant on 20 January 1935 as a week-long storm ravaged Scarlett Point. ''It sure was Blowing and snowing,'' he remarked, with the understatement of nearly thirty years' experience of storms. The maniacal wind uprooted a huge Douglas fir which crashed down, flattening the boathouse. The kitchen window broke loose. Hunt sallied out into the maelstrom to salvage what he could. ''While I was working saving things from the Boat House, I fell off from the top of the cement foundation and struck A

Boulder on my back, I think one of my ribs is Broken close to my Back Bone, I might have to get A purmit to see A Docter from you as it pains me some. Outside of that,'' he reported, ''all O.K. here.'' [7]

Hunt turned sixty-nine that winter. That summer he and Vivian rebuilt the boathouse from the foundation up, and the superintendent of lights pronounced the station to be ''in a neat and clean condition.'' In August 1935 Wilby received a letter from Ottawa, pointing out that Hunt would be seventy come January, and asking the agent to report on the keeper's physical and financial condition. ''I have six Grandchildren, three Boys, three girls, to take care, aged from 7 months to 13-½ years old,'' Hunt disclosed. ''I am well able to do my work here yet, no I have not saved any money, six kids to care for.'' [8]

One December night in 1936 he noticed a door to the storeroom was hanging open and went out to fasten it. Hunt knew the station well enough by now to go about blindfolded, but some errant ''kid'' had left a set of wheels on the boardwalk and he tripped over them. ''I fell right on one of the flanges on my right Breast and Broke one of my ribs in two places,'' he wrote Wilby. ''To Date I havent seen a Docter about it yet. On the first part of last month I asked for three weeks leave of Absence but to Date I have had no answer to it yet.'' Otherwise, things were ''all O.K.''

By 3 February he was still waiting for permission to leave, coughing blood and crabbing around the station like a wounded beetle. The mission boat *Columbia* called that night with a nurse. Besides his splintered rib, the old man allowed he had been ''pretty sick'' for eight days—''the stomach flu is the sickness that had me.'' The *Columbia*'s nurse implored him for over an hour to come away to hospital. ''I told her I could not leave here without a permit from you,'' he told Wilby. Hunt finally received permission to go on 8 February, but by then the flu had immobilized him. ''It has shifted from my stomach to my head and eyes,'' he wrote Wilby March 2, ''but I can get along without a Docter yet. To Date all O.K. here.''

He held on for another two years, but in December 1939 Ottawa ordered Wilby to proceed with Hunt's superannuation, ''inasmuch as there . . . [was] no authority whereby he may be paid following the 31st of this month.'' On 21 July 1940 the citizens of Port Hardy gathered at a public meeting to pay tribute to William Hunt. Their mayor presented him with the Imperial Service Medal. Vivian Hunt stayed on at Scarlett until February 1941 when someone wrote: ''I left Scarlett Point Light station today, Feb. 9/41'' for him, and Hunt scrawled his signature, bringing the family's thirty-three-year stewardship to an end.

George Smith was certainly no stranger to lightkeeping when he arrived at Scarlett Point from ''neighbouring'' Pine Island in 1941. His father had been first keeper of Nootka light on the West Coast. During his three-year stint at Pine, George had taken only four days' leave. There had been an avalanche of trouble with assistants during that time, and he longed for transfer to a more accessible station, like Scarlett Point, where he might also get fresh food. Soon after arriving, Smith charged that Scarlett Point was ''a combination of an Indian Reserve and the Black Hole of

Calcutta, the rooms were impregnated with the odour of smoked fish, clams, etc.etc.'' Though he was toiling sixteen hours a day there was still "sufficient work to keep three assistants and two charwomen busy for months."

But Scarlett's new keeper ought to have held his nose and copied the Hunts' seafood diet. He had eaten out of cans for the past five years and "had reached the stage where he approached a can of meat with a feeling of revulsion." In those days, revulsion was the least fearful symptom. In January 1941 Smith began suffering acute gastric attacks and told Wilby, "The pain got so bad that it would double me up at times." Fortunately, the *Columbia* called, took him to hospital in Alert Bay, and brought Vivian Hunt back to man the light. The doctor certified that Smith's condition arose "from exclusive consumption of canned goods," and warned that it was "imperative that he should have a varied diet of fresh food." Armed with a doctor's certificate, Smith requested a leave of absence until he could be transferred to Nootka, where there was a store. "At present I am degenerating into a baking soda addict," he confessed. "I would like to cure the trouble, not relieve it." On 25 January the addict wrote Wilby from on board the *Princess Adelaide*, enroute to Kelsey Bay, advising he had left Vivian Hunt in charge again. He had been living on a vile mixture of canned soup and baking soda.[9]

Since everything had been "O.K." at Scarlett Point for thirty years while the Hunts were there—in spite of broken bones and hearts—Wilby had little patience

Scarlett Point Lightstation.

with Smith. H.V. Anderson, chief of aids to navigation, wrote from Ottawa demanding an explanation for the keeper's strange conduct. Why could he not fish and grow his own vegetables? Wilby replied that the waters around Scarlett Point teemed with fish "only waiting to be caught and eaten," and "the odd deer might be shot." Smith could also raise carrots, cabbage, and lettuce, "although," Wilby admitted, "very possibly it can be truly said that there are considerable difficulties in this regard."

George Smith had another compelling reason for going back to Nootka. He had originally bid for Scarlett Point, a one-man station, as a result of his endless friction with assistants at Pine Island. "I figured a man was better off running a station himself," he explained. After a few weeks at Scarlett Point, however, he "figured

Scarlett Point 1981. Jim Ryan photo.

different. . . . Although I am doing my best,'' he wrote Wilby, ''I realize that I am not running this station efficiently as far as watches go, that is, a single man cannot maintain a watch *indefinitely without sleep*.''[10] Better they should place a family man there, someone whose wife or children could relieve him. Besides, just before he left Pine, George had finally found a compatible assistant in Joe Mikas, who was now eager to go to Nootka with him.

Smith finally moved over to Nootka with Mikas in March 1943, but no one could claim that he hadn't left his mark at Scarlett. All through that soup-and-soda winter when he gagged at the thought of opening another can, Smith rebuilt the interior of the kitchen at his own expense, installing a new sink, counter, and cedar cupboards with alternate dark and light panels. Not wanting the government to think he was ''getting extravagant,'' he had purchased his own paint and varnish. ''I feel a little pardonable pride in the job, it looks nice and with the new stove, the kitchen looks clean and modern,'' he boasted.

There is no better measure of the Hunts' endurance than the experience of those who followed them. Smith and his successors balked at conditions that William Hunt either endured or overcame. The Mountains, who followed Smith, protested the lack of regular mail service. Raymond Stockhand spent one winter there in 1952. ''Now that I have recovered from the affects of the seasonal fogs, I have come to the conclusion that it will be to the best interests of the service and myself if I tender my resignation,'' he wrote in December. ''Doubtless, next Season will be less strenuous than the one just past, but I don't care to experience another.''

Pulteney Point

Malcolm Island was reserved by the Dominion for Finnish immigrants, members of the Kalevan Kansa Colonization Company, who came to carve a viable agricultural base out of its thickly wooded terrain. It was hostile country, even for the sturdy socialist Finns. The soil proved fertile enough after the back-breaking chore of clearing the land, and there was seldom any shortage of rain, but there was also no convenient market for their produce. As time went on, more and more of the colonists boarded up their homesteads and drifted to Shushartie, Port Hardy, and Sointula, turning to fishing or lumbering. A few moss-covered frame buildings and corrals, scattered herds of ornery wild cattle, and people and places with tongue-twisting Finnish names, are the last vestiges of their agrarian utopia.

In early May 1905 Colonel Anderson approved plans for a manned light at Pulteney Point on Malcolm Island. He sent duplicates along to James Gaudin in Victoria and advised him ''to have buildings erected by days work under the charge of Mr. G.H. Frost, nominated by Mr. Sloan, M.P., as foreman.'' The plans were identical to those of Discovery Island light. That June the *Colonist* hailed the new beacon as ''one that mariners. . .[had] long been anxious to secure,'' a boon to seamen southbound between Vancouver Island and the mainland ''with the intervening archepelago of Queen Charlotte Sound,'' and likewise for vessels steaming north who would ''make out the light'' as they neared Alert Bay.

Pulteney Point light, standing on the extremity of a low gravel spit, went into operation 15 September. It was a square wooden lantern, rising thirty-five feet from the centre of the cottage roof. The fixed white dioptric-type beacon was visible for eleven miles in an arc sweeping 230 degrees, clearly setting the mouth of Broughton Straits apart from Queen Charlotte Sound. The station was supplied with a hand fog horn in November 1906.

''Austin McKela'' took up his duties as Pulteney's first keeper soon after. The name was an ingenious and doubtless a prudently anglicized version of ''August Makela,'' die-hard socialist and founder of Kalevan Kansa. McKela had attended university in Finland, and in Helsinki had written for *Tyomies* (*The Worker*). His wife Elli had been an actress in Finland.

In October 1910, with winter coming on, he asked for a stove. Gordon Halkett replied, ''Owing to new regulations, the Department does not furnish stoves to Lighthouses, they have to be provided by the Lightkeepers.''[1]

There was no lack of heat during ''a long spell of drought'' the following spring, unusual weather for that corner of the coast which was usually blanketed by rain and fog. McKela spent a parched, breathless week fighting persistent brush fires. On 16 May the wind suddenly turned. The flames devoured a nearby farmhouse ''in incredibly short time,'' then marched toward the lightstation. ''The camp and boat house both surrounded by bush and in the lee of the wind, were doomed from the start,'' he wrote. McKela dragged two boats down to the beach, but had to flee the choking smoke and searing heat before he could secure them. The tide came in and claimed them in the night, while the fire consumed the boat house and advanced on the oil shed and light tower. Both were ''in grave peril'' all that afternoon and the following night, but McKela saved them.

Right: *Pulteney Point keeper Austin McKela.* Left: *Pulteney Point Station inauguration 12 September 1905.*

In July 1913 McKela resigned, claiming, "I have not obtained the leave of absence asked for." He left Toivo Aro, a fellow Finnish settler, in charge. The department hired Aro full-time in 1915 and installed a mechanical fog bell to replace his hand horn. F. Cullison went up to demonstrate the intricate workings of the bell, and Captain Robertson, mindful of the poor record of George Watson's clockwork bell at Portlock Point, wanted "no complaint as to the non-ringing of same when it is required and necessary."

Fog bells were never an acceptable substitute for a horn. Their range varied with the wind, and ships often had to run close in, take soundings, then shut down the muted grumble of their engines while officers listened outside the wheelhouse for the faint sound of the bell across the water. As early as 1921 the Union Steamship Company drew the department's attention to this danger. Wilby noted, however, that there had been no mishaps before the bell had been installed, which probably said more about the hand horn's effectiveness. After meeting with "various Steamship Companies," the agent conceded that a mechanical horn would be superior, but recommended against it until there was "a very increased amount of traffic." The pestering "Marine interests" never gave up easily, however. In October 1928 the Canadian Merchant Service Guild called for a horn at Pulteney and also recommended the power of the light be increased. They wrote Wilby again in September 1929, pointing to the fact that "the number of ships of all Classes passing this point. . .[had] greatly increased in recent years." Three times that foggy summer their passenger steamers had to kill their engines "for a considerable time—none less than an hour"—to take a fix on Aro's elusive bell. Time, after all, was money. Wilby finally gave in and installed a fog alarm at Pulteney in April 1931.

Aro's selection, like McKela's, marked a curious departure from patronage. He was a fervent social democrat who had participated as an agitator in the Finnish General Strike of 1905—a man hardly in sympathy with Borden's Bay Street Tories. However, he lived on the island, and if his opinions came to the notice of local politicos there may well have been a tendency to brush them off as the aberrant quirks of an immigrant. One expected queer politics from people who chased each other out of saunas into the snow with birch branches.

In November 1917 Aro pointed out that living costs had skyrocketed 50 percent since the war. His annual salary of $600 was barely enough to scrape by on, and he received nothing for winding the bell every three hours. He asked for an increase of ten dollars a month. "I would say I have done my duty well and satisfactorily because there has not been any remarks," he claimed, adding, for good measure, that he was contributing to the Patriotic Fund. Two weeks later Ottawa turned Aro down, ruling that Pulteney Point was "correctly classified."[2]

Gordon Halkett was disgusted with conditions at the light when he inspected the station in the autumn of 1920. He said as much to Aro, which prompted a letter from the Finn headed "Rather privately." Aro explained that the disorder was temporary. He was in the habit of receiving mail Saturdays and hoarding it until

Pulteney Point station with one of Toivo Aro's "paying hobbies" in foreground.

Sunday, putting off his housework until the next week. Halkett and his wife had landed without warning on a Sunday morning, while Aro was helping a neighbour launch his skiff. "At the same time I honestly confess that I have been sometimes tired to keep allways very rigid order in the house," Aro apologized. The light and the bell left him little time for sleep. Besides, the place badly needed a woman's touch but there were few fetching or eligible females around. "There has been no women around here of proper age, and I have had no time to go seek further," Aro lamented. "Such women I like, for instance, the lady who was with you here, are not easily found."[3]

In September 1925 Ottawa asked Wilby to rank his stations by levels of isolation as a prelude to reclassification. His reports are a valuable measure of the decline of once-hopeful transplanted communities like the Finns. In 1918 Robertson had pronounced Pulteney "not an isolated" station, but almost all the Finnish farmers save Aro and his brother had moved to Sointula, seven miles away with no connection by road. Like the other Finns, Aro could farm, but there was no ready market for his produce, so he was "practically dependent on his salary."[4]

Always eager to prescribe any cure for penury other than a pay raise, the department suggested that Aro take up a "paying hobby." He began building boats with his brother. The two produced a small armada, working out of their boat shed on the neighbouring property, turning out everything from clinker-built dinghies to purse-seiners like *Orca G.*, still operated by Ocean Fisheries sixty years later.

In 1922 Kyllikki Jaakola landed in Sointula, bringing Toivo Aro's quest for a woman with charms comparable to Mrs. Halkett's to an end. They married soon after, and their son Vic was born within a year.

Most of her sisters on the lights would have envied Kyllikki. With family and friends nearby, a ready supply of fresh vegetables, and enough room to graze sheep for mutton and wool, Pulteney Point light was a paradise compared to some of the barren outposts to the north. It was still a long, lonesome way from home, though, and the young wife and mother began to fear she had plunged into a new life in a new country and gone out too deep. In her private moments with the boy on the beach and Toivo making shavings over in the boatshed, she would dress herself in elaborate traditional costumes as if trying to salvage at least the outer wrappings of a mislaid past.

Keeping the light was grinding Toivo down too. After ten years' effort he had yet to master the lightkeeper's art of catnapping, only managing occasional snoozes stretched out on a mat behind the kitchen stove after lunch. He could not sleep during the day, and this disability hit him hardest during the long winter nights' watch. He would soon learn, to his horror, that these nights were the worst time for Kyllikki—especially after word came of her father's death, when the wind sucking at the shutters and the flat crunch of the swells on gravel provided background for the bell tolling out the seconds of their lives.

Like most other lighthouse kids of his generation, Vic Aro's memory is free of the blemishes of a tough life, though he allows that ''life at the light. . . as an only child was at times lonely'':

> I particularly remember the lonely winters when it was too wet and stormy to venture outside. Other times of the year were not so bad as we often had company, particularly my uncle and aunt and their daughter who was the same age as I. If I was alone and the weather was good I would prowl the beaches and the woods with my border collie who was my constant companion. It was probably there that I became interested in marine life, which ultimately led to me becoming a fisheries biologist.

As he approached school age, Vic obviously was ready for something more than a dog and a stretch of beach. It was the same dilemma facing all the keepers up the coast, made worse by Toivo and Kyllikki's lack of English. She had had no need for

Pulteney Point station from landward.

Toivo and Kylikki Aro of Pulteney Point Light.

"Joy at Christmas," "strength in the year 1927"
reads Aro family Christmas card for 1926.

Toivo and Kylikki with their son at Pulteney Point.

it; he always had his Finnish-English dictionary within easy reach to communicate with the ''big shots'' in Victoria. He got it out early in 1930 to appeal over their heads to the Department of Finance, asking if he could withdraw his pension contributions in a lump sum. When Wilby got wind of his plans, he asked for an explanation. Aro replied, ''I will need the money sorely when I will build a house for my family. I am not yet wholly incapacitated but really speaking the nerve strain is growing too hard to me caused by lack of sleep during foggy times at summer and the stormy periods of winters. So I thought to leave the job before I will be a total nervous wreck,'' He recommended another Finn, a friend named Sula Wartie, as a replacement, and quit Pulteney in November.[5]

First they settled for a few weeks in Rough Bay, across from Sointula, then moved in with Toivo's brother and sister-in-law in the village. ''Later my father remarked once that he should have remained with the lighthouse service and should have built a small house in Sointula,'' Vic recalled. ''It is possible that another reason father left the light was to get my mother away from there. He later told me that the continual wind and the wash on the beach bothered her.''

Wartie served briefly as a substitute until Oliver ''Shorty'' Maisonville took his place in June 1931. Late that fall, much to the delight of Malcolm Islanders, a southbound U.S. freighter loaded with canned salmon gave Pulteney Point too wide a berth. She ran aground at the mouth of Cluxewe River across the way. In a feckless attempt to refloat, deckhands began dumping cases of cargo over the side and stacked the rest ashore. The crew left the ship unattended to seek a tow, and a whole flotilla set out from Sointula. ''The local ladies didn't have to can their own salmon for some time,'' Vic Aro remembered.

Maisonville's experience confirms that some men freely chose the exile others complained so bitterly about. In August 1933 a party of evangelists visited Pulteney. Most keepers had long supported the Anglican and United Church mission boats which, aside from the Red Cross, were often their only connection with the outside world—welcome voices in the wilderness. In addition to offering low-key spiritual comforts, the crews called at isolated communities up and down the coast with news and companionship, a tradition which the *Thomas Crosby* continues to this day. The preachers Maisonville encountered were missionaries of a different stripe. Though they lacked the polish of latter-day T.V. evangelists, their message was virtually the same—a heady mixture of morality and literal interpretation of the Bible.

Maisonville invited them in, though ''their decorum smacked of the gangster.'' In the course of their conversation, one of the party was ''so feared that he might forget something that he made pencil notes.'' Before leaving he offered up a prayer ''that would insult an ordinary intelligence—not to mention a Diety.'' A few days later they called again to inquire if Maisonville had seen ''the Light'' yet. ''I had—and ordered them off the Island,'' he informed Wilby. Next he received ''a literary epic'' from one of the party, R.J. Walker, a stipendary magistrate, who castigated Maisonville for ''living at a Government Station with a woman to whom . . . [he was] not married." Walker offered his services to make an honest woman of her since, he insisted, "It is neither wise nor right that you should continue as you are."

Maisonville related to Wilby that many people, hungry and in need, called at Pulteney. "Up to date I have fed about three hundred," he said. But he wanted no truck with "sky walkers" who came uninvited, with "no business on this reservation in the season of fog after the light is lighted." He threatened to sue Walker and forward his "epic" to the attorney-general, and wanted to know the "law regarding trespass on Light Stations" so he could harry them off if they ever came back.

In May 1935 the evangelists returned and found Kalle Kaisla in charge while Maisonville was away. The shore party asked Kaisla if he was a Christian. According to Maisonville, "When he replied in his quiet way that he didn't know, they asked him if he wanted to die like an animal"—a prophetic insult as it turned out. Once again the keeper wanted to know about laws of trespass so he could fend off "these gentlemen of the cloth." Shorty had been alone three months, and at a station "where one sleeps where he can," he believed he was "surely entitled to some protection and peace."

On the afternoon of 21 February 1937 Maisonville's friend Kaisla set out for Sointula in his gas boat with his daughter Ann. They came back through a blinding snowstorm around 10 P.M. Kaisla ran in close to their home, put Ann ashore, then went out to moor his boat behind the thick membrane of snow. On shore Ann and her mother could barely see his lantern moving feebly as he let down his skiff and climbed in. Then the light went out. Ann ran down to the dock, launched Maisonville's dinghy, and rowed out, screaming for her father. Only the howling wind replied. "After an hour's rowing she managed to get back, how, God only knows," Maisonville related. She ran up to the lighthouse, hysterically pounding her fists on the engine room door although it was unlocked and Maisonville was inside tending the horn. It was now past midnight.

Ann beseeched him to begin emergency signalling for a steamer to turn in and join the search. Her request posed a dreadful dilemma. With less than a few hundred yards' visibility, should he risk hundreds of lives in what might well be a fruitless search for his friend? Maisonville refused. In despair and disgust, Ann struck out on foot for Sointula at daybreak. Unable to dissuade her, Maisonville gave her a jar of rum and some matches. The storm had reached its peak. She reached the first deserted house three hours later, then pressed on, barging into Sointula's Co-op store at 4 P.M.

The weather cleared an hour after Ann ran off, and Maisonville began to summon help with his horn. Ann's mother, "crazed with grief," wandered aimlessly up and down the beach in search of her daughter. "When Ann staggered in, I damn near wept," Maisonville reported, "her feet [were] so swollen that she couldn't get my gumboot stags on her. Her shoes had given out halfway to Sointula." The two keening, disheveled women spent the night with Maisonville, ''but there was little sleep for anyone.'' Next morning Ann's sister and brother-in-law took them away, and the police began the grim task of dragging for Kaisla's body. ''This I think is enough grief for one letter,'' Maisonville closed his account, ''will try to write Mr. Halkett tomorrow, but believe me, the way I feel etc.!''[6]

In and around Sointula, Maisonville paid a heavy price for his fateful decision. The conviction quickly became current that the keeper had cruelly sacrificed his best friend rather than risk his job. They were Finns after all; he was an outsider. Maisonville soon became a pariah. Letters railing at his ''spineless cruelty'' went to Wilby, MPs, the Finnish consul, and the minister of Marine and Fisheries. Wavering under a barrage of indignation, Wilby asked Maisonville to explain his actions. The keeper brushed aside these calumnies coming from people forty miles away—one of whom was ''familiar with the Police blotter in Vancouver. . . .I take it that the Department relies on keepers to use deductive reasoning, in running their stations, instead of violent emotion,'' he argued. ''The sore spot seems to be that I didn't start signalling blindly when they thought I should. Had Mr. Kaisla been drifting in his gas boat or some craft, I would have signaled; but an hour or more after the accident, when he had nothing but a three board straight sided 'coffin,' it was too late.'' As for the widow and her daughter, hadn't he sheltered and fed them for two anguished, sleepless nights, and lent them ''Thirty Dollars to tide them over''?[7]

By 1940 commercial shipping in the area was in sharp decline and the waters around Pulteney were ''used extensively by fishing boats,'' each one with an anchor light showing atop its mast after dark. It was fatally simple to mistake Pulteney's fixed white light for a fish boat riding at anchor on a smooth sea, so the department installed a new revolving apparatus to give a distinctive flash.

The new lens worked well until the summer of 1942, when orders came to black out the West Coast after the shelling of Estevan Point. The Alaska Steamship

Alaska Steamship Co's Columbia *aground on Pulteney Point 1942.*

Company's *Columbia* hit the spit in the dark and ran a third of her length up on the point, towering over the lighthouse. There she stayed, like a cartoonist's vision, for three weeks, until tugs took her off on a high tide.

On 2 May 1945 a fisherman reported a burning gas boat making for the beach about three-quarters of a mile northwest of the light. Maisonville struck out through the bush with a lantern, and came upon the smouldering craft and its crew. "There were three men, two women and a small child on beach," he reported. "One man was burned about the face, hands and one foot. We brought them up to the light and gave him first aid with burn dressings etc. After coffee and food we made beds for them in the engine house." Next day he helped them refloat their charred boat and they proceeded to Blunden Harbour.

That December Maisonville reminded Stamford he had turned sixty-seven. He wanted to give ample notice of his intention to resign the following June, after fifteen years' service. The *Berens* called in May to install a radio telephone. Her chief engineer wanted to know if Maisonville had found a temporary replacement until his successor took over at Pulteney. "Why all the rush?" Shorty asked, "Unless it is to get me off the Station before I get in my fifteen years." He wanted it "clearly understood" he was not quitting until June 10. If necessary he would stay on a month longer. "I thought the Wilby technique had passed out of that office along with his weighty signature and his prostate gland of sacred memory," he snarled.[8]

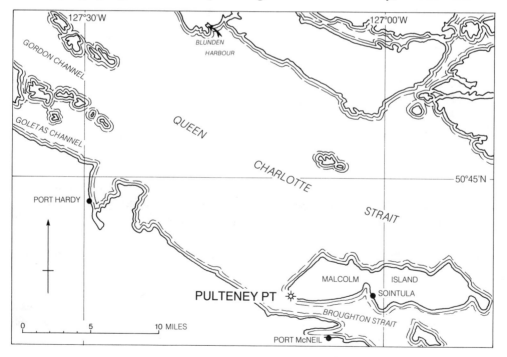

Pine Island

In 1860 Captain G.H. Richards of HMS *Hecate* sailed through the northern entrance of Johnstone Strait, en route to map the coastline of the Queen Charlotte Islands. He passed a small, heavily wooded island, some hundred acres in area, with trees towering two hundred feet. For centuries pines had been transplanted from Baltic forests to the decks of British ships as masts, and in those days before forestry became a science in its own right, most coniferous trees were dubbed pines. Richards scrawled the name "Pine Island" on his chart, although no pines can be found among its cedars, fir, and hemlock.

Pine has a precipitous, rocky shoreline, pounded incessantly by swells curling around Cape Scott. Rough weather and fog are frightful, constant companions up there. Before he moved over to Scarlett Point, George Smith, Pine's keeper in the 1930s, left behind a vivid description of the temper of one winter gale.

> On the eighth of this month we had a storm, it reached such an intensity that the A frame platform (for the Winch) was floating up and down by the wind pressure underneath, the paint shack lost about two square yards of shingles, one inch boards were flying through the air like paper.

So much foam shot past as the seas battered the rocks that visibility dropped to near zero. Smith went out to crank up the horns.

> That trip to the Fog station was interesting if not graceful, one serious blast pinned me against a building so tight I couldn't get off. I realized it was not good judgment to try until it slackened a bit, as I did not know where my next destination would be, however I arrived at the Fog station by a combination of crawling and clawing.[1]

The same weather harried construction workers in 1907, but in spite of the problem of landing supplies and keeping them there, the work party managed to erect a square wooden light tower with an attached dwelling on the southwestern point of the island. The tower supported a red polygonal iron lantern, and there was also an engine room and oil storage shed. The department put William Hunt ashore as caretaker during the construction phase. S. Montgomery, the department's mechanical engineer, went up to Pine Island that June to install the engines. Disgusted at finding an Indian and ''half-breed'' acting as caretakers he complained, ''It was impossible for myself and two men to eat what they cooked in the filthy condition of the cook-house.''

Once the engines were installed and run in, he went back to Victoria. Gaudin instructed him to return aboard the *Cascade* with Arthur Broughton Gurney, the new keeper, and his assistant. Montgomery went to Nanaimo where the steamer rode at anchor in Departure Bay. ''This is what was aboard,'' he caustically reported, ''an engineer and mate rotten from whiskey, a lightkeeper just over the D.T.s from whiskey and his assistant, an imbecile from the same cause.'' It was an inauspicious beginning for the strategic new station, but one that Gaudin might have anticipated. When he first met Arthur Gurney in the marine office after the Parksville shopkeeper secured his nomination from William Sloan, MP, Gaudin had ''detected an odour of spirits'' about his person, ''and thought it advisable to give . . . [him] a timely warning.''[2]

Gurney's patronage plum soon turned sour. On New Year's Day 1908 he wrote Sloan to advise that his assistant threatened to quit by the first of May if no increase in wages was forthcoming. Gurney earned $1260 and paid his assistant $500. ''Now regarding myself,'' he explained, ''I find it is quite out of the question for me to live on *$700 per annum* and keep my family . . . the wages is altogether out in proportion to the amount of work to be performed and to the drawbacks connected with a station like Pine Island.''

There were drawbacks aplenty. Other than Rhinoceros Auklets there was no game on the island, and no leaving it without risk to go fishing. The keeper had recently lost $35 worth of provisions, ''also nearly . . . [his] life through it being such a diabolical place to land.'' Gurney sheepishly asked Sloan not to consider him an ingrate but, he asked, ''I want to know as soon as possible am I going to get a *raise in wages* or am I going to have to *have the station with my wife as assistant*.'' If the latter, he demanded a job back ''in Civilization.''[3] The MP took up Gurney's cause with Colonel Anderson, who refused an increase. The salary, he decided, was ''a fair one and . . . the highest given at any station in B.C.''[4]

Undaunted, Gurney wrote directly to the minister that May, itemizing his grocery list. With potatoes running at $5.00 a sack and butter at 40 cents a pound, it cost $800 a year just living hand to mouth. ''I also would bring to your notice that the Government wage in British Columbia is three dollars per day for eight hours labour,'' he concluded. If B.C.'s workers had been required to stand twelve-hour watches, even on weekends (and without an assistant Gurney must have fought off sleep for much longer), they would earn $1575—more than twice his salary!

Gurney's permanent appointment was approved that August. At Pine Island, though, it seemed little cause for celebration. He asked Gaudin sarcastically what his position had been for the past year, and wondered how he was "going to obtain a competent engineer and live. . . at the wage of $1260 a year. When an engineer would at the smallest wage. . . want $2000 to live on a place like Pine Island?"

Within a year Gurney was obsessed with escaping. The relentless winds, heavy surf, and continuous fog were wearing down men, women, and machines alike. In early October 1908 he had toiled forty-eight hours without sleep, trying to replace faulty ignitors in his gas engines, and finally gave up in disgust when he discovered the wrong parts had been shipped. "I have conscientiously tried to carry out my duties here," he told Gaudin, "and this sort of thing that I have gone through in the last 48 hours is making an old man of me." The engines cried out for expert attention, a complete overhaul—and they would have to get it if the department wished to retain his services on Pine Island.

Gaudin seems to have disliked Gurney from the start, right from the day he stood in his office exuding that sour aroma of "spirits." His continuous flood of ink about wages to MPs and higher-ups (even the minister!) could only have sharpened the agent's disdain, and the issue of the engines seemed to offer a solid pretext to be rid of the gadfly once and for all. Gaudin forwarded Gurney's complaint to Ottawa, attributing the engine's mechanical troubles to the keeper's "ignorance in handling it as well as his incompetency and disinclination to work." Sack Gurney, he recommended, and find a replacement "of some mechanical experience."[5]

William Hunt over at Scarlett Point soon supplied another reason for getting rid of Gurney. He charged that Gurney was working an ingenious, if unorthodox, way out of his dire financial straits: hawking government supplies to passing boats. He informed Gaudin that his "neighbour" had sold gasoline, cotton waste, and other government property to the sloop *Repentance*, as well as selling twenty-five pounds of white lead, three gallons of mixed red oxide, and other supplies, in Shushartie Bay. Moreover, he had foolishly confided to Hunt his plans to market more gasoline and coal oil if he had an opportunity.[6] Gaudin referred Hunt's charges to Ottawa, advising that he would spare no effort to uncover proof. The deputy minister asked for the nomination of a man to succeed Gurney. As it turned out, however, no concrete evidence was ever brought forward.

The matter of the engine failures hinged upon competence, but the acting chief engineer studied Gaudin's and Gurney's exchanges and laid the blame squarely on policy rather than personnel. No inspector of fog alarms had been assigned to British Columbia, even though each installation had to be examined by one of the department's "expert mechanics at least once a year." It was absurd to place unqualified men in charge of sophisticated power plants, and just as stupid to expect any qualified engineer to work for a lightkeeper's wages. Ottawa was wasting money to save it. "The Department could undoubtedly save money and reputation by

Arthur Gurney in Pine Island engine room.

appointing only thoroughly qualified men to such places and give the same salary that similar services are worth in the vicinity,'' he recommended.[7]

Meanwhile, up at Pine Island, the Gurneys' morale was sinking fast. In February 1909 the lightkeeper wrote another MP: ''I cannot stay here longer than the beginning of the summer as the two years' confinement on this island has broken down my wife's health & I have to get my children educated.'' All his savings had evaporated. After a year's toil and trouble, he found himself ''in a worse predicament'' than when he landed there. Gurney reminded MacDonald that he had "worked all. . .[his] life for the Liberal Party." Surely he deserved some richer return for his zeal. "Give me a billet," he begged, "—any small billet in civilization by the end of June 1909."[8]

A month before his deadline he had a reprieve, though Gurney was so disenchanted with his fog-bound surroundings that it must have seemed a hollow triumph. William Peter, an engineer for the department, landed at Pine Island and soon confirmed the keeper's complaint about the sorry state of his overworked engines. Peter told Gaudin that the lightkeeper was no slouch—he had done as well as could be expected under very trying circumstances, and had proved helpful in assisting with overhauls. Gaudin wrote his deputy in Ottawa to withdraw the earlier charges of incompetence, sloth, and neglect.

Now that he was a full-time lightkeeper, with the shadow of incompetence dissipated, Gurney wrote Gaudin with an imaginative, if outlandish, proposition. He offered to stay through the summer, then take leave from September 1909 until April 1910, standing by somewhere on Vancouver Island, "placed in such a position that if necessary at any time. . .[he could] proceed to Pine Island." Gaudin scotched that scheme.

Their fourth winter at Pine Island proved too much for the Gurneys. Over at Scarlett Point, William Hunt was puzzled when the Pine Island horn blasted away for three days in clear weather. He rowed over on Boxing Day and Gurney explained that he wanted Hunt to take charge while he went off to Victoria. Hunt replied it was out of the question without Gaudin's say-so. Next day Gurney left his wife and children anyway, rowed over to Scarlett Point, spent the night there, then boarded the *Camosun* bound for Victoria. Hunt dispatched two of his sons to Pine, and sent an indignant letter to Victoria.

Gaudin was incensed when he read about Gurney's desertion. He stormed out of his office and spent an afternoon checking hotel registers, but Gurney had gone underground, perhaps staying with friends or using an assumed name. This was the last straw. Gaudin again wrote the deputy minister, recommending Gurney's dismissal.

As if Gurney did not have enough problems, his creditors were hot after him too. George Pearson, despairing of ever being able to contact Gurney, and knowing that no claim could be made against a government employee, wrote the minister as a last resort. Gurney, he explained, had incurred a debt of $249 with Pearson's firm, then "quietly slipped away to Pine Id. Lighthouse to a position secured him by Mr. Sloan leaving his affairs in such shape that his creditors found almost nothing to liquidate."[9] Stanton, the deputy minister, instructed Gaudin to warn Gurney that the department expected "him to settle his indebtedness," and would not "tolerate such action. . .on the part of any of its employees." The lightkeeper's indebtedness also aroused the ire of Liberal circles in Victoria. Ralph Smith, a local MP, wrote Brodeur, the minister, pressing him "to insist on these men meeting their obligations." As they were patronage appointments, it would "bring discredit upon the party" if they did not pay their bills.

Fortunately for Gurney, the Victoria Liberal Association promised him the nomination for the new Sheringham Point lighthouse Colonel Anderson was building west of Sooke in Juan de Fuca Strait. Things were looking up, and just in time, too. That winter had seen record fog. After running the alarm non-stop for 276 hours, Gurney finally had to hire an extra assistant, a luxury he could ill afford.

In 1911 Gaudin left the department, and with him went any lingering ill feeling between Gurney and the Victoria agency. Gurney wrote Captain Robertson, reminding the new agent of the Sheringham pledge and suggesting some improvements to be made there. "If the Dominion gov't expect respectable people to take charge of their stations," he declared, "they should treat them as such, not as *siwashes*." At least they could install a toilet. Carrying steaming buckets of excrement from the house to the sea, "in winter in a gale of wind, rain and snow," counted among Gurney's "many other pleasant occupations on Pine Island." Since there was "no dirtier job than the running of a fog alarm," they might as well build a bathroom at Sheringham too.

Late in September the long-awaited letter arrived from his MP, confirming that Sheringham Point was his. "If you have any pity in your heart," he told Robertson, "have us moved as soon as possible as the 343 hours of fog has quite broken down my wife."[10] Robertson replied that he would do his utmost to assure that Gurney went to Sheringham soon.

Weeks dragged into months. Another winter lay siege to Pine and still no word came. It was worse than ever—this time the Gurneys were marooned, unable even to row out for mail and supplies. Twice that fall the keeper lost his mast and his mail, including much-needed money sent from the "old country," when he went out to fetch supplies. H.L. Kemp, the mail carrier, had capsized his boat in the surf on Christmas Eve 1911. Gurney lent him the lighthouse boat to row over to Port Hardy for a new battery. Neither Kemp nor the boat was ever seen again.

There was also a political storm: Wilfrid Laurier and free trade went down to defeat that October, and Liberal patronage shriveled and withered on the vine. Gurney, lifelong Liberal though he was, went through a striking political metamorphosis that winter in his isolated cocoon, and emerged a true-blue Conservative in the spring. He began pestering Tory MPs. At first they seemed cool. Francis Shepherd, who had won Sloan's Nanaimo seat, merely advised that Gurney's transfer would receive "due consideration," and referred ominously to "several applications in." Sheringham seemed to be slipping away.

After a fifteen-year famine, competition for spoils among B.C. Tories was fierce. Gurney pulled out all the stops. He wrote Captain Robertson, binding him to his earlier promise to write Shepherd and recommend him for the coveted nomination. For his part, Gurney boasted of "other conservative friends, among them the Prime Minister who knew . . . [him] in Halifax when . . . [he] was a soldier."[11]

Robert Borden's acquaintance sent his wife down that spring to plead in person with Nanaimo's new MP. Shepherd had her in to tea on 26 April. H.C. Killeen, the department's engineer, was there too and could testify to the insufferable plight of a lightkeeper's wife at Pine Island. Shepherd, in his first encounter with a lightkeeper, was obviously touched by Anna Gurney's desperation. He wrote Captain Robertson immediately, asking him to revoke the Sheringham appointment—which had already gone to a Mr. Robinson—"with as little friction as possible." For his part, Shepherd would stroke the ruffled feathers of the Sooke and Otter Point Conservative Association.

Anna Gurney was ecstatic. The dreadful din of the fog horn, the week-long stints in the engine room, the hours worrying about Arthur battling the angry surf in a skiff—all that seemed behind her already. She penned a chirpy note to Robertson from Vancouver, describing her meeting with Shepherd. "I am in great hopes it will be finally settled before I return to Pine Island," she crowed. She wanted to know when the tender might sail for Pine so she could buy supplies for their move. A wire confirming Arthur's appointment was forthcoming, and she wrote, "Altogether it looks as if we might possibly succeed."

It must have been a jubilant homecoming at Pine Island when she landed with the news. Once their excitement abated, Arthur and Anna began crating their belongings. Two weeks later Gurney informed Captain Robertson, "I have all my personal effects packed and Pine Island Light Station is ready to turn over to the incoming Light Keeper at a minute's notice. I am most anxious to move at your earliest convenience to Sheringham via Victoria."

They kept aside the coffee pot and just enough food to make meals, and sat on their crates awaiting their deliverance. The mail boat finally came in mid-August and Gurney immediately ripped open the embossed department envelope. He read:

Victoria, B.C. August 6th/12

Sir:—

I regret to inform you that Mr. Shepherd has notified me this morning that the Association of the constituency of Comox-Atlin, in which Sheringham Point is in, has nominated Mr. E.T. Arden for the position of lightkeeper.

A copy of Mr. Shepherd's letter is herewith enclosed.

Yours respectfully,
Agent. [12]

It was a crushing blow. Crestfallen, they began prying their crates apart and set up house again, with furniture which should have been standing in a parlour with a spectacular view of Point-No-Point, at the end of a road leading to Sooke and a school.

There was still a crumb of hope. In his letter to Captain Robertson, Shepherd held out the prospect of Gurney's exchanging places with the keepers at Sisters or Ballenas. Gurney's letter dated 1 September betrays his despair at losing the prize once in his grasp. He asked to be considered for transfer. Naturally he preferred

Ballenas over Sisters. Besides, its keeper was not even a constituent, had less seniority, and was a bachelor. "Do try hard to get it for me," Gurney pleaded, "but get me one for sure." The prospect of a sixth winter set to pounce upon that wild and windswept place was more than they could bear. When the Gurneys' ship finally came in, it loaded their effects and set a course for Ballenas, delivering them from Pine's clutches in 1912.

Donald McPhee inherited Pine from the Gurneys. The bachelor advertised in the Vancouver papers for a housekeeper. A widow, "well educated. . . from a very fine family in Australia," came up with her two teenaged children, Violet and Percival Pike. Within a year she became his common-law wife and they transferred to Estevan Point. Percy Pike and his new bride Mary, seventeen, stayed behind.

In stark contrast to the Gurneys before them, the Pikes embraced the place and had a ten-year love affair with Pine Island. Their career on the lights would span forty-five years. Toward the end Percy boasted they "would do it all over again." They seemed virtually to thrive in isolation, and Pike's surviving correspondence is free of Gurney's bitter spite and biting sarcasm. One wonders if they were actually at the same place for the same length of time.

If they had no regrets, however, the Pikes also had a rare capacity to put the past behind them. Whether they knew it or not, Mary was expecting their first child in February 1920. As they prepared for bed on the nineteenth, she complained of a slight headache. By 11 P.M. "she was taken with convulsions and unconsciousness," and the child was born at 2:30 A.M. Percy had his father-in-law as an assistant, and both became increasingly alarmed when Mary's coma stretched into its third day. They wired for the doctor at Port Hardy but received no reply. The *Leebro* called at the island on 23 February. Percy wisely decided, "It was death to remove my wife." The tender hoisted anchor, steamed back to Port Hardy, and returned next morning with a nurse aboard. The crew attempted to take Mary off, but turned back in the heavy swell and carried her ashore. They finally wrestled her aboard shortly after noon, and took mother and baby away to hospital in Alert Bay.

Captain Wilson reported that the nurse had found "arrangements for looking after her were very bad in spite of her parents being on the station." Wilby sent off a scathing letter to the new father, demanding an explanation, "concealing nothing, as to why such conditions were allowed to exist, why this office was not advised, and why, apparently, no efforts were made for the proper care of mother and child." According to Percy, the whole incident had come as a complete surprise! Neither he nor Mary's father had detected "any change in any way, shape, or form" in his wife. "Should I have known of her ailment," he claimed, "I would at once without doubt, taken proper measures for her safety."[13]

This was a bit much for Colonel Wilby, who was encountering lightkeepers for the first time as marine agent. He expressed his amazement and disbelief at "how any man or woman arriving at years of discretion and understand[ing] could have the ignorance which" Pike professed regarding his wife. Still, one had to keep an open mind about these things. He could hardly establish the ''absolute incorrectness'' of Pike's statement, so Wilby sternly warned him not to let it happen again. The whole affair, he concluded, ''does anything but improve your record in the service.''

In June 1921 the Pikes suspected that another child might be on the way. This time they took no chances of incurring the wrath of Wilby. Mary went to hospital at Alert Bay in plenty of time to give birth, but the infant contracted pneumonia on the boat ride home and died eighteen days later.[14]

Slinging a supply of oil ashore, Pine Island, circa 1930.

Instead of trying to escape their surroundings in Arthur Gurney's fashion, the Pikes set to work planting gardens, raising chickens, and slashing hiking trails across the island. Shushartie Bay, a grueling fourteen miles away by rowboat, was their closest source of supplies. Whoever stayed behind could never be sure when, if ever, the other would return. Often Percy arrived only to find landing impossible in the seething surf. He would turn around and row back to Shushartie. In January 1921 (the worst month in the north) he wrote Wilby an apology for having been ''held at Shushartie Bay for the past twelve days on account of weather conditions, making several attempts to land with failure.'' With a woman like Mary left behind, though, no one need worry.

John Muir, a master on one of the Union steamships, marveled at Mary Pike's courage and strength. ''She would run that light and she would row her boat into Shushartie Bay and get anything she wanted,'' he recalled. ''I used to roll up newspapers and when it was a fine day, I'd blow the whistle and they would know us anyway, coming along. You can go right in close to Pine Island and throw the bundle of papers over to her. Whether they were wet or dry, she didn't care. That was the Pikes.''

The waters between Pine Island and Shushartie Bay reared up in swells within arm's reach of a rowboat's gunwales. In the 1950s a launch service ferrying supplies from Shushartie was discontinued as too hazardous, and the department forbade lightkeepers to make the trip themselves. This was after the Pikes' time, though; they had made the journey as a matter of course. Mary Pike thought nothing of striking out for Port Hardy, a round trip of forty-four miles!

In 1921 the Red Cross sent Rhoda MacKenzie to Pine Island in the course of their lighthouse survey. Her reports provide a rare insight—the first impressions of an outsider. She praised Mary as a fine housekeeper who kept ''her home and her baby in excellent condition.'' The child had been suffering from rickets but appeared to have recovered. ''They have a launch but seldom leave the place as their duties demand most of their time,'' the nurse reported. ''The landing is rather dangerous, so Mrs. Pike gets out very little.'' Their dwelling was warm and well lighted, she noted.

> They have a few houseplants and more would be appreciated. Have a good breed of hens and plenty of eggs. Rabbits run wild. They have a good Victrola. Mrs. Pike has a rug on the floor which she made on a wooden frame and with a hook modelled by her husband, who is of an inventive turn of mind. He paints with oils.... When a young man he went to sea as a bell-boy on various boats and there learned many things of assistance to him now.

In sharp contrast to the Gurneys' torment, the cozy scene could now be captured in a needlework sampler titled ''Home Sweet Home.'' Forty years later, when interviewed about working conditions on the lights, Percy Pike declared that he ''never regretted a minute of it.''

As the most isolated station in the Victoria agency, one which bore the full brunt of every gale that barged down Queen Charlotte Sound, Pine was a forcing house for "green" newcomers to the lights. "If they can handle Pine, they can handle anything," deckhands remarked as they ferried supplies and furniture for new arrivals, and stole sidelong glances at the men and their wives for any betrayal of sentiment about their new home.

No place could be further removed from the safe and stuffy life of Rex Pendril "Pen" Brown, who had spent twelve years as a bank clerk behind cages in Toronto and Vancouver. Pen, his wife Elizabeth, and their two daughters, came on the lights as assistant keepers at Fiddle Reef and Cape Mudge, and took a promotion to Pine in July 1957. Up there, far from the incessant clatter of typewriters and telephones, the Browns hacked out an agrarian paradise on the edge of the rolling North Pacific, trading mortgage seekers and auditors for monthly shore parties and occasional birdwatchers.

When a *Colonist* reporter visited Pine in 1960, he encountered a "truly happy man" standing there amongst his squawking flocks of chickens. Pen had set ducks and geese to work eating slugs and mowing lawns. "The long winters, isolation, mean nothing to either of them," the journalist wrote. And so it can seem when time is measured in seasons, when one gale breathes hard on the heels of another, when one can hunker down and stroll through horrendous weather, then come home to curl up with a book or pore over a hobby while logs crunch and grind on the rocks below and wind whines up the stovepipe like a violinist going up the E string. Such was the idyllic life of the Browns of Pine Island until their dream turned to a nightmare one wild night in February 1967.

The storm was conceived, like all its kin, deep in the swirling mid-Pacific womb of weather fronts, familiar today in satellite photographs on the television news. By late afternoon its winds had mustered hurricane force of one hundred knots off Cape St. James. They rushed headlong into the strait for an assault on Pine, driving a heaving sea before them. At 11:30 P.M. the Browns lay sleepless "on account of heavy sea noise." Then they heard chains clanking against the fuel tanks. They dressed hurriedly and groped their way to the engine room with Lewis, their assistant. The sea had risen up the full length of the fog alarm building and smashed a window. Hastily filling the breach with plywood, they "left the engine room as unsafe."

Minutes later, as they sat at the kitchen table sipping coffee and composing a damage report, there came an ear-splitting roar and the lights snuffed out. Pen ran to the window and stared transfixed at the engine room, taking in the full measure of their peril. The very floor where they had been standing was now open to the sky, a scene of total desolation, mangled and mauled beyond all recognition by a wave, fifty-feet high, which had plowed the building right up to their front steps. They "got the children up and with the Lewises and a lantern and some kerosene left hurriedly for high ground," where they "made a fire and spent the night." Pen ventured back to the house twice in the night for food and clothing.

Pine Island before and after the tsunami that struck in February of 1967.

The first thin streaks of wet dawn filtered through a tangled mass of metal, mud, and rubble. The station was ''a complete wreck'' except for the two dwellings. Pen's catalogue of the chaos provides a sobering measure of a killer wave's awesome power:

> Helicopter pad. . . timber section torn out, concrete pads torn out by the roots and scattered. . . .
>
> One fuel tank full on stand but pipes torn off and it all leaked away. Could not get near it to save it and no tools anyhow.
>
> One empty fuel tank nearby, the other two gone. All piping, walks etc. ripped to bits.
>
> Fog alarm building swept off clean to the floor, wreckage in a pile at the inner end. . . .
>
> Most of the inventory can be considered a total loss. Fog alarm engine probably on or under the wreckage. . . .
>
> One power plant almost undamaged, the other had air tank smashed against it and it may be in poor shape. Alternators OK except for water damage. . . .
>
> Paint shop wrecked, contents can be salvaged. . . .
>
> Oil shed wrecked, some contents can be salvaged. . . .
>
> Tower OK except for hole smashed in bottom sheeting by sods and soil swept over top of oil shed. . . .
>
> Boat house in one piece up against winch house, contents salvageable.
>
> Winch house damaged but not too much, machinery OK, but boat in way of use. . . .
>
> Beacon antenna is dislodged from base and must either be taken down on guys or adjusted immediately.
>
> Aerial mast, cable and carriage appears OK except for broken off haul-back line.
>
> Wreckage of course is scattered across the whole front of station. Some things from the engine room were carried into the gulley.

Brown recommended that ''the whole station except for principal keeper's house and landing facilities . . . be relocated on much higher ground.''

As Pine's keepers picked their way through the ruins like shell-shocked refugees, they pondered the miracle of their survival, wondering if the Pacific, vengeful and frustrated in its grab for men and machinery, might come after them again. ''I wasn't really scared,'' Pen said years later. ''What affected me most was seeing all those years of work wiped out in a few seconds. It was very depressing.''

The Browns left Pine Island soon after for Victoria, where Pen served as a lightkeeper-in-residence at the Coast Guard base, coordinating supply and services to the lights. Pine Island lightstation was rebuilt on higher ground.

Views of Pine Island damage 1967.

Pine Island from the air, 1981.
Jim Ryan photo.

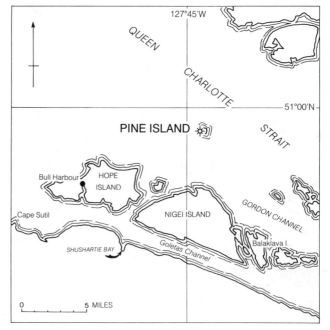

The Northern Lights

Captain Norman MacKay wondered out loud where all the smoke was coming from when he steered the *Alexander Mackenzie* through Metlakatla toward her berth at Digby Island one Friday afternoon in the 1960s. None of his officers knew and the crewmen, already delirious with Friday night fever, were eager for a glass of beer and a woman's touch and couldn't have cared less. MacKay threaded his way past them, down the corrugated gangplank, and sauntered over to the parking lot to see what the clerks were dumping into their bonfire. Files. The agent had ordered them to burn all outdated files. They had started first thing that morning, glad to be outside away from their desks. Fanning away the smoke, the veteran captain hitched up his trousers and squatted down, squinting teary-eyed for a closer look. Some labels still stood out on the charred, curling folders: Green Island, Lawyer Island, Boat Bluff, Cape St. James . . . all the rest of the northern lights. Half a century of human history was going up in smoke.

Norman MacKay knew all the names and most of the events sandwiched between those frayed manila covers. He had married John Moran's daughter from Green Island, and here was her past feeding the fire at his feet. He implored the clerks to stop, to think about what they were doing, but they merely shrugged, said something about "just following orders," and went back for more. In a week the movers were coming to truck their desks and cabinets over to the posh new base at Seal Cove. According to the agent, this was all needless bulk.

MacKay snatched up some files, limp and bulging with smouldering onion skin, carried an armful over to his car and opened the trunk. The irate agent hurried over and ordered him to throw them all back on the pyre or face a written reprimand. When the wind bore their ashes aloft over the trees and across the harbour, it dispersed such an appalling record of human suffering and sacrifice that future historians might wonder if some other motive than mindless efficiency was at work that day.[1]

Luckily, one side of the correspondence from a few of the northern lights remained unviolated in Ottawa. Something can be reconstructed, but unless more pioneer keepers or their offspring come forward to share memories and written records, little more will survive than a few dates and photographs. The gaps in the north are cavernous and leave no choice but to leap across whole decades of blotted-out human experience. Among the obliterated lights are Lawyer Island, Barret Rock, Holland Rock, Cape St. James, Boat Bluff, Dryad Point. Life on the rest can be partially revived from miles of microfilm and second-hand memories passed down to the more recent keepers. What remains, though, is more than enough to measure the mettle of people pitted all alone against the most trying conditions of life and work ever. Daykin, Watson, Hunt, Erwin—all the pioneers of the harbour lights, the Inside Passage, even those strung out along the forbidding West Coast, lived sheltered lives by comparison. Even in the world of helicopters and radio, the north remains a proving ground. A man must take his family up there or abandon all ambition on the lights. The course of careers which end at Point Atkinson, Albert Head, Active Pass, or East Point—all the "in stations"—detours way north of Egg Island.

Like the lights of the Inside Passage, they were the offspring of the Klondike Gold Rush and the Grand Trunk Pacific Railway, two speculative ventures which laid siege to the imaginations of table waiters in San Francisco and barons of Bay Street. In time, both faded away, leaving the lighthouses behind as permanent fixtures of dissipated dreams.

Once the iron sinews of the new railroad reached Prince Rupert, the gigantic Triangle Island beacon off Cape Scott would summon inbound traffic headed north to the projected superport, or south to Victoria, Vancouver, or Nanaimo. Northbound traffic veered away from Pine Island for the Egg Island light, then steamed into Fitzhugh Sound and on to Prince Rupert, sheltered all the way by island breakwaters.

Captain Oliver, missionary and master of the mission boat *Udal*, was among the most familiar hands at threading the Inside Passage, since his calling took him into virtually every settlement along the way. ''We used to run straight up the middle of Fitzhugh Sound until we had that white cliff on the east side of the Sound right abeam of us,'' he recalled. ''Then put the wheel hard over and, with the cliff dead astern, we ran right into the mouth of the pass.'' The land lay low at the entrance to Lama Pass and a vessel could easily go aground. Further inland the hills cast dark shadows far out over the water blanketing the shoreline. Near the end of the channel, above Bella Bella where Lama Pass empties into Seaforth Channel, the only bearing was a cluster of three treetops higher than the rest. According to Oliver, ''You could see them on the darkest nights. When we got them exactly abeam, we put the wheel hard over and run right into the channel. If we went farther ahead without turning, we would have piled up on the rocks. There is a lighthouse there now—at Dryad Point.'' It was a route as convoluted as it reads, a serpentine maze impossible to clear without steering along the kinked chain of lights, link by link, listening for bells, handhorns, or diaphones.

Madness, murder, suicide, and disaster punctuated the life and times of men and women stranded on these, the most isolated lights of all, though there were degrees of solitude, even up there. Addenbroke Island was a short and sheltered row, even in the dark, from Safety Cove and Rivers Inlet—all too convenient for a deranged killer. Klemtu lay close by Boat Bluff. Bella Bella could be reached from Pointer Island and Dryad Point. It was possible too, in fair weather, for a man with good arms or a jury-rigged sail to cross over from Lawyer Island, Lucy Island, and even Green Island, to Prince Rupert. All the others were cut off: human contact consisted of a dark smudge on the horizon that marked the path of a tramp freighter. And so they remain, little islands scattered along Canada's western approaches. Some can be walked around in a few minutes, but at Triple Island no one dares venture out at high tide in rough weather.

Egg Island

There were few places on the planet more isolated than Egg Island at the turn of the century. The station was built in 1898 at the entrance to Fitzhugh Sound, the most strategic point for the burgeoning gold rush traffic pouring through the funnel into the northern reaches of the Inside Passage. Three deadly clusters of rocks—Pearl, Hanna, and the Virgins—surround the hundred-acre island like jagged stumps of rotten teeth, reaching fifteen miles out into Queen Charlotte Sound. From the south the island resembles a hen's egg on the horizon, and over the years the island with the unlikely name has hatched a dark brood of disaster and death.

William Brown was the first keeper appointed. His wife died suddenly just weeks before he embarked. The widower spent his first winter on the light with his three-year-old son and an assistant named Wilson. Together, the trio watched in mounting terror as the seas came surging at them. Streaming away before the wind, spray smoking from their crests, the mountainous waves smashed and carried off the boathouse and ways, came clear up to the house, then broke and entered the basement windows.

James Gaudin inspected the battered station in the spring of 1899. He pronounced it to be "in fairly good condition," though all hands were surly and sick. He recommended building a sea-wall across the gap on the north shore to blunt the great gouts of water funnelling through. But that last winter was too much for Wilson. The two men were "very hostile" and Brown "was equally anxious that he should go." Gaudin refused to give the assistant passage until a replacement could be found. He immediately wrote Colonel Gourdeau, spelling out the hazards of leaving anyone alone on Egg, relating how Brown had set out to row across to Rivers Inlet for mail a few weeks before. A sudden southeast gale caught him in the open and swept the boat up on False Egg Island a few miles away. For six days and nights Wilson and the little boy watched and waited. On the seventh they could see the boat. After a week without food, Brown was at the outer reaches of his endurance, and every pull on the oars seemed like his last. Fortunately, the tide ran with him. "He was so exhausted as to be unable to manage his boat," Gaudin reported, "which was swamped and destroyed on the rocks on landing."

The department paid Brown $500 a year. Gaudin calculated Egg's keeper could hire no competent assistant for less than $420, and "that would leave nothing for poor Brown but the glory of being lightkeeper." There was only one solution: the department *must* hire and pay qualified assistants, or at least provide the keepers with a substantial increase in pay to hire their own. As for Wilson, he was typical of the sort who would stoop to work under such conditions for such wages—"a broken-down dissipated law student" who was "only fit to smoke and drink when he could get it." That summer Wilson somehow made good his escape to the world of drink and smoke.

By 1 October, with winter on its way, Egg Island was running perilously short of lamp oil, and Gaudin waded ashore with a dozen cans. The workboat swamped and the wet agent was furious when he learned Wilson had absconded. The image of Brown and his toddler all alone up at Egg would haunt him at his desk and in bed all winter long. The father was neither strong nor in good health. The agent wrote Colonel Anderson: "With his little son aged three, should any accident happen... the little fellow would starve to death before any assistance could be rendered."

Before the month was out, Gaudin's prediction very nearly came true. Brown fell sick late in November. Without medical attention his condition steadily deteriorated until he was unable even to crawl upstairs to light up and wind the clockworks. In desperation the keeper flew the station flag, "union down," as a distress signal, then took to his bed. It was all he could do to feed himself and his child.

Brown languished for nearly a month, watching in disbelief, then dismay, as each vessel passed him by. One day his spirits soared; deliverance seemed at hand when a steamer altered course and veered close in. For once the sea was smooth enough to land, but his hopes were dashed when the captain just blasted the whistle and steamed away. Finally the *Quadra* arrived—on Christmas Day—and took them away to Victoria. The light had been out twenty-seven nights.

Back in Victoria the *Colonist* published Brown's experience, expressing disgust that "none would send a boat in the cause of humanity." Hewitt Bostock, a prominent Victoria Conservative, took up the issue with Louis Davies, minister of Marine. Pointing out that the matter had been "taken up very vigourously" by the American papers, Bostock declared, "There should never be less than two men in the Light House." The keeper, he had learned, earned only $40 a month, "while

James Forsyth, Egg Island 1909 – 13.

Damaged seawall, 1913.

the man at Cape Beele gets $100.'' Egg's keeper should be paid at least $1000 a year to hire an assistant. ''There is no sense or justice in an unfair discrimination of this kind,'' Bostock concluded, warning Davies, ''You would be well advised if you attend to this matter at once . . . before the meeting of the House.''

Davies demanded an immediate report from Anderson. ''Matters are not quite so bad as Mr. Bostock's letter would indicate,'' his chief engineer explained. Making no mention of Gaudin's repeated and fruitless pleas for paid assistants, Anderson sidestepped the scandal by blaming the victim for the crime. The whole episode stemmed from Brown's ''utter incompetence.'' Conceding that it might not be desirable to keep a man alone at Egg Island, Anderson explained the practice was hardly unusual. It went on at other stations equally isolated. While ''not very high judging by British Columbia standards,'' Brown's salary was still twice what the department paid on the East Coast! As far as the unjust discrepancy in salary between Egg Island and Cape Beale was concerned, it was no problem for a man of Anderson's genius to reconcile fair play and fiscal responsibility. Immediate steps would be taken to assure parity in future: the salary paid at Cape Beale was ''altogether too high,'' and would be cut accordingly. The chief engineer also instructed Gaudin to pay Indians at Rivers Inlet $5 every two months to check on the Egg Island keeper's health.[1]

Colonel Anderson fortified his bizarre interpretation of the Egg Island episode a week later, with a special memorandum to Davies. Once again omitting any reference to Gaudin's stubborn opposition to single-manning, he pilloried Brown for

Colonel William Patrick Anderson, CMG MICE PPCS CE FRGS, 1851 – 1927.

"utter uselessness." As a result of his shiftlessness, "blame was placed on the Department." Moreover, Gaudin had recently reported that the revolving apparatus at Egg "had been rendered unworkable" by G. Shunn, the temporary replacement. Clearly, better men were needed. The harried minister was easily swayed by his engineer's warped logic. In future, he ordered, the department must insist that all lightkeeper nominees be capable and fit. However, instructions from Ottawa turned out to be very malleable indeed when thrust into the firepits of local patronage.

After Shunn departed, Gaudin hired a former sailor named Nicholson, who was eager to take over at Egg Island. The new keeper soon "proved himself thoroughly competent, helpful, adapted to the station." After breaking up his home to go to Egg on short notice, he had "worked hard in its improvement" and wanted to stay, but patronage gave Nicholson short shrift. The local MP nominated William Scarlett for the position that September. Consistent with the new policy, Gaudin went to interview him and take Scarlett's measure. Unimpressed, the agent pronounced the candidate "altogether unfitted for an isolated and distant Station like Egg Island." Judging from the man's appearance, he was best suited for "very light labour." Scarlett seemed hardly capable "even of supplying fuel for domestic and heating purposes." He intended to leave his wife and family behind, taking his sixteen-year-old daughter with him. "I shall always feel considerable anxiety on their account during the long winter months," wrote Gaudin, who knew the queasy feeling only too well by now.

He assured Anderson his opinion was in no way tainted by his appreciation for Nicholson, whatever his merits. He denied any intention "of interfering with Mr. Maxwell's [the MP's] privilege." The agent sent the letter off, doubtless relieved that he would be spared another winter of worry about Egg Island.

On 3 October 1900, however, Gaudin was aboard the *Quadra*, steaming north for Egg Island with the Scarletts. Maxwell had agreed with Gaudin that Egg was "just the wrong place to send a man to experiment with, with the winter coming on," but what could he do? His constituent was in "bad shape," and the MP "had to find the poor fellow something to do." He had asked Gaudin to send Scarlett "a strong letter" to frighten him off, but Scarlett "did not scare much," even when the agent related that a barrister friend, after passing Egg Island on his way down from Skagway recently, claimed he "would much rather be sent to the Penitentiary than be transported to Egg Island."[2]

Full of foreboding again, Gaudin wrote a confidential letter to Anderson. "It is cruelty to send a man like Scarlett to Egg Island," he declared. No one knew the lights and their keepers better, and James Gaudin did his utmost, even dipping into his own pockets, to ease the suffering that resulted from Ottawa's meanness. "Goodness knows, I do my best for them," the agent wrote.

> I have stocked both [Egg and Ivory] islands with rabbits and given Egg Island a few goats at my own cost, so that in a little while they should be able to procure fresh meat. Would you recommend sending a couple of goats at Ivory Island, also a pair of pigs at each station for a starter. I ask this because the people appointed so far have been the hard up sort and have not the means.

As it turned out, the Scarletts owed their lives to James Gaudin's generosity. At the prevailing wage the new Egg Islanders must have been very hard up indeed to embark on this strange new career. It was hand to mouth at best, with the *Quadra* dropping off supplies in March and October. October 1904 came and went with no sign of the tender. The Scarletts grew uneasy, then desperate, as their stores dwindled away. They slaughtered Gaudin's goats, then ate all their hens and boiled all the bones. The last of their provisions ran out on 18 November and the famished castaways waited for the ants to carry them out the keyhole. They had no way of knowing that the *Quadra* had been delayed over a month, loading construction materials for the new light at Lennard Island off Tofino. When she finally arrived on November 20 her crew found the Scarletts "were in a state of starvation." Scarlett bitterly explained, "We were on short rations for over a Month, if it had not been for what we raised in the Garden and our hens and Goats, we would have had to raise the Flag of Distress or Starve."[3]

It was a rough day, typical for November that far north. The workboat swamped, spilling Scarlett's wife into the surf. After weeks in the hold, all their fresh meat was "completely rotten." Most of the other supplies came ashore damaged and soggy. Scarlett's loss totalled $100, nearly a quarter of his yearly pay. "I trust you will get me the allowance of damages from the Government," Scarlett wrote Gaudin, adding his "compliments of the Season." They had only three gray hams to last the winter.

That same day the outraged keeper wrote a friend in Vancouver, attributing their "privation and hunger [to] Culpable Neglect or Maladministration of Affairs of the Government." He implored him to show his letter to R.G. McPherson, the MP, or to anyone else he "saw fit." Anderson replied that the department did its "best to deliver supplies in good order," but insisted that "the Keepers always take the responsibility for loss or damage."[4]

The Hartins were as starved for human company as their predecessors were for food. William Hartin wrote the agent in September 1919, asking to be relieved at once—"my wife has gone crazy," he said. When the agent met them aboard the *Quadra*, he learned that lack of mail was the main cause of the woman's "breakdown." They had received letters four times in the last year. After a week in Victoria she seemed "perfectly normal with exception of being somewhat nervous." The agent predicted that a brief rest and change of environment would "complete her cure."

The lights were always a man's world. The only adult company for women—besides rough-hewn crewmen from the tenders—was provided by the rare visit of a mission boat, which might offer a few hours' talk with the clergyman's wife or a nurse. In 1923 Rhoda MacKenzie, a Red Cross nurse, landed at a number of northern lights and found to her astonishment that some keepers' wives had not set eyes on another woman for as long as fourteen months. Their only release was the mail, and though the Red Cross tried to establish a correspondence exchange, letters were few and too far between at Egg Island.

Arnold Moran knew better than anyone else what life up there on the northern lights had to offer. He had grown up on Green Island, the most northerly one, and was the first to follow in his father's footsteps at the Prince Rupert marine agency. As a result, he could speak with more authority than any other keeper about the issue which always weighs heaviest upon lightkeepers: the effect of the life on women and children. Sooner or later they must grapple with the dilemma: should they rear their children far away from the real world, or should they "bring them in," even if it costs their career? It means many crying jags and long sleepless nights, watching the beam sweep across bedroom ceilings, wondering what kind of a life they can make for their children. Some couples resolve their dilemma by asserting, almost as a litany, all the rewards they reap from a life apart from the decadent and seamy side of civilization, living and working together, tucked away from society's values and vices. Many more, as a century's plaintive letters to Victoria confirm, hold out hope for transfer to an "in station." Others just resign. The middle course is to break up the family; to send children, with or without their mother, off to relatives or boarding schools.

The Morans started out on the lights at Barret Rock near Prince Rupert harbour, then transferred to Egg Island and soon succumbed to "one of the most isolated off-shore stations." As their oldest son approached school age, with no friends or relations "to whose custody. . .[they] felt justified in intrusting. . .[their] child," they faced "a problem that called for grave consideration." Neither federal nor provincial government provided for the education of lighthouse children. They weighed the boy's future against the only life his father had known. In the end, his mother decided the issue.

> In addition to the above, I found that the cruel isolation of Egg Island affected my wife's health. It is no light thing, Sir, for a woman to be cut off entirely from all social and religious contacts; to be immured in what is virtually a prison during the term of her husband's service. Should she be blamed for trying to induce me to seek a position where conditions of life are more human?[5]

Arnold Moran quit and bought a poultry farm in New Westminster. His brother Tom took over at Egg Island. Sophie Moran, Tom's wife, had suffered a nasty mauling five years before when she was dragged into a winch at Triple Island. Her health continued to decline at Egg. On 27 January 1934 the mission boat *Thomas Crosby* landed supplies, "with much difficulty owing to the rough seas." Dr. Austin came ashore to check on the Morans. He found Sophie in bed, wracked by a series of excruciating heart seizures. He ordered her to stay there for ten days, and wrote William Stamford, the department's agent in Prince Rupert, advising, "She ought to be removed from such an isolated place." Tom suggested they take her away to stay with his parents at Green Island, but the doctor decided it was impossible to move her with such a heavy sea running. "The situation is rather precarious," he warned. "Death is not an improbable outcome of one of the attacks such as she experiences."

Moran nursed his wife for a month before the *Newington* arrived off Egg on 9 February. Captain Ormiston deemed it too rough to land, but, much to the crew's astonishment, Tom Moran launched his rowboat, hauled his way out, and climbed

Egg Island 1941.

aboard. He asked permission to go to town with his ailing wife since he had engaged a friend, Dan MacDonald, to relieve him.

Captain Ormiston called Jimmy Flewin, his sixteen-year-old mess boy, up to the wheelhouse and explained Tom's situation. Flewin "seemed quite pleased to be going ashore" to assist MacDonald. Tom Moran always insisted he had an ominous premonition that he would never see the two again when he shook hands farewell. "Remember, Dan's the boss," were his parting words before helping to carry his wife and children to the workboat.

The Moran's passage took much longer than planned. The *Newington* had to steam all the way over to the Queen Charlottes to relight a buoy, then tend to the broken-down fog alarm at Langara Point light. A month later, on the night of 12 February, there was much confusion on the bridge of the Union steamship *Catalla*. According to the charts, Egg Island light should be flashing right off her port bow. There was nothing but darkness ahead. "What's the matter with the light?" Captain Dixon wondered aloud, shuffling through his charts, double-checking compass and chronometer. He rang STOP on the telegraph and shouted down the tube for Eric Suffield, his chief officer. "How come there's no light?" Dixon demanded. "Well, we're in the right place," Suffield replied.

Every seaman knew that only injury, sickness, or death could account for a light's going out. The *Catalla* altered course and deftly picked her way through the Pearl Rocks, playing her searchlight all along the shore. The beam danced over the darkened dwelling, engine room, and tower, all eerie and as still and pulseless as a corpse above the crashing breakers. "Something's wrong," Dixon declared. "We better get ashore."

A lifeboat was quickly launched, with four crewmen at the oars and Suffield holding the tiller. Landing was impossible in the swell. Suffield stripped, tied a rope around his waist, dove over the stern, and swam ashore. He went into the house and saw a table set for two, with the rancid, petrified remains of a meal on the plates. Above the stove sat a pan with a mouldy sponge of bread. Suffield called out. No reply. He climbed the stairwell to the tower, pumped up the vapour tube, lit the lamp, and wound it up. The only clue to the keepers' disappearance was their boat, upside down in a cove, rising and falling in the surf. Suffield retied his lifeline, swam back to the boat, and they returned to the *Catalla*. Dixon sent a message to Prince Rupert and resumed course with a very quiet crew.[6]

To this day, the fate of Dan MacDonald and Jimmy Flewin remains a mystery. Their bodies were never found. By the time the *Newington* returned with the Morans, the boat had disappeared as well. The best clue lay in the discovery that much of Tom's fishing tackle was missing. Flewin's father offered a theory from his anguished imagination. ''I would respectfully ask you to create a personal picture of the case,'' he implored the minister of Marine. ''An island in the midst of nowhere, food supplies seriously diminishing, an overdue relief boat 'The Newington,' a row-boat and fishing lines coupled with a knowledge that sea food can be obtained, a natural desire to maintain ones self physically, and the attempt to obtain these supplies of sea-food with its disastrous result.''

Flewin, a widower, held a temporary post with the Department of Fisheries at Rivers Inlet. It was a precarious toehold on the slippery slope of the Great Depression, and young Jimmy had been ''of great assistance'' in providing for his younger brothers. Now his father brooded over the loss of one son and two incomes. He informed the minister, A. Duranleau, that his MP had already made ''strong recommendations'' on his behalf for compensation, and implored Duranleau to hack through ''existent restrictive red-tape [to] relieve the added burden on the victim's relatives.'' Stamford reported that Jimmy Flewin had signed off the articles of the *Newington* and was, therefore, Moran's employee rather than the department's— the department had no responsibility in the matter. A week later, however, Captain Ormiston showed Stamford that Flewin's name remained on the ship's muster.

The issue of compensation for the relatives of Flewin and MacDonald went all the way to the Justice Department, where the minister ruled that the Government Employees Compensation Act did not extend to lightkeepers' assistants. Though his officials were unaware of a single case where compassionate allowances had ever been awarded to keepers' families, they betrayed some sympathy for Flewin: after all, the boy had *volunteered* at Captain Ormiston's behest. His grieving father finally received an undisclosed award, but had little time or chance to enjoy it. As soon as he heard about Flewin's application, Dr. R. G. Large of Prince Rupert instructed his lawyers to file a claim in Prince Rupert court against him for $415 in overdue medical bills.[7] MacDonald's family received nothing.

The British Columbia Provincial Police investigated the disappearance and came up with no answers. They did, however, recommend that all isolated stations like

Egg be supplied with rockets and flares in case of emergency. Stamford decided against it, though, claiming that four short blasts on the horn, or an irregularly flashing light were adequate distress signals. The agent's decision very nearly cost the lives of an entire family at Egg Island.

It seems the sea has always held a grudge against the place. After Brown's first frightful winter, workmen constructed a wooden breakwater to blunt the crashing surf. The following winter it was casually swept aside. Two years later the wind and sea came calling at the house, snatching away the porch and smashing windows. Over the next fifteen years the

Egg Island survivor R. Wilkins.

front porch was washed off again, along with a good portion of the roof. The wind tore up a wooden walkway, demolished a fence and steel derrick, and stove in the fog-horn building, but these were all just parries and jabs as the sea probed its victim's defenses before delivering a knock-out blow.

For three days and nights the winds had shrieked, moaned, and sobbed down the Hecate Strait. T.R. Wilkins, his wife, and ten-year-old son kept inside while the sea seethed, white and hissing all around them. Wilkins continued to radio weather reports to Bull Harbour, and kept the horn blaring.

Shortly after midnight on 2 November 1948, the outside world lost all contact with Egg Island. Anxious radio operators at Bull Harbour tried time and again to raise Wilkins, then notified the marine agent in Prince Rupert. Gordon Odlum, Triple Island's keeper, recalled the atmosphere at the agency as he and his wife sat cooling their heels, waiting for the storm to blow itself out and let them go home. "The opinion was that they had a mechanical failure, and finally someone decided the batteries had got wet in the basement." Little did they know that basements were all that remained of Egg Island light. The rest of the station was a shattered mass of flotsam churning about at sea. The Wilkinses were cowering in their pyjamas in a chicken coop across the washed-out bridge on the main island, with no food, water, or spare clothing.

They had remained in the house as the fury of the storm mounted. Then water gushed in through their bedroom window. With a sudden gust of fear they heard a thousand nails twist in their wooden sleeves as the house teetered on its foundation. All the windows shattered in a mad chorus as the family dashed to the door. For a few desperate seconds Wilkins tried to force it open, but it was jammed tight in its shifted frame. They climbed over a jagged sill and fled for their lives across the bridge. Halfway across Wilkins heard his wife scream. He looked behind as a big foaming sea roared wildly out of the mist and made for their abandoned home with all

Egg Island after tsunami demolished lighthouse, 1948.

the fury of a madman with an ax. Everything was submerged in the raging acres of surf, and in retreat it carried off the entire station—including six months' provisions landed three days before—leaving only hollow concrete foundations full of curdled foam behind.

Colonel Keith Dixon, marine agent at Prince Rupert, broadcast urgent appeals to all shipping in the area to investigate and report on the condition of Egg Island. The fishpacker *P.W.*, and the tug *Ivanhoe*, put bravely out of Takush harbour fifteen miles away, but were unable to fight the distance through the heavy seas. Later that night Captain E.B. Caldwell signalled from the swaying bridge of the CPR steamer *Prince George* that no light flashed at Egg. Next morning the tug *Edward G. Coyle* veered in close enough to confirm that the tower and buildings had disappeared. There was no sign of life, but the *Coyle*'s crew was unable to land.

Foraging about for food, Wilkins stumbled upon a kerosene lantern. He hung it from a branch after dark and the shivering threesome huddled together, praying that someone out there in the black turmoil would see their pathetic little beacon before its fuel ran out. At 7:30 P.M. the steamer *Camosun* radioed: LIGHT OF NATURE STORM OR EMERGENCY OIL LIGHT AT LOW LEVEL SIGHTED ON EGG ISLAND AS WE PASSED NORTHBOUND WITHIN THE PAST 15 MINUTES. The fishboat *Sunny Boy* was their savior. On 7 November, their fifth day in the bush, the fishermen picked Wilkins and his family off the rocky shore. "Another day and they would have been dead," one of the rescuers predicted. They took them to the B.C. Packers' fish-buying camp at Finn Bay. ALL SUFFERING FROM EXPOSURE. REQUIRE HOSPITALIZATION, the manager radioed Prince Rupert. LIGHTHOUSE DEMOLISHED, ONLY CEMENT FOUNDATIONS LEFT. The tender *Bernie* picked up the refugees on 10 November and took them to hospital in Prince Rupert. When they left hospital, the Wilkinses never returned to the lights. The entire station was rebuilt on higher ground.

Above: fifty-foot swells breaking in the gap at Egg. Below: Bringing supplies through the gap.

If they had any reservations about living on Egg Island after the Wilkinses' harrowing experience, Laurie and Peggy Dupuis smothered them under layers of romance and adventure. Peggy had left her husband in Victoria to take up with the handsome, full-bearded lightkeeper, and brought her fourteen-year-old son Stanley with her. "When we decided to leave the whirlpool of the city and my husband was appointed to Egg Island Lightstation, our friends thought us mad," Peggy wrote in a feature article for the *Vancouver Sun.* But as far as Peggy was concerned, ''everything the songwriters, poets and philosophers have ever said about the paradise of isolated islands'' was true.

> The view of the sea on three sides is unsurpassingly lovely and to watch the sun sink into the horizon over the white-capped rollers is a never-to-be-forgotten experience. And just think, no time clock to punch and no bus to catch! If you want to go fishing on a nice day, as soon as routine chores are done, you go; everything else will keep—and then there's always tomorrow!

No end of tomorrows. Those lines could be, and often are, written with the same passion by people fresh to the lights. The Dupuis filled their tomorrows with gardening, painting, taxidermy, and a ham radio. They made a swimming pool in the foundation of the original dwelling. Both tried their hand at writing. Peggy was ecstatic when she saw her story printed months later in the *Sun*. Another article appeared in the *Colonist* headed ''Wife of Egg Island Lighthouse Keeper Finds Life of Isolation Fascinating.'' Laurie also had a piece printed in the English magazine *Wide World*. ''How many of our readers in crowded cities, we wonder, would care to exchange jobs with him?'' its editor asked.

They would soon learn, if the switch were made, that lovers on the lights face special challenges undreamed of by those who muse behind their jackhammers, desks, and steering wheels about escaping to an idyllic island. There are no friends out there who can offer advice, no marriage counsellors, not even a bar in which to drown one's sorrows behind a barricade of bottles. There is only a boardwalk to tramp, back and forth, alone, rerunning stale arguments. A sinking relationship can only be salvaged by falling in love all over again.

So Laurie Dupuis and his common-law wife discovered during their stint on Egg Island. As days slipped into weeks, weeks into months, one season into another, a dreary malaise settled in like the endless fog hovering around and over the island. The weather offered no relief. The winter of 1950 was a bad one. In late October the gale season was ushered in by a storm which wiped out the winch-house and derrick (mounted on a corner of the foundation of Wilkins's house), swept the boat-house off the island, and wrenched fuel tanks from their footings thirty feet above high water. The pair shipped out to Port Hardy on leave. Laurie sulked with jealous rage whenever deckhands or townsmen danced with ''his'' girl. On board the tender on their way back to the station a few days later, he poured out his woes to a radio operator. She had threatened to leave him, he muttered, perhaps even return to her ex-husband. Dupuis ended his harangue by threatening suicide. His listener, after trying to reason with him, kept his ears cocked for a splash.

Back home, Laurie and Peggy picked cruelly away at the last threads of their unravelling affection until it rent. Peggy needed minor surgery and left in April aboard the tender for Vancouver, taking Stanley with her. As soon as they were gone, Laurie sat down to write her, hoping to smooth over the roughened edges of their relationship. A letter a day for eight weeks piled up at his elbow, waiting for the mail boat or Peggy's return. Then one morning, after passing on his weather report, the radio operator at Bull Harbour asked Laurie to stand by for a personal message—a message that cost eighty-five cents and a man's life. "I MUST HAVE A PICTURE OF YOU," the operator read. "RECEIVED YOUR LETTER. JUNIOUR, GOOD LUCK." Laurie thanked him and looked down at the note in despair. A simple error in punctuation—the period and comma rearranged—had altered the whole meaning of the telegram from the boy's father, making it sound as if the man was responding to a letter from Peggy herself (in fact, the telegram was addressed only to Stanley). Laurie was sure now that if Peggy came back at all, it would be to pack up her things.

He must have re-read it a hundred times, sitting alone, weeping over his lonesome meals, imagining her back in her husband's bed in Victoria. Laurie's sense of betrayal and rejection puffed up like a cyst. He would show her, the rotten cold-hearted bitch! He arranged all the tools for his grisly project at the kitchen table: a .22 calibre rifle, pen and paper, shells, and an envelope. He wrote out his will and a note, folded them up, slipped them into the envelope with the fateful telegram, then licked the gum and ran the heel of his hand over it. Slipping on a windbreaker, Laurie picked up the rifle and walked down to the rocks near the boat-house on the island's east shore. He put the cold steel muzzle between his lips in a kiss of death, looked along the barrel one last time at that "never-to-be-forgotten" view, and jerked his thumb.

If he had only waited till next morning, he would have seen Peggy and Stanley waving excitedly from the deck of the USS *Coquitlam* as she steamed by Egg. The captain was happy to oblige when the lightkeeper's wife asked him to blast his horn. No reply. They landed at Namu where they spent the night. Next day at Bull Harbour, Peggy learned to her horror that no scheduled weather reports had come from Egg Island for two days. In her mind's eye she saw Laurie sick in the house, or down on the rocks crippled by a broken leg, or worse. A radio operator handed over the telegram, the last message acknowledged at Egg Island, with a terse note scrawled across the bottom that the station had been silent ever since it was transmitted. When she saw the error in punctuation, worry gave way to dread.

She ran down to the wharf and begged Captain Cloke of the B.C. Packers' *Theresa* to take her out. Cloke and a crewman went ashore, leaving Peggy and Stanley in the skiff. They knocked at the house, opened the door and saw the stack of letters on the table. Cloke brought them back aboard. The last letter was stamped, so he never expected her back! When she read, "I would sooner die than live without you . . .," Peggy ran ashore and searched frantically through the house for Laurie's rifle. On their way back to the boat to collect their luggage, Stanley spied the corpse sprawled over the rocks. The fishermen covered it with a tarpaulin and went to report the mishap, leaving Peggy and Stanley behind.

The naval tug *Clifton* took them away to Ocean Falls the next night to testify at a coroner's inquest. They came back with his coffin aboard the *MacKenzie* next day. Deckhands lay it across the thwarts of their workboat, steered under the hook, and

Peggy winched it ashore. They dug a grave behind the house, then Darby, the United Church missionary, read the burial service as seamen stood fidgeting in their raingear beside Peggy and the boy. A deckhand stayed behind to assist her, and Peggy sent off an application for the post, declaring Egg Island was ''the only life'' for her, but she remained only until a replacement could be found. Laurie Dupuis still lies behind the house, his white wooden cross a sinister and enduring testament to the ultimate response to isolation.

Laurie Dupuis' grave at Egg Island, 1979.

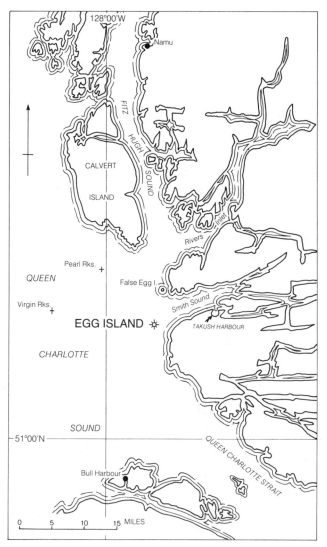

Pointer Island

James Codville came around the Horn with the horde of starry-eyed clerks, labourers, and dreamers who rolled up their sleeves and shoveled muck for gold in the Cariboo Rush of 1858. Like most of them, he went home to Woodstock, Ontario, seven years later—no wealthier, but captivated by the lure of the Coast. In 1887 he and his wife Fanny came west with their five-year-old son Ben, detraining at Vancouver's "Stumptown" when it still lay under a pall of ash and smoke after the great fire. Three years later Codville found work with the Department of Marine and Fisheries as a guardian on the Skeena and Nass Rivers. In the course of his work he smashed his right hand—a mishap which spelled ruin in those days before Workers' Compensation or disability pensions.

In the spring of 1894 James plowed all their life savings into a tract of land on King Island, across Fisher Channel from Pointer Island. Somehow he had learned that King Island would soon be selected as the terminus for the new Grand Trunk Pacific Railroad. He gambled that within a few years he could subdivide and sell the land at windfall profits for a townsite. It seemed a shrewd move, but fate seldom plays crueler tricks than it did on the Codvilles. Whether from chicanery or simple error, he had literally heard wrong: there would never be a bustling railhead and port on King Island. Months before, in some far-off boardroom, Charles M. Hays, president of the GTP, had already hunted over the map for the best setting for his superport, and stabbed his finger down on Kaien Island. Opportunists better posted than James Codville were already clearing land, driving stakes, and stretching chains to lay out the present site of Prince Rupert.

The Codvilles found themselves marooned without means, on a vast tract of wilderness in the middle of nowhere. It was all over now. Having lost their livelihood and squandered their life savings, they faced a grim future as hermits and beggars. Unable even to afford lard, they subsisted almost exclusively on boiled salmon. At one point they dug up and ate shellfish every day for three weeks, playing Russian roulette with red tide after their flour supply ran out before the salmon run. Indian neighbours took pity on the white castaways and shared their food.

The desperados were reprieved in 1899 when a work party landed across the way to lay the foundation for a lighthouse on Pointer Island. The department remembered Codville, and as compensation for his injury hired him to help in construction. In November, when the paint was dry, James and his family moved into the dwelling with the lantern on top. Even today a visitor to Pointer is struck by its claustrophobic layout—all the buildings are sandwiched together on an outcropping of rock, a frustrating hundred yards from the mainland. The first light was a fixed white beacon, forty-two feet above high water. The *BC Coast Pilot* advised that "a hand-horn. . .[was] sounded during thick or foggy weather when a vessel's fog signals. . .[were] heard." When they erected the tower, Codville insisted that carpenters spare a towering cedar cradling an eagle's nest in its upper branches by trimming away only those limbs which blocked the sweep of the beam. James would watch the eagle swoop and plunge for his prey out on the water. When the bird dragged his prize back, the keeper let him pluck the eyeballs, then gutted the salmon and tossed its entrails to the bird.

There was not much in the way of human misery Captain John T. Walbran had missed in the eight years since he brought the *Quadra* over from her birthplace in a Scottish shipyard. As a seagoing magistrate, all the woes of whites and Indians alike

The Codvilles at Pointer Island, 1902.

C.G.S. Quadra.

passed under his gavel on her foredeck. He witnessed firsthand the shattered dreams of homesteaders, looked down upon the wide-eyed lunacy of the ''bushed,'' followed the scabrous spectre of smallpox into every inhabited inlet, island, and passage from Victoria to Anchorage, where the *Quadra*'s whistle brought men, women, and children running to the landing to fetch mail, settle disputes, and rub shoulders for a while with those emissaries of the outside world. None of that prepared him for the nightmare he walked into at Pointer Island when he came ashore after delivering supplies on 28 June 1900. Infuriated, he went straight to his cabin after climbing back aboard, pulled out a sheet of his embossed stationery, and dipped his pen.

''The lumber was duly delivered at Pointer Island,'' he began.

> I saw Mr. Codville, he tells me he cannot stay as the salary he receives does not provide them with food sufficient to sustain health, and really I must say a more weak looking and famished family I never came across—I was so sorry for them that I gave them a few provisions. Mrs. Codville cried and said ''better to return to King Island and live in the charity of our neighbours than be famished and keeping a government lighthouse.'' The old man is trying to earn a penny or two by writing stories suitable for periodicals but I understand to present his labours have not been successful. To look at him he doesn't seem to want very much more in this world—he is so frail and thin. Mr. Codville told me that during the heavy gale we experienced at Egg Island, the lighthouse on Pointer Island shook so that they left it and sought safety in the boat house.[1]

James's mangled hand and the inroads of malnutrition ruled out heavy work, so most of the demanding tasks fell to seventeen-year-old Ben. When his father died in 1917, aged eighty-three, Ben took over the station, tending to the light and his aging mother. Like any other lighthouse parent, Fanny Codville fretted over her son's prospects in isolation. Grateful for his care and company as she grew older and her eyesight dimmed, she also agonized over his pleasures and prospects. How was he ever to meet a woman, fall in love, have a family, in the middle of nowhere?

Ben had just turned thirty-four when his mother turned in desperation to Captain Oliver of the mission boat *Udal*. Pocketing a photograph of her son, he promised the widow to "try to interest some young woman to come and see him." Back in Vancouver, Oliver took the photo around to Reverend G.A. Raley, principal of the Coqualeetza Residential School. Raley called his female staff into his office one by one, but whether unimpressed with the man staring out at them or with the prospect of an isolated existence, they all demurred.

Undaunted, Oliver contacted the commander of the Salvation Army, who referred him to the matron of their home for girls. "She was a big woman with a wealth of white hair," Oliver recalled, "and when I told her what I wanted, she said, 'Oh, will I do?' " By this time the clergyman was doubtless peeved by people poking fun at his bizarre courtship-by-proxy, but then the matron remembered a young woman on her staff who had suffered "a disappointing and trying time." "I'll mention it to her," she promised, "for she is alone in the city."[2]

The girl was every bit as lonesome as Ben Codville; her fiance had gone overseas and married an English girl. She agreed to travel to Pointer in two weeks to meet Ben and his mother. Oliver sailed back up the coast, stopping in at a cannery managed by a member of his far-flung congregation. The manager promised to meet the prospective bride when she arrived by steamer, row her over to the lighthouse, then return and await word to pick her up in case she balked and wanted to sail back to Vancouver in a hurry. Word never came. She fell in love with the man in the picture. On his return trip, Captain Oliver came ashore to marry them. Ben and Annie Codville spent the next twelve years keeping the light and caring for Fanny in her blindness, leaving only to row ten miles to the cannery for their mail.

They tended the beacon together, scraping frost and snow off the panes in winter, pumping the hand horn whenever a fog wrapped its clammy mantle around them and ships bawled mournfully for guidance through the pass. As Codville later told Lyle Bigelow, Pointer's keeper from the 1960s, survival in those days was a full-time job in itself: bread must be baked, clothing mended, game hunted and butchered, fish caught and filleted, canned, or dried, clams dug on the beach, gardens planted, nurtured, and harvested, and all their bounty preserved. All year long they hauled driftwood from the beach and bucked it by hand for their insatiable wood-stove. During her wartime night watches, Annie Codville knit the second highest number of socks for soldiers of the British Empire. She earned a medal but paid an awful price: the work left her fingers twisted from arthritis.

Ben and Annie Codville of Pointer Island.

They never once took a holiday; instead, Ben sent for a relief keeper and they stayed home to paint the tower in the summer. After forty-six years and five months on Pointer, twenty-nine of them as lightkeeper, Ben Codville retired. King Edward VII awarded him the Imperial Service Medal, a distinction then held by only thirty other Canadians. When asked why he chose to settle in Prince Rupert, Ben explained, "Well, that is where they offered to transport us."

One can hardly imagine their mood the day the workboat took them out to the tender—when they climbed over the rails, turned, and looked upon Pointer Island for the last time. When she had left the warrens of the Salvation Army hostel in Vancouver, Annie Codville never suspected it was the last she would see of the outside world for so long. In a vocation where loneliness is a way of life, endured when not enjoyed, the Codvilles made it a passion. They had followed the strutting parade of monarchs, presidents, prime ministers, armies, and assassins, and had watched the heavy tread of fascism and the frightful dawn of the nuclear age, all on the pages of newspapers. When he landed on the dock at Prince Rupert, Ben must have felt something like H.G. Wells's Traveler when he let go the spindles of his Time Machine and stepped into the nightmarish world of the Morlocks and Eloi: he had never seen a car, a paved road, a cash register, a revolving door, nor a telephone, and seldom other women or children.

Lyle Bigelow first came over from Pointer to visit them in town in 1963, stepping gingerly around the piles of newspapers overflowing their front porch to knock on the door. The Codvilles proudly displayed the diaries they had meticulously kept on Pointer, complete with illustrations, highlighting their activities from day to day. "When Ben and Annie left the island for Prince Rupert, they had stacks and stacks of newspapers that Ben refused to part with because all the learning he had was from newspapers and books," Bigelow recalled. "They continued to live in a very similar manner to the way they had lived at the lighthouse. They still had a wood stove, and Ben was so old and feeble that he had to hire a boy in the neighbourhood to cut and stack his wood, but he would not switch to oil or gas." Convinced someone was pilfering from his cords, he marked every faggot with chalk. He would have nothing to do with electricity and its spawn of new-fangled gadgets like refrigerators.

When he took over Pointer from his father in 1917, Ben made $595 a year, with a portion paid in flour. In 1945, when he left, he earned $1590. The two pinched every penny, striving to bequeath as much as they could save to the Government of Canada. Having outlived the majority of pensioners, the pioneer lightkeepers regretted causing Ottawa an undue expense. In 1968 Annie became ill and died shortly after in a Victoria nursing home. Alone and truly isolated for the first time in his life, Ben wandered aimlessly around the city for a few months, then followed her.[3]

The department had appointed Charles McCoy to relieve the Codvilles on 30 April 1946. On 8 November 1947 Vincent MacDonald replaced him. When Lyle Bigelow corresponded with MacDonald in the 1960s, Vincent expressed his sympathies for Bigelow's posting to Pointer. Even though he played the fiddle, accompanied by his wife on the accordion, and though they had entertained occasional summer visitors from Bella Bella, the winters proved too miserable, long, and lonesome. They were glad to leave after seven years.

In 1949 the original building was demolished and replaced with the "salt block"—a concrete structure with a beacon room on the roof that was reached by a stairway inside. Shortly after the original light was installed, a captain had run his vessel aground, mistaking the beacon for the steady light of another vessel turning down Lama Pass. A new flashing light replaced the fixed apparatus, eliminating any confusion with a ship's light. The unique Aladdin kerosene lamp stood upon a small platform, surrounded by a glass chimney and a ventilating apparatus which was attached to three metal reflectors with gaps that allowed the light to shine through, all floating upon a bath of kerosene—an ingenious device for its time. Heat from the flame passed up the chimney, causing it to rotate. As it spun, the metal plate eclipsed the beam at regular intervals. The speed varied with the wind.

Four feet away, a new engine room housed a five-horsepower Briggs and Stratton gas engine, driving air compressors for a diaphone. The old hand horn, the ''Moo,'' went into storage, relieving Pointer's keepers from squatting outdoors at all hours in all weather—as they had done without fail for half a century—pumping its bellows seven strokes at a time until ships steamed out of range.

After the MacDonalds quit Pointer, sixty-year-old Arnt Bendicksen and his wife served there for two years until Ed Carson replaced them. Lyle and Velma Bigelow bid Ed Carson farewell in April 1960. ''I came there to die,'' Lyle confided. His doctor had pronounced him terminally ill shortly before. They stayed on Pointer Island twenty years, and left a rare first-hand insight into their lighthouse life, the best comprehensive account of the transition from kerosene to electricity on the lights.

''My family came with me to the lights in July 1957. We had come up the coast from Vancouver, B.C. with the Union Steamship Company's *Camosun*. It was a wonderful trip for us as the ship called at so many ports along the way. We arrived late at night in Prince Rupert, B.C. and saw Ian Campbell, who was Superintendent of Lights and met us. We drove to Seal Cove and were put aboard the CGS *Alberni*.'' Velma asked Campbell how long people usually stayed on the lights. ''We have two kinds of people on the lights,'' he replied, ''those that stay for a long time, and those that don't.'' Lyle and Velma were the right kind.

The Bigelows embarked upon their new life as assistants at Green Island, then set sail for Langara on 2 January 1958, stopping over in Prince Rupert. ''Mr. Beketov [the agent] met us and drove us about Prince Rupert in order that we and our three small daughters might see some of the Christmas lights that were still decorating the homes,'' Lyle remembered. ''Little did we realize that that would be the last of Christmas lighting of a city that we would see for five years.''

After leaving Prince Rupert aboard the *Alexander MacKenzie*, the Bigelows were tossed around on high seas for five days before landing at Langara. They worked with Ed Hart there until April, then sailed for Pointer. ''We arrived here with the *Alexander MacKenzie*. There was myself, my wife Velma, our 5-year-old French-Canadian daughter Lorayne, and our 4-year-old Japanese, Davis, and Irish twin girls, Karen and Sharon. We were the first family to have small children living on the island.'' In late September 1959 the department built a new dwelling. It was ''so much larger in floor space'' that they ''seemed to rattle in it at first.''

Four children seemed too few for Lyle and Velma. In 1967 they ''got anxious to add another boy'' to the family. They went to Bella Bella to ask the doctor to ''put in a good word'' at the welfare department. ''I didn't know you wanted more children!'' he exclaimed. ''There's a little Indian girl in here who is looking for a home.'' They bundled her up and rowed back to Pointer, much to the delight of Karen, who was waiting at home, and of the other children when they returned from boarding school in Bella Bella.

Pointer Island, 1982. Jim Ryan photo.

The winter that hit the north coast the following year was one of the harshest in memory. On Christmas Day 1968 Lyle was "feeling poorly" again, and a fisherman took him over to see the doctor in Bella Bella. The weather grew steadily worse. Back at Pointer the wind howled out of the northeast at sixty knots, driving the mercury down to minus ten degrees Fahrenheit. All the diesel lines froze. Velma dressed the children in snowsuits and gathered them around the propane stove in the kitchen. She and Charles Redhead, their assistant, heated water and poured it over the pipes, then wrapped them in old coats and managed to start the furnace for a few minutes at a time until it sputtered out again. "It helped to keep my family and food supply from freezing," Lyle recalled.

"School on the island has always been a problem," he conceded in 1980. "Over the years my wife has taught our six children for many of their grades. Each child has been sent out or kept at home according to their own personal needs. Velma has taught every grade from kindergarten to Grade Nine during the past nineteen years. Now the last one has gone out to school, and we are all alone."

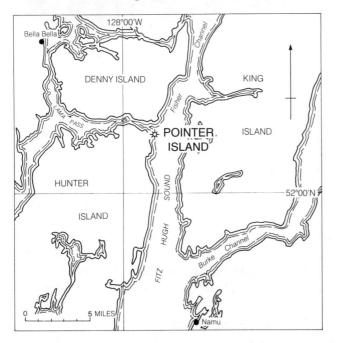

Ivory Island

T his is a tough place and I am not exaggerating," lightkeeper Thompson informed the minister of Marine and Fisheries in a letter written one October night in 1899 after bolting the shutters against yet another gale at Ivory Island. "It can be amply proved if necessary." The proof lay in the island's location off Robb Point in Milbanke Sound, at the mercy of the full-blown force of the open Pacific. Nothing stood between Ivory and Japan to blunt the "very violent" storms and mountainous, crashing swells which mauled the island all winter long.

The station was erected, with all the attendant trials of landing men and supplies, in 1898 just months after Egg Island. Peter Wylie, Ivory's first keeper, manned the station alone until Thompson relieved him less than a year later. "He could stand it no longer, it was so isolated and exposed," Thompson recalled. "He was the most overjoyed man in Canada on his release."

Little wonder. Captain Gaudin encountered Wylie for the first time on the afternoon of 24 March 1899, and pronounced him "an intelligent painstaking and helpful officer" who kept "the station in a capital condition." A succession of storms that previous November had "completely demolished" the boat house and ways. Marooned and alone, Wylie had waded waist-deep into the rampaging surf to retrieve what debris he could snag with a boat hook. Gaudin was appalled at such risk-taking. Until the agent arrived, Wylie had "not seen or spoken to any person since the 20th of December." When asked why he did not hire an assistant for his own safety and sanity, Wylie pointed out that it would cost him at least $360 out of his annual salary of $460.[1] "I am disappointed that someone did not come and take my place," Wylie confided to the agent that June. "I cannot live after this month as my provisions will be out."

Wylie's logic was obvious, a matter of schoolboy arithmetic, and Gaudin's innovative turn of mind came up with the ideal solution. Since the department would neither hire nor pay for another man, why not hire married men and thus enjoy the benefit of an unpaid assistant in the keeper's wife? Colonel Gourdeau quickly underscored Gaudin's recommendation, affirming that it should be easy to find middle-aged family men grateful for a permanent job with free housing. Otherwise, he pointed out, the salary must be increased "to a sum sufficient for two men, say $700." He blithely assumed there was not work enough for two at Ivory, thus the department "would be paying them only to keep each other company." The appointment of Thompson and other "grateful" family men would solve the twin problems of money and morale at a single stroke.[2] Although women had been helping their husbands as unofficial assistants since Rosina Davies landed at Fisgard in 1860, this was the first time the practice was expressed as department policy.

Within a year, however, Thompson was as despondent as Wylie. Two could hardly live as cheaply as one up there, especially since he had been hired at an annual salary that was $60 less than Wylie's. "Is this just—is it fair to me?" Thompson asked. He and his wife had "no encumbrances." "[We are] emminently fitted for the position," he said, "and are willing to take upon us the onerous duties entailed, which if one has a conscience is no sinecure (& I have a conscience) for the lives of many fellow men depend upon our properly accomplishing the duties required, not to mention the property at stake." The keeper attested to his devotion to his calling, declaring that the masters of steamships "who go bye to Alaska" always reported "perfect satisfaction as to the exhibition of...[the] light." Why, then, should he earn less than Wylie?

Thompson's missive was one of many flooding the in-trays in Ottawa and Victoria, another ripple riding a groundswell of discontent. Whatever attracted men and women to the lights—escapism, vocation, romance, desperation, or the strengthened bonds of family life forged in isolation—all the keepers were sinking steadily into a quagmire of debt and ruin. The lowest wage paid by the department, $1.50 a day to "Indian labourers," amounted to $547.50 annually. "White" lightkeepers earned even less, yet were required to pay a competent assistant out of pocket. Like southern sharecroppers, these sentinels of the North Pacific faced the prospect of becoming credit vassals to local merchants, or, what was worse, meeting the crippling monthly payments exacted by poor nutrition.

Disturbed by Thompson's plight, and doubtless touched by the keeper's reference to a marine agent's "kindness & thoughtfulness in his endeavours to encourage and make us comfortable," Gaudin came north again in August 1899. Upon landing he was horrified to discover that the contractors had made no provision for fresh water cisterns. Two feet of stinking stagnant water stood in the cellar. "They have been using water that gathered in the holes of the rocks and what I tasted was scarcely fit to drink,'' he reported. Colonel Anderson immediately authorized funds to build a cistern, confiding with relief that it was ''a mercy . . . the keeper and his wife were not dead from typhoid fever.'' Conceding that ''a certain amount of fitting up'' was called for on these hastily-built northern stations, the chief engineer was ''anxious to provide everything which . . . [was] absolutely requisite but no luxuries.''[3]

Gaudin portrayed Thompson as an educated man fallen upon hard times, who was compelled to accept his present position ''through the force of circumstances.'' His wife suffered from chronic angina and was hardly up to the duties of an assistant, albeit an unpaid one. Obviously, ''more robust, resourceful people'' were needed at Ivory. He recommended that the Thompsons move over to Pointer Island near Bella Bella.

Louis Davies, minister of Marine and Fisheries, was swayed by Thompson's logic and Gaudin's report. ''The keeping of that station is worth $450.00 the salary previously given,'' he scrawled across the top of Thompson's letter. In November Gaudin raised the salary by fifty dollars, and awarded Thompson his arrears. It was too little and came much too late—a pittance which hardly compensated for conditions on what was, at that time, ''the most northerly, exposed, isolated and worst situated lighthouse on the coast.'' Thompson's morale and his wife's health were deteriorating fast.

''The disadvantages of the station affect my wife just as much as they do me,'' he confessed to Davies. ''The last time the *Quadra* (supply boat) was [here was in] September & she was compelled to lie off and on for nearly a week before she was able to land supplies, it was just as impossible for us to go out to her on account of the roughness of the sea. From this you can draw an inference of the state of the weather, it being September.''

By June 1900 they had had enough. Gaudin sat at his desk and slit open Thompson's last communication, its purpose and tone all too familiar to a beleaguered bureaucrat, charged with maintaining the lights on a shrinking budget, making bricks with no straw.

> I am sorry [to resign] but my wife absolutely refuses to leave unless I go with her and it would be unkind on my part to stay against her wishes. We are so far from medical assistance and she dreads so her attacks so far from a Doctor. You saw her yourself this Spring and she is still very sick. The fact of it is I should never have brought a sick woman out here.

Sick as she was, the wife outlived her exhausted husband who died late in 1904, leaving her ''entirely destitute.'' As an ''unofficial'' assistant at Ivory she had never been placed on the department's pay list, so was regarded as a non-person. Even if she had worked as an assistant, she would have been Thompson's employee rather than the department's, so there would be no pension. Frantic, ''alone in the World and Penniless,'' she wrote the minister in January 1905 reminding him that

Ivory Island Light in its new position, 1905.

her husband had been "a great worker for the Liberal party here & in Ontario & since the days of George Brown of the Toronto Globe of which...[he] was a proof reader." Surely such stalwart loyalty merited *some* reward. Had he lived, she was confident the party would have found him "some situation." As for her, all she wanted now was for the Liberals to help her "financially to...furnish a small house and rent rooms." Two weeks later Gaudin replied that the department had no funds for such a purpose.

The same day that Walbran wrote Gaudin, laying bare the stark and horrid plight of the Codvilles at Pointer Island, the harried agent took the unorthodox and risky step of writing privately to Maxwell, his MP, hoping to bring some underhanded political pressure to bear in Ottawa. With Thompson's letter to the minister in hand, he reviewed the difficulties of getting men to take Ivory and Egg Islands: "They are in very isolated places...a man cannot possibly get out for six months." Yet, owing to their importance to navigation, "they should be in charge of good men, and...a liberal increase [should] be granted."

As a stop-gap Gaudin recruited an Indian couple from Bella Bella to take over at Ivory for a lower wage than Thompson's. He hastened to point out the danger to Colonel Anderson. Although he did not want "to establish a precedent in the appointment of Indian lightkeepers," he allowed that Carpenter had "so far given satisfaction at Dryad Point," since he was "one of the old fashion Indians that cannot speak English, they are the most reliable as a rule." But the new keepers at

Ivory thought their time was "just as valuable as that of white men under equal conditions." Gaudin doubted they would stay long after learning Thompson had received a higher wage.

James Forsyth replaced the Bella Bella people in March 1904 and soon sank into pitiful financial straits. He was earning $500 a year. Freight shipped the sixteen miles from Bella Bella to Ivory Island cost $5 a load. He wrote R.G. McPherson, his MP, pointing out that over the past two years the price of "almost everything" had "so materially advanced" that it was "indeed hard to get on." McPherson told the minister that his constituent had "a very good case here," and recommended a $100 raise. Surprisingly, Gaudin argued against it, insisting that the light was small, there were "no living expenses entailed," and the salary was "amply sufficient for the services rendered." Moreover, Forsyth's salary equalled those paid keepers at Cape Mudge and Pointer Island. If the department gave Forsyth an increase, it must raise all the keepers' salaries. The minister agreed.[4]

In December 1904 the contaminated water supply caught up with Ivory's keepers. Ellen Forsyth and her baby were wracked with dysentery, their bowels on fire. Luckily, the *Kestrel* responded quickly to James's distress flag and took them off and away to hospital in Bella Bella. A shaken Gaudin wrote Colonel Gourdeau that if the *Kestrel* had not altered course, it was "probable the child would have succumbed." Forsyth resigned, but he would be back on the lights at Egg and Langara.

The following April, William Sloan wrote Gourdeau, recommending "a decided acquisition to the service" in the person of a Mr. Reuter, a carpenter and machinist who "as a boatman" had "few equals on the Pacific Coast." Reuter seems to have departed from Ivory's tradition of addressing plaintive appeals for money to everyone from the minister on down. Very likely it was his difficulty in English rather than an adequate cash flow which stilled his pen. At any rate, he stayed ten years at Ivory, a welcome lull for Gaudin and his successor, Captain George Robertson. His past caught up with him in 1916.

Owing to his isolation, Reuter had no way to seek out a notary public and take out naturalization papers, as thousands of other Germans were doing in that anxious summer of 1914. Instead, as war approached, he began checking off contributions from his meagre salary to the Patriotic Fund to prove his loyalty. It was not enough. In June 1916 the only keeper to last more than two years at Ivory Island was summarily dismissed "on the ground that he . . . [was] an alien enemy subject."[5]

The bureaucratic warfare between Ivory Island, Ottawa, and Victoria waged back and forth in concert with an equally futile struggle against the elements. Owing to its site, Thompson had complained, "We suffer from storms and bad weather from West and South continuously and they are very violent." In 1904 the violence reached a crescendo when most of the station was swept away by a tidal wave. There was a lesson here if Colonel Anderson would only heed it: anything built less than fifty feet above high tide was a temporary structure at best.

On the night of 24 October 1963 a wave came roaring out of nowhere and smashed into Ivory Island, ripping away the seaward wall of the fog alarm building from the roof-line to its foundation. The roaring cauldron of water shoved the compressor fifteen feet across the floor, drove the stove from the centre of the room out the far doors, flooded all the generators and machinery, and retreated with a twenty-gallon day tank and six sections of metal siding.

On Christmas Eve 1982 the keepers at Ivory listened in disbelief as McInnes Island's keeper passed his barometer reading with his aviation weather: 29.88 and "falling rapidly." Within two hours the mercury column plunged to 29.25. Something big was headed for Ivory. By midnight the dwelling, the oldest in the Prince Rupert agency, "was groaning in every rafter like an old barque as the wind swung from the south-east, climbed past 60 knots, and came with all its 'Force Ten' from Cape St. James to. . .[the] back doorstep." By early morning Gordon Schweer noticed the kitchen windows "resembled a plastic which was expanding under heat."

The tide was on the rise. Andy Findlay, Gordon's assistant, radioed his weather report at 6:30 A.M. and advised that they might soon be "off the air." Waves were sweeping the decking so Findlay sounded the old hand horn to wake up the Schweers. . .just in time.

> There was no warning a moment later from the wave that gained the sea wall and flooded the station. Our only indication that we were "over our heads" came when the outer door to the radio room filled entirely with white sea water. For a second the door seemed to resist—then the dam burst, flooding sea water and debris into the kitchen, pantry, basement, living room and cistern. Neither keeper was injured by flying glass, even though I had bare feet and fled the room while it was still awash. Mr. Findlay followed abruptly, since the same wave in uprooting small trees and severing larger limbs had stripped the radio room bare of shingles.
>
> With an outer kitchen window shattered, we moved back into the safety of another room, but were again interrupted while ebbing the flow of water. There is no way of knowing whether the metal tower was knocked down by the same wave or one succeeding it, yet the. . .mainlight shone [its] search beam hard through the living room windows for several minutes before burning out.

Aside from the dwellings, only the radio antenna remained. The fog horn trumpets were sheared clean off at their concrete base, their reinforcing steel stretched and bent like pretzels. Schweer reported: "Our water tank containing 1000 gallons slid 20 feet before hitting the house; boulders in excess of fifty pounds removed siding from the house and the platforms, stairs, and railings were either damaged or entirely missing. Later in the morning the subsiding swell removed various sections of the bridges behind Robb Point." It was all "ample proof," if any more was "necessary," that Ivory remains "a tough place."

Ivory Island Light from the Coast Guard helicopter, 1982. Jim Ryan photo.

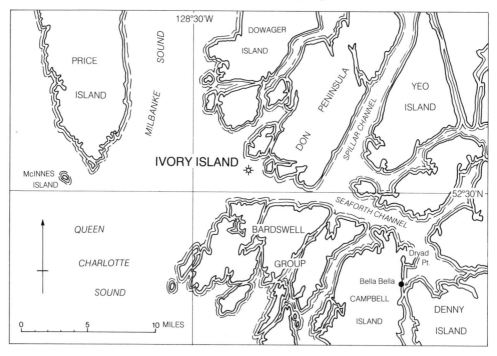

Green Island

I t's an old saw on the lights that only the ignorant or the ambitious take on Green Island. Furthest north of the lights, lying 1½ miles east of Dundas Island, it is a barren, windswept, treeless hummock cringing above a shingle beach. The winter wind whistles down the Portland Canal from Alaska, and seas lash away at the tower and dwellings, shellacking them with ice so thick that the whole station resembles ice sculptures at a bizarre winter carnival, and the keepers need a hammer to open a door. Windows were nailed shut long ago. For many who serve at Green, their primary concern is getting somewhere else, soon. One wild winter there is bad enough. Two or three, with the prospect of another, might make or break a keeper. Some have succumbed to despair, cast away years of seniority, crated their belongings, and steamed away, never again wanting any contact with the lights or people from them. Others relish the challenge of Green Island in winter, and are captivated by the spectacular vista across the settled seas of summer.

Such a place generates its own mystique. When they report their weathers to Prince Rupert marine radio, Green's keepers often bear the brunt of black humour from the operators, who know that fifty-knot winds are a light breeze up there. Legend has it that one assistant hired "off the street" was jarred awake in his bunk aboard the *Sir James Douglas* by the rattle of anchor chains and the humming winch. He climbed up to the wheelhouse at sunrise. "Where are we now?" he asked, watching a workboat plowing over the swells toward Green Island. "Well, that's it, your new home," he was told. "Bring it back," he muttered, thus ending the shortest of all careers on the lights.

Green Island light went up during the Gold Rush construction boom in 1906, a typical square frame house and tower standing eighty-one feet above sea level on the southwestern point of the islet, with a flashing white light that was "slightly interrupted by a chimney to the northwest." S. Baker went out to Green first, and like the Scarletts down at Egg Island two years before, he and his family nearly starved. For nine days the Bakers subsisted on cornstarch and water while waiting for the *Quadra*. Then the lamp oil ran out, and the keeper wrung one more night's light out of their domestic supply, draining the last drop of kerosene from every lamp in the house.

There was no light the next night when the steam tug *Goliah* approached with the barge *Quatsino* in tow. Captain Bailey had no inkling he was over foul ground until the barge snagged on Lincoln reef, nearly ripping the capstan off *Goliah*'s afterdeck. Bailey ordered the engines reversed, cut his tow, and stood by until daylight, when he and the crew were amazed to see the silhouette of a light tower take shape against the sky.

Bailey lowered a skiff and went ashore, but immediately sent a party back to *Goliah* to fetch "a generous portion of eatables." The Bakers' state was etched with outraged clarity in the captain's mind. When he docked in Seattle he told reporters "it was a lucky wreck for the lightkeeper," and revealed how "the lightkeeper and his family were on the verge of starvation." Bailey invited the public to ponder the full measure of the Bakers' peril: if the keeper's oil had outlasted his dwindling reserve of cornstarch, his lopsided determination to keep the light might have killed them all.

M. Turcotte took the Bakers' place in 1909, but turned the station over to Alexander Dingwell less than a year later, in December 1910, when he moved to neighbouring Lucy Island. John Moran came in December 1918 and was still there a decade later when he risked his life attempting to save two fishermen, in one of the most dramatic one-man rescues in the North.

Moran grew up in Liverpool and went to work setting type for the *Manchester Guardian* and the *Times* of London before emigrating in 1909. He took up his trade in the cellars of the *Victoria Colonist*. The atmosphere there, as in any composing room in those days, was redolent with fumes rising from cauldrons of molten lead. Shortly after Armistice Day 1918 John Moran woke up blind from irisitis. Three days later, when he regained his sight, his doctor warned him to get away from the poisonous press room. Fortunately Moran had a friend in Ralph Nicholson, inspector of lighthouses, who found him a job as far as one can possibly get from Victoria: Green Island. "We had just 3 days to pack, procure 6 months supply of groceries and be ready to sail on the *Estevan*," his daughter Rose remembered.

Keeping a lighthouse was a rigorous transformation for a man accustomed to setting type. Green was the coldest of all the lights, yet the department landed a paltry half ton of coal a year to heat the engine room. Rose recalled that one keeper had brazenly ordered a full ton and received a buck saw instead! John and his two boys foraged constantly for driftwood delivered on the tide, bucking all they could salvage and hauling it up to the house.

At sunset Green's keeper lit up and joined his nocturnal comrades on watch. "Green Island was a vapour light," his daughter explained. "A speck of dirt or dust lodged in the tiny hole at the top of the vapour tube could cause a 'black up' if not attended to immediately. These 'black ups' were to be avoided at all cost, as in a few minutes the entire lenses and inside of the tower itself could be covered in black, foul smelling soot. It was a task of many hours to clean the soot away, and often left the inside of the tower requiring a coat of paint."

The Dingwell family at Green Island Lighthouse.

John rigged up a mirror in his parlour so he could look up from his book at the spokes of light spinning outside the rattling windows, his ears attuned to "the slightest variation of the 'hiss' of the mechanism" upstairs. It was a ritual he performed every night for eighteen years on that bald outpost—a record likely to stand.

John's wife, a "meticulous housekeeper" and unofficial assistant, also put in long hours. According to the terms and conditions of service promulgated in 1918, "the place was always 'available for inspection' " by the brass or the public, and Mrs. Moran was always ready for them. "All visitors were very welcome, and were given a meal if time and weather permitted," Rose Moran recalled. "Often the gift of a pie or homemade bread was offered. In turn the fishermen kept us supplied with fresh fish."

But that was just routine. As proprietors of lightkeepers' "whole time," the department expected as much from every keeper. However, John Moran went far beyond the shore of Green Island and the call of duty. On Christmas Day 1925 he rescued the American consul, cast ashore on Dundas Island, and received an engraved set of binoculars from a grateful President Coolidge.

On 24 April 1929 the weather was fine, and Harold Dahl and William Cummings of the *Grier Starret* reckoned they had plenty of time to pay a call on the Morans at noon. They set their "big hook" in what seemed to be good ground, reeled in their skiff, and rowed over to the station. "I was on the boatways when the men came ashore, and remarked upon the unseaworthiness of their dingy which was then half full of water," Moran wrote the marine agent in Prince Rupert that evening. They tipped the craft over to empty it, John fetched a rope from the boathouse, tied a bowline to the cleat, and ran the boat out, hoping its leaky seams would swell and tighten. Then he escorted his callers up to the house for lunch. A gentle southeast wind blew, rare and welcome at Green at that time of year.

When Moran walked back down to the landing with them, he was appalled to find the skiff full to the gunwales with water. He implored Dahl and Cummings to take his station boat instead. They refused, convinced they could make it back to their packer. But she began to drift while they were on their way out, dragging her anchor. "By the time I had closed and fastened the boathouse doors and returned to the house, the *Grier Starret* had drifted about halfway to Grey Island, and the two men were about halfway to the boat," John wrote. "I came indoors for a moment or two, and then went to look out again. I was horrified to see that the boat had overturned, and the two men were in the water."

John knew as well as anyone that in April the water temperature of the North Pacific hovers around a bone-chilling 8 degrees Celsius. Once overboard a man has less than fifteen minutes' life in him as hypothermia spreads its icy tentacles through his thrashing frame, beginning its caress at the extremities, then seeking out the armpits and crotch, condemning him to a sluggish, delirious descent to the crabs' platter.

With adrenalin giving him the strength of two men, Moran sprinted to the landing in his slippers. He dragged his boat out of the boathouse, down the ramp, and into the water, all within five minutes. As he shoved off, he could see that one man had reached the overturned boat and had hauled himself up to sit astride its keel. The other was thrashing a few feet away. "I could plainly see his head and shoulders and surmised he had hold of the painter, and was treading water," Moran reported. "The sea by this time had become very rough and I made all possible speed to the aid of the unfortunate men, I often lost sight of them when I was in the trough of the waves. However, some few minutes before I reached the overturned dinghy, I could see only one man, I was fortunate enough to make a good position for effecting the rescue of Mr. Cummings, who was in a state bordering on collapse, I got him into the boat with a little difficulty, and he lay in the bottom in a state of utter exhaustion while I rowed around for a few minutes in the hope of locating Mr. Dahl."

Meantime, *Grier Starret* had drifted perilously close to Grey Island. With Cummings sobbing and shivering at his feet, Moran rowed alongside and managed to hoist him aboard. Just in time, too, as his "own boat was by this time carrying quite a quantity of water," and he was "glad to get aboard the *Grier Starret*." Cummings soon revived enough to crank the engine to life. Moran took the wheel and steered the boat over a zig-zag course, scanning the rearing waves for Dahl. Abandoning the futile search, he tried unsuccessfully to find safe anchorage on the northwest side of the station in order to get Cummings to warmth ashore. By this time Cummings insisted he could make Canoe Pass alone. Moran let him go and rowed back to the lighthouse.

Moran paid tribute to the "heroic behaviour of Mr. Cummings," who, though "suffering extremely as he was from grief at the loss of his friend and skipper, and shock from his immersion in the ice-cold water . . . did all that a man could possibly do to save his vessel. . . . I am afraid as a 'green hand', I was of very little real assistance to him." Moran concluded his tragic account with a complaint as common today as it was fifty years ago, launching a "vigorous protest" against fishing craft leaving port with unseaworthy dinghies or "life boats" unworthy of the name. "The latter term is a farcical one in reference to some of the craft that have come ashore here from time to time," he claimed. "They are simply deathtraps, and little safer, even in calm weather, than a basket would be."

John Moran left Green Island in 1936. His legacy of nearly two decades on one of the roughest lights placed him up in the ranks with Daykin, Erwin, and other pioneer veterans, but he paid an even handsomer dividend to the service. Two sons, Arnold and Tom, followed him on the lights and made the Moran name synonymous with service in the North. It is a name still recalled with respect by the thinning muster of old salts in Prince Rupert.

Left: *Green Island Light from the sea.* Right: *The landing.*

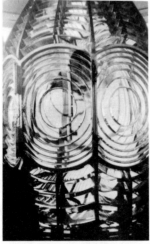

Above: Green Island Lightstation. Below: Green Island lens.

Lucy Island

Prince Rupert was a gamble right from the start, a chip on the felt in a far-off game where the players held their cards very close to their chests indeed. The stakes were glamorous, so high that only the most exclusive gamblers (with the exception of James Codville) sat in—men who would form the directorship of the new Grand Trunk Pacific Railroad.

They had every reason to think the deck was stacked in their favour. It had all come so easily to the CPR decades before: the keys to the Treasury, massive land grants amounting to every other square mile along the main line, the Mounted Police to break strikes with their Winchesters—and the new line, to run north of the CPR, would have a distinct advantage if it could only acquire and build a port north of Vancouver. As boosters in Prince Rupert never tired of proclaiming, they were at least two days closer to the Orient. S.M. Newton, editor of the *Prince Rupert Empire*, gloated, ''Prince Rupert has the finest harbour to the north of San Diego; the entrance to the harbour is no more dangerous than the entrance...at San Francisco, and is safer than that of Vancouver.'' The ''existing jealousy'' of Vancouver, Victoria, and Port Essington up the Skeena River could never retard its development, Newton predicted. Besides, he bragged, ''the climate is good, as good as that of Vancouver or Seattle.''

Dogs might bark when the sun came out in ''Rupert,'' but no one could seriously deny its worth as a port. Some tried. In October 1908 the *Vancouver Province* quoted officers of the survey ship *Egeria* to the effect that ''DIRECT RUN FROM SEA TO PRINCE RUPERT IMPOSSIBLE.'' This distortion sent an indignant Newton fuming down to the wharf where he learned from *Egeria*'s captain that ''no officer...[had] made or...[was] likely to make such a remark.'' As in love and war, all was fair in the fierce competition for waterborne commerce.

The year before, the Department of Marine had poured $100,000 into surveying the harbour, building lighthouses, and anchoring buoys. The cash would hardly have been spent, Newton concluded, ''if the harbour was not to be used.'' Conceding that it ''might be well to get an expert...in no way interested in the

Grand Trunk Pacific Railway,'' he cornered W.J. Stewart, hydrographic surveyor for the Department of Marine and Fisheries. Stewart assured him that the largest Atlantic steamships (the standard of comparison as ''no one at Ottawa'' knew ''anything about the steam ships on the Pacific Ocean'') ''could steam right into Prince Rupert harbour in the middle of the darkest night,'' guided by ''two lighthouses and a half a dozen blinkers.''

The two lighthouses stood on Green Island and Lucy Island, their intersecting beams bracketing the entrance to Metlakatla Channel. Lucy was Prince Rupert's Race Rocks, drawing traffic bound north and marking the eastward turn. Green was the northern marker. From there the blinkers and buoys would point the way to the celebrated harbour.

If ever there was a settlement whose destiny was tied to the sea, it was Prince Rupert, but the dream would be holed and sunk on another ocean, eight thousand miles away.

Charles M. Hays, president of the Grand Trunk Pacific, was a can-do sort, every inch the captain of industry (some called them robber barons), a spade-bearded figure cast in Carnegie's mold, supremely confident of his capacities in the corporate jungle. All the town plans, tables of track miles, wage bills, financial connections, lists of Grits and Tories whose doors swung open smoothly on hinges oiled with campaign contributions—every facet of the grand venture was locked away in his memory. Only the sketchiest details had been committed to paper. In April 1912 he set out for home after a hectic sojourn in London cultivating English investors. The homeward voyage was to be the highlight of his tour, a pinnacle of privilege, an opportunity to travel in superlative luxury that was new even to the likes of the Astors and other plutocrats whose company he would enjoy aboard an ocean liner so new her paint was still tacky: *Titanic*.

So Prince Rupert's dream of becoming Canada's door to the Orient went down with Charles M. Hays in the frigid unwrinkled waters east of Cape Race on that ''night to remember.'' Reeling from the implications of the ultimate marine disaster, the local press vainly tried to prop up the townspeople's sinking spirits (and the drooping real estate values), trumpeting ''HAYS ALIVE,'' while its readers stood about waiting for confirmation from the IMM-White Star line offices in New York. The final casualty figures had already confirmed their worst fear however. Hays's name was on the list.

There would be no railroad until the Canadian government opened its coffers and came to the rescue of the bankrupt Grand Trunk and Great Northern Railroads in the 1920s. Even then, Prince Rupert lay at the end of a mere branch line stretching west from Jasper through the Rockies and down along the Skeena River. There was only the ocean highway left, and it was busy enough to justify the Department of Marine and Fisheries' establishing a sub-agency there in 1913. Prince Rupert, though reeling, was a town too tough to die.

Octave Ouellette, whose name would be synonymous with Lucy Island, was as tough as his adopted home. Isolation always weighs heaviest on those who dwell upon what they might be missing over the horizon, but it can be a certain balm to others who have seen and done enough. Even as a child Octave had the wayward, turbulent nature of a born eccentric. His mother gave him up for adoption at the age of eight. He was taken in by an Italian couple who were trapeze artists in the Barnum and Bailey Circus. So began a boyhood beyond the wildest dreams of his Quebec-bound peers. They took him all over the globe, taught him their "death defying" art, showed him the coronation of Edward VII, the colosseum in Rome, Eiffel's new tower. Fifteen years later something drew him home. He stowed away aboard a ship bound for America and wound his way back to his first family in Quebec. He stayed put, went to night school, got married.

It could not last. A man who had performed high above rapt, gaping audiences, who once sat sipping wine in Europe's sidewalk cafes, and remembered Renaissance splendours of Florence, could hardly fit into the tight little world of rural Quebec at the turn of the century, a society propped up by the twin pillars of the Catholic Church and Laurier's Liberal party. When news of the Klondike discoveries broke, there was no holding him back. Octave uprooted his family, now a boy and a girl, with a third on the way. Their odyssey ended in a dank sixteen-by-sixteen foot clapboard shack in Prince Rupert, with "the stork bringing my sister . . . refusing to venture any further into the frozen Arctic," his eldest daughter recalled.

Tharsyle Ouellette began keeping a journal at the age of eight. It offers surprisingly eloquent insights into pioneer life in the Pacific Northwest through a child's eye. Her mother succumbed to a "black depression" as they sat on their crates around the feckless stove, with only a bed for furniture, listening to the rain pound the tin roof. Contrary to her globe-trotting husband, Therese Ouellette "knew nothing but the calm and bourgeois life of her native village, amidst a family of wealthy farmers." She felt cornered and betrayed, held hostage by "black misery" instead of enjoying the riches they expected to find.

Octave drank. He could easily hold his own among the legions of fishermen, failed prospectors, lumberjacks, and trappers, yet his own bitterness grew until "he was crying in his heart as he . . . was 'doing it on the town'." A labouring job for the GTP paid enough to live (at 37½ cents per day), but they knew they could never save their way out of Rupert—a hard-nosed company town where workers and bosses faced each other like snarling cats across class lines. In April 1911 the simmering conflict erupted in the Battle of Kelly's Cut, when the Prince Rupert Industrial Association fought a running battle against truncheon-swinging police and special constables backed up by a local detachment of Earl Grey's Rifles.

Lucy Island provided an escape from this life, saving the Ouellettes as surely as it saved the seamen who made their way past in the dark and fog. One sunny Sunday in June 1910 Prince Rupert's tiny French-Canadian community packed hampers and struck out for a picnic on Lucy, eighteen miles away. For Tharsyle's mother it seemed a release, "like a lifebuoy in the storm of anxiety in which her soul was sinking." They landed on the expanse of beach on the north shore, pulled up their boats, waded through the surf with their baskets, and knelt in the sand while their priest said Mass in front of the rocks that formed a cathedral of stone, festooned with starfish, barnacles, and chitons. After lunch, their spiritual and material needs sated, they hiked through the forest, laughing and singing as they plucked swollen salmonberries off the bushes. Finally they reached the lighthouse, where they were pleasantly surprised to find one of their own—M. Turcotte, a bachelor, first keeper of Lucy Island light.

He was overjoyed by the unexpected company, especially at meeting a man like Octave Ouellette, who held them all spellbound with his tales of life under canvas with Barnum and Bailey. For his part, Turcotte could only confide the loneliness and despair he suffered in the endless empty weeks between mailboats. He could never get to town since no one wanted to relieve him. He wanted off.

That Sunday's sliver of happiness changed their lives. Turcotte's plight had an electric effect upon Octave and Therese; it charged them with the possibility of escape at last from their carousel of drink and depression. Though Tharsyle's account must lose something in translation, there is no more stirring description of the romantic allure of the lights:

> An idea is a plant which sprouts quickly, especially in ground as well prepared as my mother's ear. In less time than I take to write it, she saw the possibility of coming to establish in this enchanting place, far from the moral and material ugliness of the town she abhorred. She was seeing her children grow in the clear morning spaces, the happiness of her family safe, hidden in this asylum under the eye of God. She looked at my Dad. Her eyes must have been quite eloquent, as he read them like an open book. He also had had enough of this hopeless life he was living for the past months, and for him to become a hermit would only be another feather in his cap. It was worth the try. Back on the boat . . . the little flame of hope lit in their heart made their eyes shine almost as much as the stars, lighting up one by one in the sky.[1]

Next day they called at the marine depot on Digby Island with an offer to relieve Turcotte. A month later they were unloading their meagre possessions from a workboat on that same beach, and packing them up to the light. Lucy Island was theirs!

Anyone who has landed there knows Lucy Island is a magical place, a miniature Tahiti, surrounded by white sand beaches in front of the swaying trees. To this day Lucy remains, as Tharsyle Ouellette found it, "a corner of Eden." The forest floor is a shag carpet of moss, dappled by sunlight that filters through the needled branches, tunneled and mined by rhinoceros auklets for burrows. Nothing could be further removed from Prince Rupert with all its warts and worries.

The dwelling was anchored by masonry to a rock sixty-five feet above sea level, linked by a post and plank bridge to the main part of the island. It looked much the same as others of the Klondike generation, a frame house with a tower on top. A storage shed for oil, paint, and supplies stood across the bridge. Around the back of the island was a boat house and tracks. "The new Robinsons," Tharsyle recorded, "found everything in a broken-down state." Together they scrubbed, painted, and polished the buildings and equipment, built furniture to replace their crates, blasted and burned stumps, and cleared a 300-by-150-foot garden tract with mattocks and shovels. They built a chicken coop and slung nets over the run to keep the bandit eagles out. Lucy became a piece of rural Quebec transplanted onto the muskeg. Next summer, when the marine agent came out on his annual tour of inspection, he was astonished by the transformation. All the buildings had been freshly painted. Their entrances were flanked by half barrels and seashell planters overflowing with flowers. Ouellette's records and logs were impeccable, he reported.

Like all successful keepers before and since, Octave Ouellette reckoned being master of his own time and place as fair compensation for isolation. Year after year they slashed and burned deeper into the grudging forest. His diary boasted of the fruits of their labour: 230 head of cabbage, 300 celery plants, a winter supply of potatoes and turnips—all coaxed from the soil they fortified by peeling back the outer skin of muskeg and dragging kelp up from the beach. With his father-in-law's help, Octave laid a boardwalk clear across the island, three-quarters of a mile to the boathouse. The children had their own playground with hammocks, swings, miniature tables, and benches. He constructed a glass box and dangled them, giggling, over the rowboat's gunwales to watch and wonder at "all creation feeding on itself" below. In August 1913 Octave delivered his fourth child, a girl. They named her Lucy, of course.

The finest feature of Lucy Island is its beaches—spectacular tracts of fine sand like Big Sur or Long Beach off Tofino—and when the tide flows out, the table is set with clams, mussels, cockles, and abalone, a veritable "feast fit for the table of kings." From the sea itself the Ouellettes harvested salmon, rock fish, ling cod, halibut, and octopus. This was the golden age of the North Coast fishery, when no one needed search planes or sonar to find the silver cascades of running salmon. Octave once spent four exhausting hours landing a Chinook which tipped the scales at 123 pounds! From June onward, Japanese fishermen anchored their skiffs over a "glory-hole" just west of Lucy, and pitched their tents on shore at night. Every time they called at the house for fresh water, they dragged another salmon up and flopped it into the salt box.

There was no lack of company, and the lighthouse soon evolved into a flourishing centre of Quebec culture, a francophone island awash in an English sea. All through the summer Lucy lured the picnic parties from Prince Rupert. They sailed out from Rupert through Metlakatla Channel, just as their hosts had done that magical Sunday. An aunt and a grandfather came to stay in 1914, and the aunt tutored the children until she married a Prince Rupert man at a gala wedding ceremony on the island. In April 1917 the bishop of Vancouver landed to celebrate a huge outdoor Mass. The supply tender anchored north of the island twice a year, and the bearded sailors, tattoos spilling out their cuffs and collars, spent the whole day rowing back and forth with provisions—everything from lamp oil to chicken feed—to be packed up the rocks and stored. Weather permitting, mailbags were dropped off every week in summer. Even in winter there were occasional visits from mission boats like the *Thomas Crosby*.

It was an idyllic life. The Ouellettes' only worry was the weather and the sea. So powerful were the winter swells that they broke like thunderclaps down on the beach, splintering logs like toothpicks. The water excavated all the sand from the beaches in a single night's work, leaving behind a polished stone basin twenty feet deep, only to fling it all back next day in a meaningless routine. Sometimes the waves threatened to claim the house and tower too, but Lucy's keepers could always look through the drenched window panes to see Green Island light flashing to the north, and know that their experience was a shared one.

People with less faith and determination than Octave Ouellette might well have cleared out after one winter, especially after the storm which ushered in 1913. Thanking Reverend George Raley of the *Thomas Crosby* mission for his "delicate attention towards my wife m[y]self & my little family which enjoyed a beautiful Christmas tree with the presents you sent," Ouellette praised the Protestant missionaries for their thoughtfulness in visiting them:

> Beside our lonliness we have to stand the storms which are very frequent since last fall. We were visited by a fearful one on New Year Day morning. Also today is a very bad one—on New Year day it rain so heavily that water was running on floor of sitting room & Bed Room by buckets ful. per chance it cease by one o' clock. tops of waves washed the southeast part of lighthouse from eight o'clock till one P.M. It is in a place like our that we behold the power of God & Elements, sometimes we think the house may upset by force of Wind. It is a reason why we need the prayers so that God may preserve a family which are so exposed to be Wreck. Ever since I put a foot on the Island I put my trust on Him who Has suffered for us. & We never fear the elements and try to keep ready to meet our Maker at any time He may choose.

The storm finally pried half the roof from the walls, and a torrent of sea water drove them out to shelter in the storage shed where they crouched shivering in the dark, "terrorized with the thoughts that it might go next, swallowing...[them] forever."[2]

Through it all, Ouellette hauled himself in a crouch, hand over hand, over the bridge to the broken house to check the light and fetch blankets and food. They huddled together in the trembling shed for three days and nights while the gale held sway. When it died down, a fish boat came in close enough to take away a hastily pencilled damage report to Prince Rupert. A work gang spent a full month making repairs.

There were also the killer waves, the dreaded tsunamis, racing unnoticed across the open sea at five hundred miles per hour; announcing their arrival when they reared up in the shallows. One slammed into the island, ripped up the tower

Lucy Island circa 1920.

platform, surged over the rocks, and carried away all their precious topsoil, destroying years of toil in seconds. They had to start all over again—but there were no hard feelings. The ocean gave; the ocean took away. "But when wearing its silvery coat, Ah! was she ever beautiful and how sweet did she seem, our great ocean!" Tharsyle exclaimed.

Octave kept careful watch and plucked a good many men out of "her" clutches, too. He once spotted a drifting derelict lifeboat without oars. Rowing out to it, he peered inside and recoiled in horror at the sight of three shriveled corpses lying in the bottom. As he lashed its bow to his stern, he detected some movement. The desiccated, shrunken seamen were alive! He towed them ashore and carried them one by one, like rag dolls, up to the house. Though they were Japanese, they somehow made the Frenchman understand that their ship had foundered at sea eighteen days before. They had survived by lapping rain water, yellow with urine, from the bottom of the boat, and by sucking on barnacles scraped from its hull.

There were frantic, frightening times, too, which hammered home the vulnerability of their isolation. Tharsyle discovered a bottle of pills up in a cupboard one day, and divided them out among the other children. Putting one in her mouth, she was overcome by a foul taste and spat it out. Her little brother Noel swallowed two and began retching and heaving, vomiting blood. Lucy, the baby, swallowed the rest and slid quickly into a coma. Tharsyle ran screaming to her mother. Therese immediately pumped the hand horn to summon Octave and a visitor, Father Wolfe, from their work in the forest. They tried everything—made Lucy throw up, forced an antidote down her throat—but all seemed in vain as her lips turned a ghastly blue. The priest had just administered the Last Rites when she revived. Octave always swore it was a miracle.

For nine years the Ouellettes fulfilled their escapist dream. There were nagging worries, of course: constant concern about the children's education (Tharsyle left for school in Quebec); lonely, drawn-out winter days slipping into the past with no human contact; perilous nights when they cowered inside around kerosene lamps as the sea came headlong at them. Yet through it all they were secure, content, and eternally grateful for their voluntary exile as they anticipated the birth of a fifth child.

In the summer of 1919 Octave Ouellette had every reason to count his blessings. The next baby was due in a matter of weeks (who knew?—maybe days). An esteemed public servant, he was also a pillar of the local French community. He had a rich storehouse of memory to draw upon as middle age approached. After that a brace of grandchildren, *certainement*. He had proven himself a capable midwife, too, when Lucy came, but this time Therese insisted on going to town. She could stay with her sister, go round and see their suppliers about groceries, be a guest for once rather than a hostess, combine business with pleasure.

As he climbed up to the house after kissing her goodbye, and stood watching the boat make for Metlakatla, Octave was as fulfilled as any man could be—a spectacular success by the standards he prized. Time would drag, of course, while she was off the island, but it was merely an expectant prelude to the day she returned with another child in her arms. Meanwhile, there was always work to be done in the day, and evenings to wile away tossing out names for approval, then a story for "les enfants" and off to bed, each with a kiss in turn, though sleep might not come easy for him in bed by himself.

When word finally came to break their delicious suspense, it was the worst news possible, and Ouellette's perfect world came crumbling down. It was a girl, fit and healthy, "all there." Her mother had walked into the hospital with the confidence of giving birth for the fifth time, but she entered a hospital understaffed and under siege by the Spanish influenza. They carried her out in a coffin.

It was as if something evil had reached into Octave Ouellette and ripped out his flourishing faith by the roots. He crossed over to Rupert for the funeral and found parents willing to adopt the baby (Tharsyle tracked her down in Saskatchewan twenty years later). He resigned, came back to Lucy, packed up all their belongings, and sailed away. Back in Quebec the widower abandoned his remaining children at the orphanage in St. Hyacinthe. Uprooted and alone, Lucy pined away and died soon after. Octave found himself back in the depths of alcoholism, disappearing for seven years into the nether-world of sawdust floors and barflies.

The matron called Tharsyle into her office at the orphanage one day in 1926, and handed her a long-awaited letter. "His miserable life seemed to want to anchor itself," and Octave had found a sheltered berth as a nurse in a sanatorium at Lake Edouard in the Saguenay. Tharsyle pinched every penny to "realize a dream which had been close to . . .[her] heart," and boarded a train, "crossing woods and lakes

Above: Tower under construction. Below: Boat house, Lucy Island.

[which] brought me to the area of Maria-Chapdelaine and finally into my father's arms.'' As his life drew to its close, Octave had taken refuge at the convent of the Gray Sisters, Mothers of Charity. Reunited with his family, he became a celebrated raconteur. ''He spoke six languages, had a memory of an elephant and an imagination as large.'' He passed his time reading, writing, smoking ''like a chimney,'' until he died at eighty, so far away from his corner of Eden in the Pacific.

Tharsyle set out on a pilgrimage in the summer of 1953. She took the train to Prince Rupert, and the Department of Transport arranged a visit to Lucy Island, where she stayed with its keepers, Frank and Elenore Glynn. As the *Katherine B*, a fishpacker converted for supply purposes, steamed through Metlakatla, she could see the light flashing and saw, too, that the island was just as she left it under a pall of misery almost forty years before. The house still stood; in fact, she was given the bedroom she shared with her little sister as a child. As she hiked over the island, Tharsyle found relics of their work, rotted and sinking into the advancing carpet of moss. The forest had reclaimed the vast gardens and flowerbeds, the playground and chicken house.

Great changes had been wrought in the living conditions of the keepers as well. A gas-powered winch hoisted supplies out of the workboats and deposited them on the landing. The fog alarm no longer needed a hand on the crank. The Glynns earned four times her father's salary, and even had paid holidays! Supplies arrived every month rather than twice a year. Perishables could be stored in a refrigerator. It was ''luxury absolutely unknown to'' the Ouellettes!

Tharsyle left Lucy for the last time that summer, choked with memories of a lighthouse childhood rediscovered. She remembered best being tucked into bed at night, begging and bartering for one last story, and her mother, to end the ritual, would always oblige:

> Once upon a time there were four little children who had parents who loved them very much. They were living on a marvelously beautiful island full of birds, flowers and tasty fruits. The trees were so high that their hands disappeared in the azure sky. Three beautiful beaches of fine sands; one red, one grey and one white, lent themselves for their games. The immense ocean was their swimming pool. . . .

At that point they all squealed with delight, knowing *they* would be the characters in her makeshift fable. ''But did we really believe to that extent we were living a fairy tale?'' Tharsyle wondered in her diary, striving like any middle-aged adult to penetrate the shimmering veil of childhood from the other side. ''I almost think that we did. At least, we were so perfectly happy that I can't remember any bitterness, or that any desire for change ever crossed our children's hearts.''

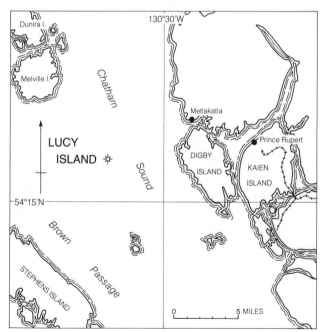

Lucy Island 1982. Jim Ryan photo.

Addenbroke Island

Captain George Vancouver christened Addenbroke Island late in 1792. The island lies in Fitzhugh Sound, only eight miles from Safety Cove where Vancouver, with Lieutenants Puget and Whitby of HMS *Discovery* and *Chatham*, anchored in the course of his coastal survey. Construction of a light on the island started in March 1914, and the beacon began turning at nightfall on 20 May. The lantern room stood upon the roof of the standard square frame house, thirty-eight feet above ground and eighty-one feet above water. The foghorn building was erected 150 feet south of the tower.

W.A. Guthro and his wife Edith moved up from Nanaimo that May. Guthro resigned temporarily due to illness in August 1917, but came back Christmas Day. Perhaps Addenbroke proved too lonesome; in any event, the Guthros resigned in August 1918, leaving the station to the Smiths from Cape St. James light.

F. Smith "took sick" in March 1922 and died shortly after in a Vancouver hospital. His widow chose to stay on at Addenbroke, and the department hired her to run the station. The *Newington* was her only regular connection with the world beyond, bringing mail, papers, and supplies every two months. "Time did drag sometimes," she allowed, but "every now and then, fishing boats would call in for a visit. I used to fish often. . . there were many things to take my mind off the solitude and loneliness." Though lacking human companionship, she managed a goat herd, several dogs, and a large flock of chickens. Her nearest neighbours lived in Safety Cove. She often rowed over for a visit, on seas that sometimes proved too much for men in motor vessels. In December 1924 a fishboat lost power and smashed into the rocks. The fisherman waded ashore through the breakers, and the "lady lightkeeper" fed and sheltered him for two weeks.

After three-and-a-half years alone she brought her second husband, W.F. Brydon, ashore. Mrs. Brydon continued as lightkeeper, moving up to Lucy Island in 1928, and finally retired to Victoria in 1932 after fourteen years' service. ''While I was in the lighthouse work, I liked it very much,'' she told a *Times* reporter a year before she died in 1942. ''To tell you the truth, I was sorry to leave it.''

Ernie Maynard swapped with the Brydons, trading Lucy Island for Addenbroke, and served until 15 August 1928. On the morning of 16 August, Calvert Thorpe chugged his trawler past Addenbroke, surprised the light was still burning an hour after sunrise. Maybe Ernie had ''slept in.'' At 8 A.M. he steered within a few hundred yards of the island, searching in vain for any sign of life.

Cal had lived at the station for a few weeks that summer and knew Ernie's habits well. Like any other keeper, his friend kept diligently to his maintenance routine. Perhaps he was sick, or hurt and helpless. Cal clambered into his skiff, steered into North Bay, and climbed the rocks. Maynard's door was locked and the windows were too high up to peek in. He yelled and was answered only by the squawk and clatter of ducks scared into flight off the kelp beds, and by the gulls (more than usual) wheeling and screaming above. Now he knew with sick certainty that something was very wrong.

Above him the light continued to turn in the tower. Down below he could make out the wharf with its winch and fog bell, and Maynard's skiff lashed belly-up in front of the coal shed. Scanning the cleated ramp's course to the wharf, his gaze was arrested by a man's form sprawled face down. Rushing to it, he recognized his friend—though half his head was gone.

Overcome by his horrible find, Cal fought off spasms of nausea and was relieved to see Hub Shotbolt, another fisherman, cruising by. He frantically signalled him to

Left: *Mr.and Mrs. Walter Brydon.* Right: *the Smiths from Cape St. James.*

come ashore. Shotbolt immediately set out for Rivers Inlet to fetch the Provincial Police, leaving Cal to keep a grisly vigil over Maynard and the flies. Rough weather delayed Coroner George Hill, Corporal Arthur Stone, and Constable J.B. Brown until 5:30 next morning. They immediately set to work reconstructing Ernie Maynard's last watch.

Suicide is the ultimate response to isolation, and Cal had been a reluctant witness to the steady deterioration of Maynard's marriage, right up until the awkward, sorry day when Maggie Maynard left with the kids. But no weapon lay at hand, so the police turned their attention to finding the identity of a murderer. The investigators concluded that the lightkeeper had been to the dock and was headed back up the ramp to the house when a bullet fired from a high-powered rifle struck the left side of his skull from behind, spewing blood, bone, and brains in a long ropy splatter forty-five feet up the boardwalk. Maynard's corpse was clad in pants, shirt, and underwear, with unlaced shoes over bare feet. His sou'wester hat lay down on the rocks below, near a kerosene lantern. Keys to the house and tower were on the boardwalk near his right hand. The keys to the wharf shed were still in his pocket. Nearby lay the only clue: a single white shirt button, with no mate on any of Maynard's clothing.

They entered the locked shed. Thorpe pointed out a small splash of red paint on the floor, still tacky. This was extraordinary indeed, he claimed, since Maynard shared the typical lightkeeper's obsession for order and cleanliness, stooping to wipe up oil or paint when it spilled. The lighthouse and dwelling betrayed no sign of robbery or violence. Maynard's .25-.35 rifle, returned by Thorpe four days before, leaned in a corner of the bedroom. The bed was unmade. The murdered man's socks were coiled up on the floor. Under the pillow his watch was still ticking, and ran for another two hours and four minutes. The ''Big Ben'' alarm clock beside his bed stopped at 1:52 that afternoon. Rewinding the clock, Stone determined how long it took to run its course, and calculated that Maynard wound it for the last time around 9 P.M. 15 August.

Sometime between then and 8 next morning, he concluded, Maynard had been awakened by a racket on the dock, had leaped from his bed, pulled on his shirt, pants, and shoes, and rushed out to his death. After dark the police discovered that the landing lay far below the beam's sweep. Whoever shot Ernie Maynard probably concealed himself in the dark and fired at his head as it was silhouetted against a nearly full moon.

When the photographing and measuring of the crime scene was finished, the coroner took Maynard's body away to Ocean Falls where a post-mortem uncovered a few tiny bullet fragments in the shattered cranium—useless for identification by primitive methods of the day. Stone and Brown went through the house, taking inventory of Maynard's ''estate,'' pulling and pawing through drawers, turning out pockets, checking every shirt button, reading letters, ransacking all his belongings for some clue, the merest suggestion of motive. After it all they were left feeling like frustrated voyeurs, with the remnants of a very sparse and ordinary life spread out around them. Money certainly did not figure, unless one counted a recipe for bathtub gin, carefully copied under Lighthouse Board letterhead.

So began an investigation without end. Stone's watery beat ranged over hundreds of miles of coastline, and he set about the monotonous chore of questioning all the motley crews of boats anchored in Safety Cove and along the shores of Fitzhugh Sound and Calvert Island. Enquiries over on the mainland soon uncovered the strained relationship between Ernie and his Indian wife, Maggie. Maggie's brothers had had a checkered past, including stints in Oakalla, but both had iron-clad alibis for the middle of August.

Stone steered in and out of every cove and camp. One day his fruitless search extended to a lonely bay near Safety Cove. He tethered his skiff and walked over to a tent where a beachcomber named Manuel Hannah stood waiting. By now the questions came mechanically: Did you know Maynard? Seen anybody or anything suspicious lately? Got a rifle? Where were you the night of August 15?

Yes, Hannah knew Maynard, he had even visited him at Addenbroke eleven days before his murder. The lightkeeper was in high spirits then. His only complaint was that deer were ravaging his vegetable patch. Something in Hannah's demeanor, especially his vacant and shifting eyes, triggered the coiled spring of Stone's suspicion. And then, giving him the once-over, Stone's eye riveted upon the left-hand breast pocket of Hannah's workshirt, glazed with sweat and dirt. A white button was missing. A casual search of the hermit's tent yielded nothing suspicious—except for a .303 British Enfield rifle.

At Stone's request the B.C. Provincial Police sifted through Hannah's past and unearthed a very rough diamond indeed. He had spent five years behind bars in Kingston Penitentiary for stabbing a Belleville, Ontario man. Then he served time in Saskatchewan for horse-stealing, and had been released from the B.C. Penitentiary four years before, convicted for a number of thefts at Cascade Harbour off northern Vancouver Island. At best, he was a violent man with little regard for life or property.

Stone was back at his campsite within a week. This time Hannah told a convoluted tale of being robbed of gasoline at gunpoint at 3 the morning after Stone's first visit. He gave a precise description of the thief, and an all-too-detailed description of his boat, seen by the feeble light of a match held aloft. Stone dutifully jotted down the information, but suspected a deliberate attempt to throw him off the scent.

Stone remarked that Hannah's skiff, already lumpy with endless coats of topside paint, sported a fresh coat. "Yes," he said, "I got a little green paint and fixed it up." If Hannah had bought the paint at Dunseith's at Seymour Sound, then lost the receipt as he claimed, he was a man of exquisite and expensive tastes. Heat-resistant engine enamel was top of the line; even the marine department dealt it out with a stingy hand when its lightkeepers needed some to touch up their diesels. Hannah showed Stone a gallon can, a lard pail, an Empress Jam tin, and a smaller can, containing red, green, and black paint.

Addenbroke Light, site of the unsolved murder of keeper Ernie Maynard in 1928.

A few pints of paint seemed a pathetic price for a man's life. Even so, the chain of circumstantial evidence—Hannah's violent record, the missing button, and the lack of any other leads—called for another visit. In mid-September Stone beached his boat at Hannah's landing again. He asked the suspect to get out his paint again so he could take away samples for analysis. Hannah, visibly agitated, carted out the cans. It was all different. The green engine enamel had been thinned with gasoline, the signal red was tinted pink and was in a different tin. Defiant, Hannah swore that he had not tampered with the tins or their contents. Stone left again, certain that Hannah's tale was a tissue of lies. He would wear him down, tangle and trip him up in a backlash of his own half-truths and fiction.

A week later he returned for another skirmish. Hannah's green boat was gone; it was a great opportunity for a search. Cautiously, Stone raised the flaps, stooped, and peered into the deserted tent. No rifle. Hannah's bedroll lay on his cot. Reaching under, Stone dragged out a pair of stained trousers. On the rickety table lay a note:

> Safety Cove Calvert Island B.C.
> Sept. 18th 1928
>
> B.C. Police
> To Whom It may Concern—
> To be coled A lier I will not take no more by *officer* witch I was. Or anyone For I have took it for the last time So you keep looking for The lighthouse Murder. For Im not the man But I Know You wold Get me because Im alone Without no Friends Donot look for me for I Will be in A better land By the time you get this
> You *Black Mailling Roberrs*
> this is *One Man Who is not*
> Gilty *Off Murder*
>
> > I Set my Hand for
> > last time
> > Manuel Hannah[1]

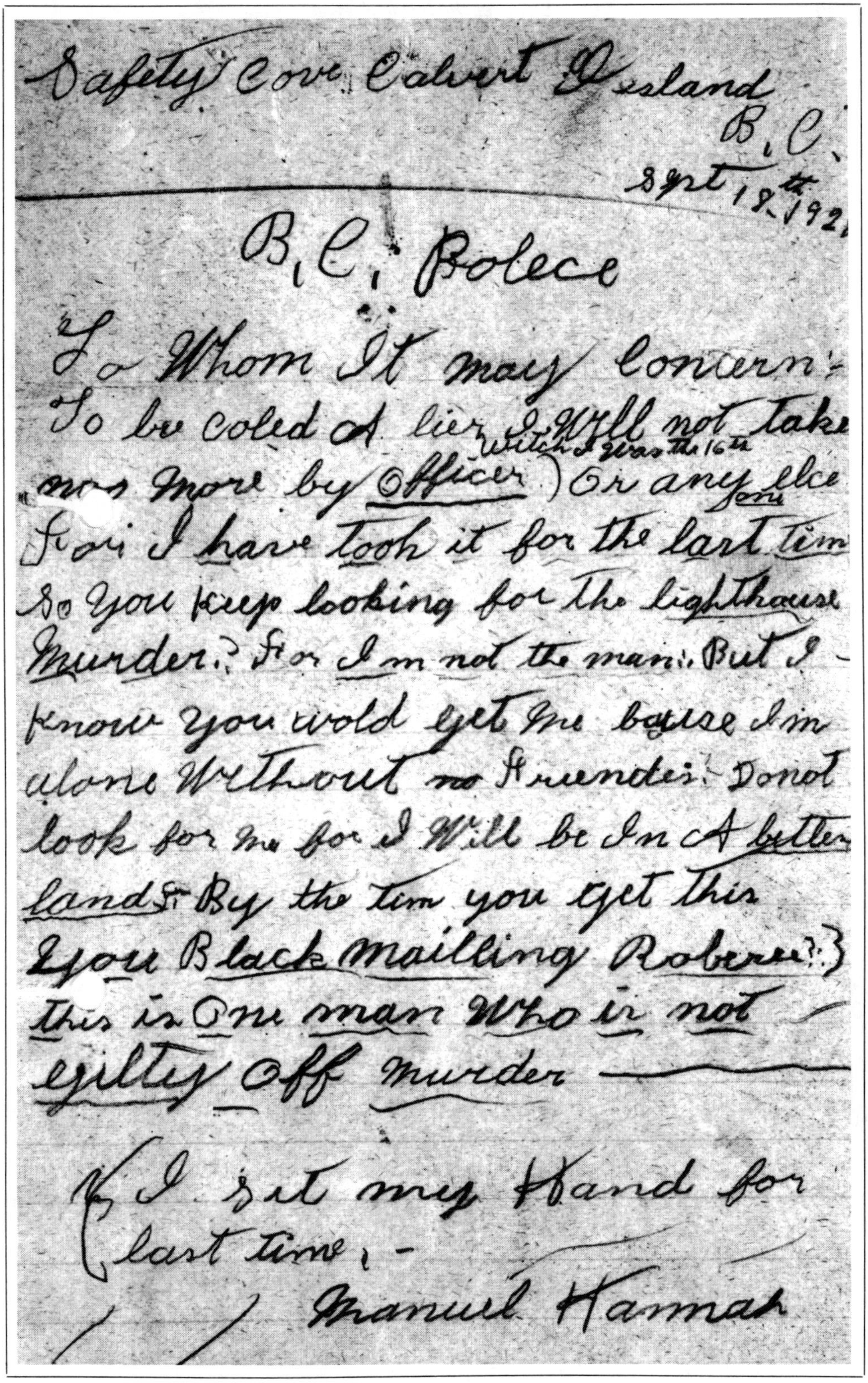

Safety Cove Calvert Island
B.C.
Sept 18th 192,

B. C. Polece

To Whom It may Concern:
To be coled A lier (Witch I was the 16th) I Wll not take
no more by Officer) Or any elce
for I have took it for the last tim
So You keep looking for the lighthouse
Murder. For I m not the man. But I
know you wold get me bquse I m
alone Wethout no fruendes. Do not
look for me for I Will be In A better
land By the tim you eget this
You Black mailling Robere)
this is One man Who is not
gilty off murder ———

I set my Hand for
last time, ———

Manuel Hannah

Manuel Hanna's last communication—but was it a suicide note?

The B.C. Police combed Calvert Island and cast a dragnet over all the shipping lanes from Alaska to Puget Sound, but Manuel Hannah had disappeared without a trace. Ten years later, detectives drove to Freeland, Washington to question a retired Alaskan fisherman named Morgan. One day in that fall of 1928, Morgan had dropped anchor in Safety Cove and met up with Hannah, whom he clearly remembered as "a sort of lunatic man with staring eyes." Hannah admired the .45 automatic pistol Morgan used to dispatch sea lions caught in his nets. Hannah wanted it but Morgan would not sell. The talk turned from guns to the recent murder. "He told me about it in such detail, even acting out the part of the murderer, that if he didn't do it himself, then he must have stood by while it happened," Morgan recalled. Hannah tried once more to get Morgan to part with the pistol, then left.

Left: *Addenbroke fog bell.* Right: *Police mock-up of Addenbroke vapour light.*

There is no statute of limitations for murder. Technically, the Lighthouse Murder Case is an open file, but Manuel Hannah remains out of reach in his ''better land,'' and Addenbroke's light still revolves above Fitzhugh just as it did that bloody summer night in 1928.

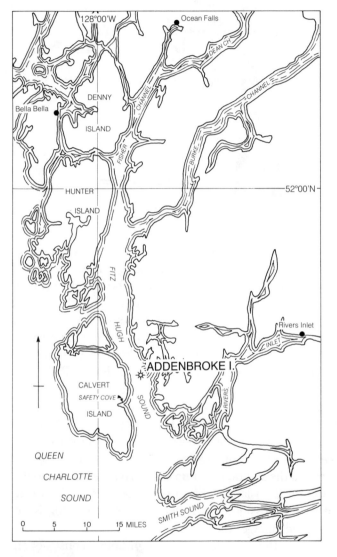

Langara

As late as 1980 Transport Canada still warned prospective keepers away from Langara light. Though it paid the highest, Langara was worth it. Fifty years' experience proved the place was best suited to someone who had already done time in isolation. Right from the start Langara was a superlative lighthouse: the furthest out, the largest island, with a full slate of synoptic weather observations to be recorded every three hours, and, after 1964, something unique—a tsunami recorder to take the erratic pulse of the earth's crust and allow its keepers to save lives ashore.   In February 1908, ''with the advent of the Grand Trunk Pacific Railway Co. to Prince Rupert in the future,'' Commander Frederick Learmonth steered his *Egeria* north to survey navigational aids needed for Dixon Entrance. In his report to William Smith, Dominion hydrographer in Ottawa, Learmonth attached highest priority to a light and fog alarm on the northernmost Queen Charlotte Island, to mark the northern entrance for transoceanic steamers bound for the projected railhead. Learmonth recommended the station be set up on ''a rounded hill devoid of trees,'' at the highest elevation on the island. ''From our experience,'' he wrote, ''the advantage of its height with a possibility of it being enveloped in fog is not great, and is outweighed by many advantages the position affords.''

Learmonth's suggestion violated the cardinal rule of lighthouse construction: never build higher than 150 feet. Incredible as it may seem, as a prelude to the Triangle Island fiasco (where the chief engineer insisted on building a station so high that clouds and fog hid the beacon from ships), Colonel Anderson was ''led to differ'' with Learmonth. He predicted that the 523-foot summit (150 feet *lower* than Triangle's light) would be far too high ''in view of the prevalence of fog on all that coast.'' Moreover, a separate fog alarm would have to be built near the shore, "entailing the maintenance of two separate stations." After landing and ranging over nearby Thrumb Island that spring, Anderson elected to build over on the North Island shore, 100 feet up on a "fairly level top (a very important thing in so rough waters)." He suggested the island be renamed Langara, the name originally bestowed by Lieutenant Jacinto Caamano of the *Aranzazu* in 1792.

Anderson dreamed in terms of concrete, and in his mind's eye imagined one of his celebrated buttressed designs planted up there on those bluffs, a mate with Triangle and Cape St. James lights to mark Canada's northern gateway. The chief engineer estimated the total cost at $30,000 and dispatched W.C. Killeen, the resident engineer for the department, to survey the site. In June 1911 Killeen reported back: "I was nine days ashore engaged on this work and could only work three days on account of extremely bad weather." Three days were sufficient, though, to confirm the wisdom of Anderson's site choice and to complete his initial survey. Killeen sketched out a fog alarm directly in front of the tower—"well above any possible danger from wave action"—and a keeper's dwelling facing north. He recommended building a 2200-foot tramway to the site from a sheltered bight to the east.

Five acres of timber had to be cleared away at a cost of $750. The tramway would cost $2 a foot, or $4400. Killeen set out from Prince Rupert that September with his foreman and eleven labourers aboard the Grand Trunk Pacific's *Prince John*. Their landing went smoothly, deceptively so, "and setting up of camp gone on with at once." The engineer drove stakes, stretched his chains, marked out the clearing, and arranged with H. Edenshaw of Masset to land supplies biweekly.

The "sheltered" landing at Langara was described as "simply Boca's de Inferno," and it took two weeks that December to land "a very small quantity of lumber and stores." Two months later a wild, ripping gale tore out the tramway and carpeted the clearing with fallen timber. There was some gravel on the site but no sand. By early October, however, the road had been rebuilt, the tower's base was poured, and the crew was hacking out cisterns and cellars.

The workers were becoming surly in their exile. Before leaving Rupert, Killeen had promised to pay them straight time. Now they discovered they were getting a much lower "subsistence" rate when weather conspired against work. They sent a petition off with Edenshaw on 13 October, claiming the reduced pay, considering their "marooned condition," was "not enough recompense." Adding insult to injury, the department paid their two foremen full wages. "In writing this you must not think we are a discontented crew of men," their spokesman explained, "but are taking this method of trying to improve our exceptional conditions on this island." For good measure he sent a copy to the Conservative committee in Prince Rupert.

"The only suggestion I can offer, " Marine Agent Robertson dryly replied, "is that if they are not satisfied they have the privilege of leaving." Robertson was still reeling from the force of Anderson's fury over expenses. After leafing through invoices in Ottawa, the chief engineer had discovered that strawberries and cream had been sent out to Langara—not to mention "$108.00 worth of fancy butter and such articles as blueberries, canned pumpkin, assorted jams, Australian roast mutton.'' This was altogether too much, and the agent had better make sure that future orders were ''made on a scale more like that in vogue in other working parties.''

The crusty colonel also balked at an order for horse fodder. How had horses ever booked passage to Langara without his knowledge? Robertson justified the ''extravagance'' by pointing out that supplies must be hauled over the mile-long corduroy road by horse-drawn sled. True, there was a landing of sorts in the gap just below the tower, but it was risky at best. Steamers might pitch around offshore for days waiting to land, as the *Quadra* had done in December. ''The cost of horse feed would not be nearly so much as the cost of time of the steamer,'' he reckoned. Unimpressed, Anderson ordered Killeen to build a winch below the tower. The winch and its control shed were flattened by heavy swells that winter, and the horses stayed.

Strange as it may seem in light of his family's brush with death at Ivory in 1904, James Forsyth came back on the lights to take over the new station. He had gone back to Ivory in January 1905 to crate up and ship out their effects, then crewed on tugs for awhile and tried farming up the Fraser, but the lights must have worked under his skin. The Forsyths continued to get letters twice a year from Egg Island keeper James Davies, Forsyth's former mate from the days when they worked the tugs. It was too easy, sometimes, to imagine themselves back up there. Those people who try the life and quit never quite purge their system of the experience, and, over time, the lights' allure can far outshine life in the real world. At least it did for James and Ellen Forsyth, who must have hungered again for the sound and smell of the sea, and that abstract ''glory of being lightkeeper.''

In 1909 Davies confided he was about to resign. His girls were getting on. Whatever the cost he wanted to send them to school. Forsyth seized the moment and wrote James Gaudin, prompting the agent's reply that he would surely like to place the ex-keeper ''in charge of one of. . .[the] lights again,'' but patronage, damned patronage, tied his hands.

Egg Island's reputation was a deterrent for many partisans, though. A man with the right political credentials won the post but backed off. Confessing his ''difficulty in getting men to take Egg or Ivory,'' the agent slyly insinuated James Forsyth back into the service. ''Be ready to leave Vancouver in 48 hours for Egg Island,'' the telegram read. They loaded their furniture into a freight car, then went to Vancouver where the *Quadra* lay at anchor, with crewmen swarming over her, stem to stern, with chipping hammers, paint, and polish, tarting her up for the Governor General's cruise two weeks away. Their freight went astray and Gaudin waited a week, then ordered anchors aweigh.

When they landed at Egg, Forsyth huddled with his old mate in the engine room, marvelling at the workings of the new kerosene engines. Davies demonstrated how to anchor the flywheel, insert a match into the ignitor, pump up pressure in the block, then ''let go the wheel and hope the whole thing. . .[goes] off at the right

Langara Island lightkeeper James Forsyth, 1914.

psychological moment to get her going.'' Davies left some mattresses behind, the crew landed some ship's furniture, then they shook hands good-bye and the Forsyths went into five-year exile.

Typically, Egg was under assault most of the time. They ''battened down the hatches and stayed put.'' ''We've seen the waves come right over that outside rock,'' his daughter Evelyn remembered. ''Every once in a while there's a super-dooper coming. It washed away part of the veranda, knocked over a couple of sheds.'' The spray lashed at the shuttered windows all winter long. ''I'd hate to see anything worse than some of the storms we weathered here,'' she said, ''but we always seemed to live comfortable.''

But James Forsyth knew that life could be far more comfortable at the grand new station taking shape north of the Charlottes. Langara had a spacious duplex and the latest first-class vapour light—much cleaner and more efficient than coal oil—perched high above the sea's reach. A first-class salary went with it. They landed at Langara on 9 September 1913.

Mr. and Mrs James Forsyth and daughter at Langara Island, 1913 – 1918.

The Forsyths stayed five years. In summer the Haidas came calling, even the church organist from Masset came, spending as much time in the parlour at the pump organ as he did setting his nets; winter cut them off completely. "You had to rely on yourselves and depend on yourselves and make your own amusements," Evelyn explained. As an advertising ploy, one of the cereal companies packed rolls of film in their boxes, and with a six-month supply on hand, James built a darkroom so she could print her own photographs—pictures which survive as the most moving visual record of early life on the lights. There were family portraits in Sunday best on the porch; James jauntily posing in natty suit and waistcoat; and Evelyn—Evelyn with the horses, in the garden, or in the engine room, making the breathtaking passage from girl to woman, recorded by her only witnesses.

The Forsyths had books, cards, and music to tide them over the long wailing winter nights. The *Estevan* came out twice a year and dropped off six months of back issues of the two Vancouver dailies. James dragged the bales into the parlour, cut the twine, then "dived for the latest paper because the war was on." Evelyn recalled, "After we came up for air and got the latest news, Dad used to have us go through them methodically and stack them week by week and we would work our way through them," catching up with July in January. One year the tender came four months late and the Forsyths, "cut right off, no mail, no boat, no nothing," moved Christmas ahead to April.

Like the Pikes of Pine Island and the Ouellettes at Lucy, they were part of the fraternity of contented keepers. Though time might slip by them in an endless and

Left: *Surf boat with supplies.* Right: *hoisting supplies ashore.*

meaningless surge, there was always the woodpile, the gardens, the ceaseless demands of light tower and engine room. Halkett landed late in December 1916 and gloated, "The machinery installed in the light-tower and fog alarm is neat and clean and in first class condition." The cruelest blow fell when Evelyn's last friend, Robertson's controversial horse, collapsed and died. As for Ellen Forsyth, "well, she was like Dad," her daughter observed, "they accepted it, that was their living and that was that."

It could have gone on forever, but five years of "that" was enough for James Forsyth. There was no mistaking the changes in Evelyn; once past twelve, books and music and cribbage were no longer enough. James wrote H.S. Clements, his MP in Ottawa, with a shopworn refrain: "My chief reason for desiring a change is that, owing to the isolated position of this place, it is practically impossible to keep a teacher any time." He hoped the cut in pay that accompanied a move to an inner station "might alone make it easier to effect a transfer." His timing was right. Frederick Eastwood retired from Race Rocks later that year.

When they climbed over the *Estevan*'s rails that December, the Forsyths set foot in the present. The war to end all wars, they learned, was over at long last. A revolution in Russia had toppled the Czar; the Bolsheviks had ousted Kerensky; British and American troops, and Canadian Mounties had landed to restore "order." The CPR's *Princess Sophia* (Evelyn had a raft of pictures of her) had blundered onto Vanderbilt Reef up Alaska way two months before. Fearing a blow to the prestige of the line and the country, Captain J.W. Troup refused American offers of aid. "JUST TIME TO SAY GOOD-BYE," her radio operator signalled through the night of 24 October. "WE ARE FOUNDERING." Next day only his aerial mast showed above the waves. Two hundred and fifty-eight cadavers littered the shore for miles, many wearing water-logged watches stopped at 7:30 P.M. The Forsyths also learned about the fate of the *Galiano*, lost with all hands after re-supplying Triangle Island light, and even Evelyn sensed the fear which gripped *Estevan*'s crew as they steamed through a roaring gale from Cape St. James to Pine

Island, their keel passing a hundred fathoms or more over the iron coffin of mates they had clinked glasses, twisted arms, and chased women with in every waterfront bar from Victoria to Prince Rupert.

Soon after arriving at Race Rocks, James hired an assistant and, as it turned out, a son-in-law. Evelyn and her husband cared for her parents until they died, then left the lights. Evelyn MacKenzie lived alone in rooms in a rambling old frame house on Victoria's Menzies Street in 1986, with her piano, her pictures, and her outspoken pride in being the oldest "lighthouse kid," eager to share a childhood five hundred miles away, seventy years ago.

In Evelyn's day there must have been a hundred or more children scattered up and down the coast at lightstations from Race to Green. Though some would settle only a few blocks apart sixty years later—in Victoria, Vancouver, Prince Rupert, or other coastal towns—most were destined never to meet in the course of their entire lives, aside from huddling together for a magic hour or two when the tender stood off and a workboat wallowed back and forth, exchanging their parents' furniture, while one set of grown-ups explained the quirks of engines and cookstoves to the other.

Still, in their solitary existences they shared more in common than their peers, who came in every night when the streetlights flickered on in Vancouver, and went to bed barely an arm's reach away in separate houses on forty-foot city lots. There was no going door-to-door Hallowe'en night for lighthouse kids, no Saturday matinees, baseball games, summer holidays, no object of undeclared affection sitting three rows over in a classroom, but neither would they ever experience the trauma of going home to find neighbourhoods shrunken with age. Instead, dream and reality were one and the same for Tharsyle Ouellette, Devina and Frances Allison, Evelyn Forsyth, and the others, whose only playmates were parents, whose finest, most durable toys were their imagination and their environment. The ocean, as Mark Twain found out, "is a success, all right," mocking time and all man's puny strivings. If time seems to reduce childhood settings to some sort of nostalgic Lilliput, how must it seem when the horizon remains the same distance away no matter how one grows or changes?

Fifty years separate Evelyn Forsyth and Eileen Hart—half a century of Langara's human history, incinerated when the marine agent cleaned out his old files that day at Digby Island. Only vignettes of the intervening years remain. The place was bustling during the war. The army set up a radar station, providing company for Gordon Odlum, a man "built to be alone." There were fringe benefits though. When Gordon twisted his ankle, a sergeant assigned a hefty private to carry the keeper piggyback up and down the boardwalk to the radio room eight times a day to make out his weather reports. It went on for weeks, with Odlum urging his mount past his snickering comrades, until the private made a night-time reconnaissance and saw his jockey walking around in the house without the slightest sign of a limp.

Often a light station's history is lost due to happiness. When outsiders hear the plaintive wail arising from hunger, isolation, injury, and death, contentment may seem an elusive quantity on the lights. The "official" correspondence filed away in

Langara Island landing showing tramway.

archives documents (only too well) the hard side of the life. Happy people do not make history, and without any written record to the contrary one must assume that most lightkeepers found some secret or inexpressible consolation. Eileen Hart set her consolation down in writing in the 1950s at Langara, and her account reads like an invitation into a special world full of discovery and delight that outweighed the burden of isolation.

The Harts were cut out for the lights. Wanderlust began with the war, which took Ed Hart out of Toronto to Alberta, then sent him overseas and back. He and his bride could not fit into that postwar generation, intent on grabbing a piece of real estate and ''normalcy'' in the suburbia of ''Father Knows Best'' and ''Leave It To Beaver.'' They sold all their belongings and hit the road, winding up, like Octave Ouellette fifty years before, in downtown Prince Rupert—a springboard to Lawyer Island, then Triple, and finally Langara.

As they stood outside on the bridge, watching the bosun winch their crates up from the workboat, the crew gave them an unsettling foretaste of the new dimension of isolation in store. The previous winter an assistant on Langara ''went off the deep end,'' guzzled some methyl hydrate, and disappeared into the bush. The other two keepers and a radio operator were organizing a search when he burst shrieking through the door, stark naked, swinging an axe. They managed to disarm and subdue him, and radioed Prince Rupert. The police smashed their boat at the landing but managed to climb ashore, and guarded their raving prisoner until a crab boat came to the rescue.

As soon as they landed and hauled their crates into the duplex, Ed and Eileen took the ritual tour, going in and out of all the buildings. It seemed a vast, far-flung complex after their confinement in Triple Island's concrete bunker. That night as they lay in bed, still rolling from their stint on the *MacKenzie*, they discovered they had plenty of company. Captain Cook had left a troublesome legacy when he stopped at the island to take on fresh water. Langara's rats are a distinct, piebald subspecies, familiar amongst the squalor of the Thames docks two hundred years ago. Without any serious predators, the ''Devil's lapdogs'' multiplied and made life miserable for humans at Langara, gnawing their way through gardens and drygoods, routing cats, invading every building, and keeping pace with the arsenal of poison, traps, and bullets. Every night Ed's traps snapped shut on eight or ten victims; every morning he flung their broken, grinning carcasses into the bush by their scaly tails. In one week he blew fifty-nine away with his revolver.

Their earlier stints had vaccinated them against cabin fever, but the Harts had ample opportunity to witness its symptoms in their successive assistants. Langara was a three-man station in those days, and three keepers could forge a tense triangle. What could be worse than coming upon two men in animated conversation and seeing them suddenly break it off?

Single men were the quickest casualties. While Ed was away on sick leave, Eileen discovered that one assistant had deliberately shut down the radio beacon. When the boss came back, he confronted the assistant, then called for the ship. "The man had been there too long, he had become bushed," Eileen related. "What really convinced Ed was the trees near the oil shed had been painted in red and white like a barber pole." When the workboat came for him, he stood down on the landing wearing "a hat he had fashioned out of an old oil strainer decorated with eagle feathers."

One couple shared their half of the Harts' duplex with a single man. Whenever the husband went out to the radio room, Ed and Eileen could hear "the click of high heels" across their ceiling, on the way to the bachelor's quarters. "We felt like we were sitting on a case of dynamite waiting for it to go off," Eileen wrote. When it blew, the explosion shattered the silence of Eileen's early morning coffee ritual: "a terrific scream of rage that raised the hair on the back of. . .[her] neck." Ed bolted for the house from the radio room, and ran upstairs into a bedlam of crashing furniture, a situation which every cop dreads. He pushed the two apart, though "both were double his size," ordering one to his bedroom and the other downstairs. First he calmed the cuckold down, then cautioned the bachelor to keep out of sight, "if he knew what's good for him," until the ship came. It took a while for the tender to arrive, and the tension mounted again, day by day, when the tapping heels could be heard on their way across the floor every time the husband left the house.

Eileen clipped an appropriate cartoon from a newspaper. It showed two lightkeepers, with a woman sitting on one's lap. "This can't be much fun for you, old chap," the caption read—a not-so-subtle reminder that single men were misplaced on the lights. Beketov, the agent, sent it on to Ottawa, and from then on only married couples came out to Langara.

One of those couples seemed amiable enough at first. "When they came down to visit in the evening, the men chatted away while Mary sat with her lips in a silent pout until John took her back to their place." Eileen tried in vain to draw her out, to find where her interests lay. "After we went to bed, she came running into our bedroom in her nightie crying that John was trying to kill her," Eileen wrote. "She refused to go back to her room. Ed had to get up and talk to John before we could get any sleep. After four or five nights of this we were having doubts if they would ever work in."

Anyone wanting to "work in" could do no better than copy the Harts, for "there was never a lack of something to do on Langara." Ed had come ashore with a home-made electric drive for the light, so there were no weights to wind up six times a night. He ordered nuts, bolts, and fittings by the crate from a junk dealer in town, and spent hours at his workbench, turning out toys for the kids: a pedal-powered car, an adventure playground, a "bucking bronco" welded from pipes and carriage springs. They laid out a pit for tossing the rusty shoes once worn by Evelyn Forsyth's horses. Eileen made jewelry in her lapidary studio. Whenever they wanted to get away from the station, they lowered the station boat for a row, or struck out into the island's interior.

"We had gone about a mile [along the telegraph cut] when an open woods on the shore side attracted our attention," Eileen wrote when they came back from a hike.

> We pushed through the heavy bush on the edge of the cut, and found we were in a lovely grove. The green moss under our feet was the thickest we had seen on the island. The trees were tall and letting in little splashes of sunlight. We made no sound as we walked down hill. It was like being in a church, so we named it Cathedral Grove. Trees that had fallen were covered with moss and young trees grew in a row down the length of the windfall.

Perched on an eyrie like Langara, Eileen had only to look up from her housework, or from lessons at the kitchen table, for entertainment and inspiration. "The winter storms were spectacular," she wrote, striving for words to describe the wanton fury down below. "Big rollers came across the wide open Pacific; as they neared the reef, they mounted higher and higher, sometimes fifty feet high before they curled over and toppled in on themselves." One winter these waves uprooted the four-foot cube of concrete for Killeen's ill-fated winch, washing it around "like a piece of soap." The grey whales came south in November, leaping "high out of the water standing on their tails." Killer whales herded sea lions into the shallows, turning the sea frothy pink with their frenzied butchery.

It was spectacular, but frustrating too. The splendour could never be shared with friends and family who visited the island only in letters. Luckily, the Harts had good assistants as well as bad, people who enjoyed the isolated life with them, upset them only by their leaving, and who remained lifelong friends through the mail. "There was a feeling of losing something good when they left," Eileen wrote, after they turned tearfully away from the *MacKenzie*'s workboat and waited with trepidation for replacements.

But life on the lights was about to change. Ed learned quite casually about the revolution which would tilt the balance towards paradise. Though Marine Agent Nicholas A. Beketov was the boss and made no bones about it, he and Ed put all that aside whenever the keeper was in town and the garrulous admiral beckoned him into his office. "You know, Ed," he confided one afternoon, "just for fun I'm going to order one of these new helicopters and see what happens."

No one recalls the historic date when "time caught up to . . . [the] lightstation"—just the God-awful noise which "brought everyone out of the house" to stand gaping at the mechanical dragonfly swaying down on the front lawn. The door swung open and out hopped Beketov, arms waving as he dashed in a crouch over to the house. He regaled them over tea with his grand design for the new toy: a pad on every light so the "chopper" could come once between every supply trip, laden with fresh food and mail.

There was a job for anyone who wanted one that summer, as crews island-hopped from one light down to the next, building "chopper pads" in the greatest construction boom on the lights since the gold rush, leaving stepping stones to

Prince Rupert behind them. Keepers and their kids strapped themselves in the seats and took their first rides, faces squashed flat against the windows of the gigantic Sikorski, as their stations dropped away beneath them. Carmanah, Egg Island, even Langara, were suddenly less than an hour away from the tarmac at Rupert and Victoria and a world with windows and aisles and muzak, overflowing with everything from fresh lettuce to new shoes.

Best of all, the choppers ferried old friends and grandparents out to far-flung enclaves which they could scarcely imagine from letters three months old. The inevitable reporters came too, and filled columns in Sunday supplements, reviving the romantic allure of the lights, coming face to face with modern-day John Morans and Minnie Pattersons at every stop.

The Harts left the lights for a school, like so many other keepers. Luckily, the department hired Ed as construction foreman for the northern agency, giving his unbridled ingenuity a free rein. As Canada's leading marine carpenter, Ed spent more time, on more lights, than anyone before or since. He became a precious institution in the bargain: a trusted confidant, better able than any clergyman or social worker to take a man aside and shepherd him through the inscrutable crises of life on the lights.

As for Eileen, every once in a while she takes out her manuscript, sits at the typewriter, and wanders back to Cathedral Grove and other lush corners of the mind, striking out punctuation, adding whole paragraphs from memory, and dreaming that one day down the road everyone will share the best years of her life—at Langara.

After the Harts left, Langara assumed a crucial role on the precarious Pacific rim, the delayed result of an event in the 1940s. At 2 A.M. on April Fools Day 1946, an earthquake had rocked the Alaskan Trench, producing a hundred-foot tidal wave that shot out seventy miles in a matter of minutes. The five lightkeepers at Scotch Cap in the Aleutians never knew what hit them when the rushing cliff of water filled the concrete tower like a test tube and swept it away. With a crest-to-crest wavelength of 122 miles, the gigantic roller headed out in all directions of the compass, moving 500 miles per hour. When it finally spent itself in the open Pacific, it left 173 people dead, 163 injured, and more than 1000 buildings valued at $25 million in ruins.

Soon after, Canada elected to join UNESCO in establishing a network of recorders to give advance warning of the horrifying tsunami, but delayed its commitment as a cost-cutting measure. Then, in 1964, a New Brunswick-sized section of the earth's plate (200,000 square miles in area) shifted under Alaska; the resulting wave killed 122 people from the Gulf of Alaska to Crescent City in California. It surged up the Alberni Canal and flooded downtown Port Alberni. Civil defense officials reckoned the total damage at some $500 million, and Langara got its recorder that year. Ironically, the recorder and the building itself were washed away by a monstrous wave in the winter of 1978, but the shed was rebuilt higher up the island to house a new recorder.

Main residence of lightkeeper, Langara.

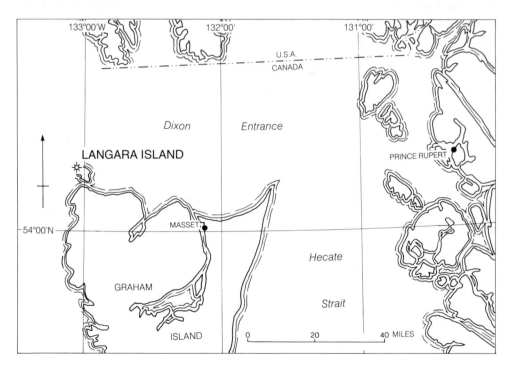

Triple Island

T riple Island—"the Rock" or "little Alcatraz"—conforms most closely to the austere image of popular imagination: a tower rooted upon a rock, a man-made bulwark against the implacable, onrushing power of the sea. Even today, when swells thunder up and pummel the concrete walls at high tide, the men inside keep calm, mindful of the motto that "she's lasted a long time so far."

The cluster of rocks juts out of Brown Passage twenty-eight miles west of Prince Rupert. The Marine Department first marked them with the latest type of acetylene beacon in the early 1900s, but an unwatched beacon soon proved unreliable. In May 1914 Captain MacCarthy steered through Brown Passage at night and reported a dull, steady light with no flash. Moreover, a light of any type was useless in thick weather. After the Grand Trunk Pacific's *Prince Albert* ran up on Butterworth Rocks, two miles away, in fog a few weeks later, the lighthouse board elected to build a manned light and fog alarm. In January 1915 Colonel Anderson unveiled plans to install a powerful beacon at Triple, thereby opening up a new northern approach to Prince Rupert, by way of Langara Island, which would shave even more precious time off the trans-Pacific run. He went out to the rocks for an initial inspection in late April 1915. Landing was out of the question, but the workboat put in close enough to the bare granite rocks—"worth nothing and probably wave-washed in storms"—for the chief engineer to pronounce them a suitable foundation for the newest prototype of his daring concrete designs. For the first time he would attempt a combined dwelling and tower in concrete, topped off with the largest possible lantern, eighty feet above high water.

Steamer Prince Albert wrecked on Butterworth Rocks, Aug. 18, 1914.

Tenders were tacked up on bulletin boards in every post office up and down the coast. Most contractors backed off quickly. In the end the job went to Snider Brothers, Brethour Limited of Vancouver for $17,449. Their foremen cleared Prince Rupert harbour on 19 August 1916 with two launches crammed full of supplies. Before an hour passed they realized what they were up against. Caught in a sudden southeast gale with heavy swells, they turned back just past Lucy Island and beat a hasty retreat. The Sniders wisely decided to postpone construction until the spring. "If I were contractor, I should not dream of bucking the Pacific Ocean in September," Anderson snorted upon hearing news of the foray.

The work force made a successful landing when they returned in 1917, and established a command post on the south rock. They hastily nailed up a combination bunkhouse-cookhouse-showers, built a bridge over to the site, and began drilling and blasting the rounded tip off the rock. Theirs was a precarious existence at best, only a toe hold. Most of the work was undertaken at low tide. When the sea rushed back in to claim another twenty feet of Triple Island, they retreated to higher ground, washed in a welter of spray. Peter Kelday was taking a cold shower one afternoon when a wave clobbered the bunkhouse, shifted it off its foundation, and sent him running barefoot over the barnacles, clutching a towel around his middle.

Kelday and his fellow workers never suspected they might be living on borrowed time as they watched the bristling reinforcing rods rise skyward. They mixed and hauled endless pails of concrete up the scaffolding, poured and tamped it down. Even if they felt uneasy the day they pulled out forms for the sluices that would allow waves to drain off the *roof* forty feet up, they might have been lulled into a false security by the placid July seas.

When it fit her schedule and a landing could be made, the *Newington* sent a workboat in on Fridays to pick up the crew for a welcome weekend in town. The men drew lots to pick the "lucky three" to stay behind, slapped them laughingly on the back, and piled into the boat. They returned one Monday morning in April 1919 to

Top: Triple Island Light under construction. Bunkhouse on right. Left: Pouring the Triple Island tower.
Above right: Triple in service. Below right: Construction finished.

find the South Rock swept clear of bunkhouse, out-buildings, and men, with no sign that anyone had been living and working there for months. As they set about pumping water out of the concrete basin, every man among them thanked his Maker it had been his turn to go to town, and wondered how long the sea would wait before claiming its due again. Another worker was crushed to death when he slipped climbing from a workboat to board the *Newington* later that summer. In October a scow and barge laden with gravel and 19,000 board feet of lumber were lost in a gale.

The builders finally escaped the rock in the winter of 1920, leaving behind a self-contained concrete bunker, with an imposing fluted tower rising out of one corner. Inside, space was at a premium. The upper floor, thirty feet square, housed the living quarters. There were three bedrooms partitioned off along the south side, a kitchen, pantry, and storeroom on the north, and the only lighthouse bathroom on the coast, complete with tub and cold water tap. Some joker put a leather patch marked ''H'' on the other side.

Down below stood the engines, pumps, compressors, air tanks, and foghorns, all joined in a twisted maze of pipes, belts, and gauges. Work benches and tool racks lined the walls. The ground floor contained another unheard-of luxury on the lights—a furnace and coal bins as well as fuel tanks for the engines. A third of the area was taken up with two hulking six-thousand-gallon water cisterns, filled by rain pouring down the gutters from the roof—one for the motors, another for the keepers. When waves scaled the walls and crashed over the roof, Triple's inmates had to run downstairs and plug the intake to keep salt water out of the fresh. The fog trumpet featured a hinged iron door outside which could be raised by cable from the roof to prevent seas gushing into the engine room during heavy swells.

Colonel Anderson designed Triple (his last station in the West) as the ultimate symbiotic environment for men and machines, with a constant background of noise. Gordon Odlum listened to the din every day and night for ten years—longer than anyone else—and described the pandemonium inside when the tower was enveloped in a gray-white plasma of fog:

> The big gas engine is putt-putting and the compressor is boom-booming and once a minute the diaphone which can be heard for forty miles on favourable occasions proclaims to all and sundry that they have ''BEE-OHH,''and the little typhoon horn sings a duet out the other side of the house. The radio power plant purrs away like a large size, extra loud cat and the lighting generator hums to itself in the opposite corner of the engine room, while down below in the radio shack the three generators and two motors produce assorted hums and whines that mingle with the various clicks and snaps of automatic switches and relays . . . .

The mad mechanical symphony would grind on and on, sometimes seventy hours or more at a stretch, with no intermission. In order to fall asleep, its conductor lugged his mattress upstairs into the lantern room, the farthest seat from the stage. Lulled

Engine room, Triple Island.

into catnaps by the low, pulsating throb of the turntable rumbling above, Odlum
would often wake to look up past the crystal prisms of the giant first order lens to see
if fog still reflected its beams back inside.

When rough weather struck Triple, it drowned out the noise inside. In January
1944 a 110-knot gale made the tower roar ''like a boiler shop'' as it rattled windows
and tried the doors. The blacksmith shop, a separate frame structure, ''lifted up its
sides and gracefully flapped its way off in the general direction of Alaska.'' Sea water
finally gained entry through windows and the tower door, rushed headlong through
the bathroom and storeroom, and cascaded down the stairwell to the engine room to
join a widening pool seeping through seams in the diaphones and furnace pipes. ''It
was lots of fun while it lasted, and no damage done,'' Odlum wrote his girlfriend in
Vancouver. ''It all sounds pretty awful, doesn't it? But it's not so bad really and the
sound of everything running smoothly lulls one to sleep. If anything stops, however,
I wake up with a start and holler, 'What was that?' ''[1]

Such was the environment of Triple Island, inside and out, in the 1940s. Three
decades had brought only one change between the winter of 1920—when Thomas
Watkins, its first keeper, transferred up there with his wife and two little girls from
Sisters—and the war years, when Gordon Odlum arrived. It was the difference
between life and death: radio.

Sadly, few sources remain to document the Watkinses' lifestyle, marooned in their
waveswept bunker. There is one letter, saved by Reverend Raley. ''It is delightful to

know that our work is appreciated and we are not forgotten in our isolation,''
Watkins's wife wrote a month after the mission boat's Christmas visit. ''During the
winter months the time seems very slow in passing sometimes and we are glad of
anything to help fill in.'' There were tide pools to explore at low tide on summer
days, evenings to wile away with dice and cards, hours spent gathered around the
kitchen table pulling together the rudiments of an education. Before the gales hit in
late fall, Watkins lowered heavy wooden shutters, one at a time, on a rope from the
roof. His wife leaned out the windows, pulled the shutters toward her, and bolted
them into place, blotting out the anaemic winter sun for months at a time.

Mail days, birthdays, and Christmases must have held out some relief from their
monotony, until New Year's 1923 when Watkins contracted pneumonia and took
to his bed. For a month, while he hacked and coughed his life away, Watkins's wife
attended to the incessant demands of motors and fog. She spent every waking minute
at his bedside or in the lantern room, like Rosina Davies at Race Rocks sixty years
before, watching and praying that some vessel, any vessel, would pass close enough
for an alert seaman to spy their flag hanging at halfmast, with ensign down in
distress. Just as at Race Rocks, no one came.

When her husband died, his widow faced an awful dilemma. There was no way of
knowing when a ship might come in, and the department had sent no shovels out to
Triple as there was no soil to move. She and her daughters had no choice but to drag
the stiffening body out by the ankles and armpits, drag it bump-bumping up the
stairs and out onto the roof to freeze. She waited another week, her mind besieged by
the sledge-hammering sea and the mental image of her lover's corpse outside,
wrapped in its thickening shroud of rime. Finally on 5 February the *Newington*
came. The grim-faced shore party chipped the brittle cadaver off the roof and took
the grieving widow and children away to Prince Rupert. The department awarded
her a gratuity of two months' pay for her trouble.

Tom Moran and his wife Sophie arrived at Triple Island in 1927 with their
two-month-old baby. Like all her sisters on the lights, Sophie was conscripted as an
unpaid assistant. Like it or not, she had to master all the skills needed to run the
station: cranking engines, pumping fuel, lighting up, and running the winch that
slung supplies up the skyline from the workboats rocking in the swells below. ''Now
this is very dangerous,'' Tom told her soon after they arrived, pointing to the
donkey engine with its flywheel, clutch arm, brake pedal, and spool of cable—all
open geared. ''You have to put on my combination overalls [when you're working
here].''

On the morning of 22 November 1929 she stood at the controls in the noisy
winch shed, watching Tom, down below on the rocks, preparing a load of wood for
hoisting. She had ignored or discounted Tom's caution about the overalls. Suddenly
the flywheel snatched and grabbed the hem of her dress, wrenching her off her feet.
Sophie tore away at the seam, then tried to crawl away, fingernails clawing the floor.
It was a tug-of-war she could never hope to win, just one woman against all that
thundering horsepower. Each turn of the flywheel drew her closer to the machine's

deadly metal embrace. Shrieking in fear, she braced her arms against the hot block, then was spun around, dragged backwards up against the flywheel, and became a human spoke.

Deaf to her frenzy, Tom waited with his firewood down below, wondering what was holding her up. He finally heard her wail of hurt and distress over the clank and roar of the motor when her right arm went into the gears. He scrambled up the rocks and grounded out the engine. ''I was right there and shut it off,'' he recalled forty years later, as though it were still happening, ''but terrible screams, terrible screams, terrible screams....'' Moran raced upstairs, snatched a knife from the kitchen drawer, and ran back down to begin the delicate, anguished task of paring fabric and flesh away from the iron molars of the machinery, dripping grease and gore. When he finally pulled her to her feet, Sophie's blood, free of its mechanical tourniquet, poured in a torrent over the floor.

For a week Tom nursed her as best he could. They had no painkillers, no antiseptic. Ripping sheets into strips for bandages, he soaked them in watered-down Lysol and bound her up. Days and nights seemed endless until the tender *Alberni* came calling a week later, in the midst of a heavy gale. The seamen wrestled a stretcher with their whimpering human cargo into a workboat, one minute high and dry, the next up to their chests in the swell, holding Sophie aloft. Afraid to manoeuvre her below decks, through narrow alleys and doorways, they covered her with a tarpaulin on deck. The captain promised to contact Moran by commercial radio from Prince Rupert with a report of her condition within twenty-four hours, but the *Alberni* had to seek shelter from the storm at a nearby fish camp overnight.

Inside Triple, Moran sat despondent next to his cabinet radio as the concrete shuddered against wind and water. After listening all day to inane commercials, the antics of Amos and Andy and the Happy Gang, his mind ran down and explored every rathole of an anguished imagination—the rasp of a bone saw, the bleak prospect of raising their son without her—until he cracked. Tom cranked up the detested winch again, lowered the rowboat into the confusion of choppy waves, climbed down, and jury-rigged a mast and sail. He climbed back, gathered up his tiny passenger and stowed him in the bow, leaped back into the boat, slipped the hook, and set sail for Prince Rupert, using Lucy Island's light for a bearing. Hours later, when the weights settled on the floor at Triple and the light coasted to a stand-still on its mercury pond, Tom Moran was desperately tacking toward Green Island light, having been swept miles north of his course. After landing at Green (kept by his parents), Moran dried himself out, then hitched a ride to Prince Rupert with a passing fish packer. The light was out of service until he returned a couple of days later.

Sophie Moran slowly recovered from her mauling and came back to Triple. When they arrived, Moran rifled his files for a Workmen's Compensation form and meticulously completed the accident report, pencilling in the exact extent and nature of Sophie's injuries on a skeletal diagram. He mailed it off by the next boat.[2]

Christmas Eve 1929 was much like any before it in the Department of Marine's nerve centre in the West Block of Parliament. The trill and clatter of telephones and typewriters subsided as the day wore on. By midafternoon, bottles came out of drawers and the deputy minister made his rounds, shaking hands with all the staff, high and low. A few loose ends remained to be tied up before Hawken quit the haw-haw of camaraderie and walked out into the Ottawa snow for a welcome holiday from running the world's farthest-flung department of government. There was, for example, the cable to be got out to William Stamford in Prince Rupert, concerning that man's wife at Triple Island:

ADVISE WORKMENS COMPENSATION BOARD CLAIM FOR WIFE OF LIGHTKEEPER THOMAS MORAN TRIPLE ISLAND NOT PAYABLE OUT OF DOMINION FUNDS IN THEIR HANDS.

It hardly needed any explanation: the matter was *out* of his hands. Sophie Moran worked for her husband, not the government. Compensation for her injuries was Tom's obligation as an employer.[3]

Even if he could do nothing for the Morans, Stamford resolved early in the New Year to make life better for future keepers at Triple Island. He composed a capsule history of the station for Hawken, pointing out that this was the second ''serious occurrence...in which a length of time elapsed before aid was obtained.'' A long-range radio phone or radio beacon would surely end the agony. Echoing Gaudin's cry of thirty years before, the agent insisted that Ottawa hire a full-time male assistant keeper.

Seal's eye view of Triple Island Light.

After the Watkinses' horror, Stamford recalled, the next keeper had transferred to a lower paying station after two years. His successor resigned after two years. Now there was this awful business with the Morans. Many more would surely quit "due to its exposed location and isolated conditions, [and the] rough water prevailing around the rock practically all the winter and part of the summer." As if to confirm the prediction, Tom Moran, who was raised on the lights, resigned 19 April after ten years' service at Barret Rock, Egg Island, and Triple. (He was back on the lights in 1934, to say good-bye to Flewin and MacDonald on Egg Island's shore.)

Hawken supported his agent, informing the minister that "the rock. . .[was] wave-swept, obliging the staff to remain indoors for days." Rather than increasing "staff," however, the department should upgrade the station, providing the keeper with more money to pay an assistant. A radio beacon and transmitter would be installed to put the keepers in communication with the agency in Prince Rupert.

In many ways, Gordon Odlum, who came to Triple twelve years after Moran, was the ultimate lighthouse keeper. A whole generation of Vancouverites will always remember him as the "lighthouse man" out at Point Atkinson, who always found time to shut down his lawnmower or put a paint brush aside to show them around the station and feed their insatiable appetite for insights into a way of life so far removed from their own. His real place in history is Triple Island: his first station, the place where he confronted the sea head-on, fell in love with the girl of his dreams through the mail, and found the peace of mind and harmony with nature which is always the stuff of lighthouse lore.

A descendant of one of Vancouver's first families, which counted a general, an ambassador to China, and stockbrokers in its ranks, Gordon succumbed early to the allure of lightkeeping when he hiked out to Point Atkinson one day. Thomas Grafton gave him a tour. Later he made frequent pilgrimages to Capilano light where he wiled hours away listening to "Captain" Alfred Dickenson's tall tales. The childhood infatuation blossomed into the longest service of any keeper on the coast—ultimately he would replace Tom Grafton—and it still flourished long after his retirement when he lived in a North Shore apartment commanding a splendid view of Point Atkinson, where he monitored the light's flash and foghorn, and the marine radio bands.

Odlum started his career relieving for Dickenson at Capilano, then went out in turn to Ballenas, Race Rocks, Kains Island, Lawyer Island, Holland Rocks, Cape Beale, Carmanah, and Langara, before he was permanently assigned to Triple in November 1942. A year later he wrote home: "I think I can truthfully say that I haven't felt at all lonesome, partly I guess because I'm built that way . . . ."

Out at Triple he had an assistant as well as a wartime radio operator. Still, there was someone he missed more than he might admit; someone who worked behind the counter at the Glass Bakery downtown on Vancouver's hectic Commercial Drive. Whenever he had been home between his relief stints, Gordon seized upon any excuse to go into the bakery, and always found it hard keeping his eyes and his mind on the tempting array of pastries. If his mother needed three loaves, Gordon made three trips. Out on Triple, the keeper seldom allowed a day to go by without conjuring up an image of the fetching girl in the far-off bake shop. He did not have her home address, yet brooded over the propriety of writing her at work. One day while kneading dough at the kitchen counter, he had a brainstorm and baked a tiny loaf in a matchbox, sending it, like a lump of coal to Newcastle, to Glass Bakery. When the tender sent his Christmas mail ashore in December 1943, her card was among the packages! As long as he lived he would never have a finer present than that return address.

Odlum celebrated New Year's by writing to her. "It was sweet of you to remember little old shabby lightkeeping me," he began. "It seems such a long time since I had the pleasure of going into Glass Bakery and saying 'Hello. Two whites please' to your sunny smile. Fifteen months it has been since I have been ashore. I wonder if you might be married and have four children by now?"

She wasn't and hadn't, and so began a seven-month courtship by mail. While Jean ran home for the mail every Tuesday, her suitor stood up on the catwalk with his telescope, scanning the choppy horizon for a mail boat. His excitement mounted when a ship steamed in sight, but more often than not it collapsed when he saw "some old scow" like the *Queen Mary* or *Empress of Asia*. Crestfallen, he would climb downstairs and take out his frustration on the daily chores.

Lying in bed, Gordon Odlum wrote reams by moonlight, describing every conceivable aspect of his surroundings, as familiar by now as the roof of his mouth. Somewhere within and between those lines lies the answer to the tantalizing question that hovers over the lights: why did they go out there? Why did they stay? His record is a rare and priceless account of a man content to live apart and contend with the rigours of weather and keeping watch on the North Coast. "I like it here on my 'inhospitable rock pile'," he confessed, "especially on these wild winter nights when the tower shakes and roars with the force of the gale and to go outdoors is to risk being blown overboard, and when the huge storm swells sweep in from the open sea and send spray shooting up 100 feet into the beams of the light as it sends its piercing beams through the night."

At least he had Jean's photograph there for company. Any technicians or seamen who came ashore passed it round over their steaming mugs of coffee with low whistles, and pressed him for her address. "Some people get all the pull," they bantered. As weeks crawled into months without mail, the man who had never felt lonesome experienced the pangs of isolation for the first time, increasingly sharp and frequent. His long letters shifted in tone. No longer crammed with technical detail and the antics of his mates at Triple, they evolved into poignant, moving monologues full of love and longing.

"You know, Jean, there are a lot of beauties in Nature," he wrote one mid-summer evening, leaning against the parapet looking south, "but tonight I'm willing to say that the most beautiful scene of all is a calm, island-studded sea on a

Watching for the mail, Triple Island tower.

breathless summer's evening.'' He invited her to take an imaginary ''walk around the roof,'' arm in arm, while he pointed out the serene vista from every point of the compass. ''Flocks of ducks fly over the water in long wavy lines and a few seagulls fly into the sunset as if entranced by its beauty. The sun has started to dip behind one of the small Alaskan islands and it is slowly going-going-gone. All the shades of colour are more delicate, more diffused and more beautiful than ever,'' he wrote. ''From now on until dark I can only watch and appreciate but not describe. It is beyond me. Just let's stay awhile and drink silently of the evening, the beauty of the sky and sea and clouds—and you.''

Month-old letters from Vancouver were never enough. However well-constructed a man might be to thrive in isolation, its attractions must be shared to be appreciated, and Gordon Odlum confided, ''The present residents of Triple don't quite fill the bill.'' He went on leave that August, and they married at St. Saviours in Vancouver on September 20. After her honeymoon on North Pender, the bride packed her bags and boarded the *Princess Adelaide* bound for Prince Rupert. At eighteen, it was her first time out of Vancouver.

The *Bernie* took them out to Triple. For the deckhands and officers, this was their first encounter with the girl in the lightkeeper's photograph, a picture which did not do her justice. Accustomed as they were to the ''odd-ball'' stereotype of lightkeepers, ground and polished by decades of anecdote and exaggeration, they were astonished that a beauty like Jean would ever go for a life of exile out on ''the rock.'' Betting ran hot and heavy in the foc's'le and on the bridge. Captain Joe Peterson and his mate, Roddy Smith, stated the odds: give her two months at the outside. She did leave within the year, and Gordon wondered for a while if she would ever be back. But no one goes home again, and Jean soon discovered that Triple had transformed her: she had grown away from her friends and become a loner in the crowd. She took the first passage back.

Life for newlyweds sharing close quarters with bachelor assistants could be awkward at best. One assistant was so convinced that Jean wanted him out that Gordon feared violence. Returning from fishing one afternoon, the keeper found him angrily packing his bags, and arranged passage for him on a fishboat. Odlum advised the agent to assign the man to a less isolated situation. Instead, he went to Cape St. James—one of the most isolated lights! Another assistant had an unsettling hobby: knife throwing. Whenever Gordon had to point out shortcomings in his performance (all too often), he would stalk off to the deck, and they heard his knives thud into a man-shaped target. In time the Odlums dispensed with assistants altogether.

Recreation consisted of rowing expeditions when the seas calmed down, or walking around the rooftop, setting a pebble on an oil drum each lap to keep track until they had gone a mile. To get the mail out, they would lower the rowboat so one could pull out to a passing fishboat, waving a shirt or scarf tied to an oar to attract attention. Incoming mail was the highlight of their lives—a bag bulging with news and merchandise culled in the evenings from the catalogues. Christmas every month.

Gordon Odlum keeping a weather eye, Triple Island. Right: *Jean Odlum rowing out for mail, Triple Island.*

Every night they climbed the tower to gather up birds hypnotized by the glare of the light. They would carry them down to the kitchen in sacks, band them, and set them free. Sometimes they shared their quarters with as many as two hundred feathered friends at a time: thrushes, sparrows, and warblers seated on chairs, clotheslines, and cold stove pipes, peeping away, each waiting its turn for banding. If one moved, they all took off for a new perch. Each morning Jean cleaned up the kitchen, ready for the next night's visitors. In June they ranged over the rocks, banding newborn gulls.

The Odlums played out more than fifteen-hundred chess games, read two hundred books a year, and sat wrapped in an electric blanket, clutching hot water bottles beside the radio after supper. Jean was a trained opera singer and spent hours at the precious pump organ she had brought with her. Still, no one is ever immune to monotony. For every month they never wanted to leave, there were days when tomorrow never came soon enough. An entry in Jean's diary for 26 February 1951 betrays her feelings of abandonment and frustration:

> Washed my hair yesterday—guess I'll have to start buying shampoo again as I don't seem to be able to get it really squeaky clean now-a-days. The sink is so damned awkward that I ache before my shampoo is over. Grrr. It makes me so cross. I guess I shouldn't let things like that upset me but when improvements could be made and are not, it makes me gnash my teeth in revolt—or something. The place is a wreck but nobody seems to think a lightkeeper needs a decent place in which to live. The floors sag—livingroom, bedroom and kitchen—the bathroom sink needs a new drain, the pantry sink is too blamed high, the plaster in all the bedrooms is falling from the walls, the windows leak

water and wind—but nothing is done. If I were in town, the landlord would soon make repairs, well we pay rent for this drafty barn so why shouldn't our landlord do something to improve the place.

Many women left the lights, but the Odlums' stamina came from knowing that once one begins finding fault in isolation, there will soon be no favour. A week later Jean re-read her complaint. "Boy, reading over Feb 26 entry—must have been really tired that night." They came out on holiday every other year.

In contrast to their predecessors, the Odlums' was a safe and happy tenure, though one day the same winch that had mauled Sophie Moran grabbed the cuff of Gordon's trousers. He managed to find a hand-hold and was left standing in his socks and undershorts while the gears gagged on his trousers. In time they began planning a family, and longed for more regular contact with friends and relatives in the south. After two years of fruitless applications for a transfer to a less isolated light, they were given Race Rocks. In late August 1952 they stood in the *Alexander MacKenzie*'s stern and watched "with satisfaction" as their "inhospitable rock pile" slipped over the horizon. While Jean was in hospital, the expectant father at Race decided to name the baby after the first ship to pass by. All that morning, while other new fathers were passing out cigars or nursing hangovers, Gordon scanned the horizon until a freighter finally veered in close enough for him to make out the script on her bow: *Joseph P. Schwelenbank*. They christened their baby girl Coral instead.

The Harts were the last family at Triple. Ed, Eileen, and their two children transferred from Lawyer Island since claustrophobia seemed a fair trade for higher pay and electric power. "It was really enjoyable because the kids loved those tidal pools and they used to go down there for hours," Eileen recalled. During the gale season they hunkered down inside, barbering, baking, teaching, reading, playing games—and inventing.

After spinning virtually non-stop for forty years, the revolving apparatus upstairs was badly worn. A few nights in the tower cranking the huge lens by hand to allow its bearing to cool convinced Ed of an idea which revolutionized labour on the lights. For a hundred years, all keepers from George Davies onward had slept in three-hour shifts, then climbed their towers to wind the weights. With electricity, Ed Hart decided, it was all a waste of time and sleep.

Parts for his prototype electric drive had to be scavenged from Eileen's wringer washer and sewing machine. After weighing a full night's sleep against going back to washboard, needle, and thread, Ed stripped the machines, cut and modified the parts, and assembled an electric drive powered by a bicycle chain. From then on, the Harts slept the whole night through. "Well you don't really sleep," Ed admitted. "If one of my engines missed a beat, I was awake." The real significance of Ed's invention lay in the fact that it was the first step in adapting modern electronic technology to serve the keepers, and it was a keeper himself who introduced it. In twenty years time Ottawa would attempt to impose automation from the top down for very different motives, with ominous results and at far greater cost.

Later that year the chief of aids visited Triple with Nicholas Beketov, the marine agent. Ed took them up the tower and pointed to his contraption. ''That's a good idea,'' the chief exclaimed. Turning to his agent, he instructed him to ''see that that goes on all the lights'' as they were electrified. Ed estimated his prototype cost $15. A few months later Beketov showed him a bill for $750 for the electric drive design the department was installing.

When the Harts left Triple Island in 1960, the department hired four men to work the station in rotating shifts for a month at a time, much like the early days of voluntary confinement at Sand Heads light at the mouth of the Fraser River. Over the years the situation sparked many anecdotes—like the one about the keeper who bisected the living quarters with tape, claiming half as his own territory. For those unsuited to confined isolation, rough weather, and their fellow keeper's disposition, however, life at little Alcatraz was no joke. Even their first month on the rock could seem like four weeks in hell.

Remite Ernest Vargas went mad soon after he arrived in late February 1960. ''A lot of people when they first came out there were really scared,'' the Harts explained. An acoustical quirk of wind sounded like men muttering and arguing in the tower. Whether these phantom ''voices,'' or something in Vargas's past or present state of mind lit the short fuse of his sanity, no one will ever know. But L.M. Clifford, his partner there, would never forget the worst week of his life.

Confronted with Vargas's disordered mind, Clifford first resigned himself to passing a month in a ''nut's'' company. Then on 28 February he came across a suicide note. Clifford immediately radioed Prince Rupert to advise his partner had ''become mental.'' Beketov brushed aside the keeper's alarm. After all, it was a strange environment which affected first-timers in strange ways. Give him a week and he would settle down.

Three days later, having heard or seen nothing of Vargas for hours, Clifford searched the complex top to bottom and finally found his assistant, unconscious and bleeding on the engine room floor, with a sledge hammer beside him. Clifford revived him, stanched and dressed his head wound, then searched his room and stashed away a .30-.30 rifle and shells. He snatched up the radio phone again. This time the agent dispatched the *Alexander MacKenzie* with two RCMP constables on board. The whole melodrama unfolded against the backdrop of a howling gale. When the tender dropped anchor, Captain MacKay radioed Clifford to advise they would send over a shore party just as soon as the rough seas abated. Meantime, he counselled, ''keep awake, keep Vargas calm until we get over there.''

For the next four days and nights Clifford endured Vargas's ravings, wrestled with drowsiness, and steered their conversation into every possible backwater to keep his companion sane. It was never enough. Vargas ripped off the bandages and pulled his head wound open again and again. Clifford finally fell asleep. While he slept, the crazed Vargas tore the station apart until he found what he was after. The explosion reverberated through the tower like a kettle drum, jolting Clifford awake. Once more he made a frantic search. When he came to Vargas's bedroom, there was a

Lighthouse tender Alexander Mackenzie decked out in flags.

grape-sized hole in the door. Mustering his courage, Clifford eased open the door, peered in and saw the assistant splayed out on his mattress with the rifle at his side and a hole in his head. "Destiny wanted it this way," his suicide note explained. Roddy Smith, first mate on the *MacKenzie*, remembered Vargas as "a very jolly lad." He told a reporter, "We were surprised, you know."

A week later an inquest in Prince Rupert concluded that heavy seas had thwarted attempts to save Vargas. Coroner George Dawes added, "Somebody has slipped up. Had preparations been made to answer Clifford's call for assistance immediately, Vargas might be alive today."[4]

Except for the helicopter pad, Triple Island still looks just as it did when the Watkinses saw it rise from the horizon, like a tombstone, on their trip up from Sisters sixty years ago. For the men inside, however, with Prince Rupert only a radio-phone away, with colour TV, a makeshift gymnasium, and changeovers once a month by helicopter, it's a different world entirely. A married man like Doug Franklin (Ernest Dawe's stepson and a veteran of Cape Beale, Lennard, and Trial Islands) finds that a month apart is a fair exchange for his children's chance to attend school and lead "normal" lives. Some bachelors like Larry Golden boast that they have the best job in town, working six months a year for full pay, with a month's holiday besides.

The sea still seems bent upon blotting out Anderson's impertinent obstacle. Doug Franklin was once jarred out of his concentration on a late-night movie when a wave smashed through the window and washed the TV set up on his lap. For weeks a huge log jutted out the bathroom window, giving rise to all sorts of scatological jokes in the cockpit and back at the hangar when the "chopper" crews returned from flights over Triple.

Those who don't fit in soon get out. Once when Larry Golden turned his mattress to make his bed, he found a cryptic note from a predecessor, recounting all sorts of abuse he had suffered at the hands of his partner, and concluding with the advice that if he never got back ashore alive, the authorities would know "who done it."

Every month they come and go in the "cage." The keeper going home cranks up the winch engine and slides the cage down the cable over the gap to the helicopter pad. His replacement climbs in, comes across, then takes over the controls to let the other down for the trip to Prince Rupert. In July 1978 Peter Redhead noticed some "hitch" in the cage and sent word to Prince Rupert. The helicopter set down next morning at high tide. Paul Pouliot clambered down the rocks to examine the cage and cable from below. Larry Golden was standing beside and slightly above him on the rocks when the wave came. Paul had just turned toward the men screaming from the pad, when a giant wall of water smashed into the rocks and burst through the gap. Someone said afterward they thought they saw the iridescent flash of a life jacket rise up in the distance, but once the monstrous suck and thunder had passed, all that remained of Paul Pouliot were his eyeglasses and trousers.

*Eagle eye view of
Triple Island Light.*

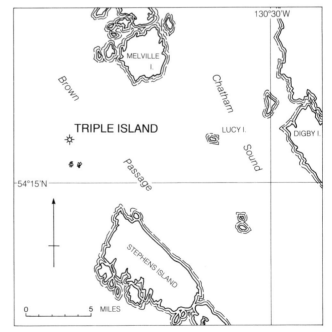

Catching Up

In late August 1921 the Amalgamated Postal Workers of Canada came away from their annual convention in Victoria with a new constitution, a new name, and a bold new mission. "Civil Servants have one master," the Amalgamated Civil Servants of Canada proclaimed, and "they should therefore have one organization." Ottawa immediately recognized the ACS of C as a "spokesman for its employees"—but nothing more. Without the right to bargain or strike, they could "speak" all they wanted. Talk was cheap.

By November 1925 the good news had reached the lights. "A Lightkeeper in B.C." (who sounded much like Capilano's keeper Alfred Dickenson) wrote the editor of *The Organizer*, the Amalgamated's monthly magazine, suggesting that each member "get the name and address of a lightkeeper and forward a copy of...[the] paper to them after they are through with it." He and his fellows were "the lowest paid and most isolated of the whole bunch," and he predicted, "As long as we are unorganized, we will remain so. Now you lightkeepers let me say that your increase in 1918-19 was brought about by the membership of this Association," he continued, "and the Vancouver branch has to my knowledge pleaded the case of the lightkeepers of B.C. at Ottawa."

When they received their well-thumbed back issues of *The Organizer* from far-away letter carriers, caretakers, secretaries, and penitentiary guards, the disgruntled "bunch" soon discovered they were no longer alone. In April 1923 the Amalgamated protested Ottawa's "attempts to water down the merit principle, to make way for extensions of patronage." At the height of the superannuation purge of 1924, *The Organizer* railed against compulsory check-offs that would be "buried in Consolidated Revenue," paying no interest and no pension at all to anyone who left the civil service with less than ten years' service. Members witnessed the infant union's ceaseless struggle for collective bargaining rights, a minimum wage, a forty-four hour week, and abolition of patronage, and they followed, blow-by-blow, the fruitless campaign against ruthless, across-the-board, 10-percent wage cuts in 1932.

If anyone on the lights still doubted the Amalgamated's role, all reservations were dispelled by the 1927 convention in Winnipeg where delegates, most of whom had never even seen a lighthouse, adopted a resolution demanding eighteen days' holiday for their brothers and sisters "employed on lonely islands, removed, practically, from civilization." From the "lonely islands" the response was ecstatic. One anonymous keeper revealed he had not taken a holiday for *twenty-five years* and hoped "the new order of things" would "mature early," before he died of old age. The "wife of a lightkeeper" related how they had to turn their home over to strangers to take a week's holiday—"and it generally...[took] until Christmas to pay for it"—adding it had been "a hard struggle to put both girls through school on

$84.00 a month.'' Another voice in the wilderness was ''most keen'' to contact the Association: ''Isolated as we are and in a pitiful minority, we have had no means of getting any of our complaints before the public with the result that for many years we have been in the position—'the World Forgetting, By the World Forgot'.''

A.W. Niell, who had a fat sheaf of lightkeepers' pathetic letters in his constituency files, lashed out at his fellow MPs in an impassioned speech in the House in June 1928. If Ottawa's six thousand civil servants had suffered so much, their demands would quickly ''be acceded to,'' but few lightkeepers had any political clout. They seldom, if ever, made it to the polls. ''I sometimes think it is a good thing to bring an argument home to ourselves,'' the indignant MP declared. ''I wonder how many honourable members of this house would like to be stuck on an isolated light station month in and month out, year in and year out, hardly able to take even the necessary exercise, because there are no facilities for walking, no chance for any kind of amusement, no hobby, no one to associate with but one's wife,'' nothing but ''the wave tossed sea'' for company, where ''it can rain more in two days. . . than it does. . . [in Ottawa] in the whole year.''

Niell spoke from hard experience—he had walked into some of those parlours and come away a shaken man. ''I visited a certain lighthouse where a man and his wife lived, and they told me a story so pathetic and so realistic that it would touch the chord of any heart that was responsive to any appeal to human kindness,'' the MP related.

> Here is the story: Every month or so the feeling of isolation and loneliness played upon them to such an extent that one or the other would get into a deep fit of melancholy. For some three years neither of them could understand the other, and they lived a tragic life until one day it dawned upon the husband that his wife was not at fault. They agreed upon a compromise whereby when either of them got into one of these melancholy moods, say, if the wife refused to get breakfast and moped around the island rock, the husband would do the work instead. This would last for a week, and when the wife would recover, the husband might fall into one of these moods. They had tended this lighthouse for six years without any holidays. Surely we are not so hardhearted as to take the attitude that those who hold the frontier, those who endure this isolation, are not entitled to a little consideration. Surely they deserve at least a fortnight's holiday without being forced to pay for a substitute out of their earnings. I am sure it would meet with the approbation of the Minister of Marine and Fisheries and everybody else who listens to the story.

Unfortunately, the minister, P.J.A. Cardin, did not respond to this plea, and no action followed Niell's speech.

When Manuel Hanna, or whoever it was, took aim at Ernie Maynard in September that year, he also triggered a new round of concerns. Under the headline LIGHTHOUSE KEEPERS' LOT, the *Organizer*'s editor hoped that Maynard had not died in vain. The Victoria Labour Council, and the Victoria branch of the Amalgamated, each passed resolutions urging the immediate appointment of assistants to all lighthouses.

While the Provincial Police scoured the coast for the elusive wild-eyed hermit, the *Victoria Times* sent reporters around to the marine agency in response to readers' questions about why his victim had been left all alone up at Addenbroke. After closeting themselves for an afternoon with Colonel Wilby, the journalists came away assured that "no man" was "safer from the assassin or hold-up man than a lighthouse keeper whose quarters . . . [were] visited but occasionally from the world outside." Wilby went much farther than that, however, and the result was a feature article which heralded (conversely): "Isolation Disappears from Life of B.C. Lighthouses"—a piece which must have been greeted with much scoffing and scratching of heads when the papers finally arrived at most lights with the Christmas mail.[1]

The *Times* article upheld the "tradition" of forcing lightkeepers to hire and pay their own assistants. While conceding that they earned less than their American counterparts, Wilby pointed out that the keepers' salaries, ranging from $1200 to $3000, compared "very favourably with salaries paid to government workers in other walks of life."

If this were the truth according to Wilby, there was little meaning left in the word "lie." An unskilled labourer in Vancouver would have taken home $2450 a year if his boss forced him to work twelve hours a day, seven days a week, all year long, and he would never have to turn a sizeable chunk over to an assistant.[2] Most lightkeepers probably placed a lesser value on their assistants' time than their own, though obviously their expenses were equal. If they paid them what they were worth, then assistants would have earned, at best, half the salary enjoyed by employees "in other walks of life." So lightkeepers could still claim the dubious distinction of being the lowest paid workers in Canada. Like "poor Brown" at Ivory Island twenty-eight years before, they had only "the glory of being lightkeepers."

There was another ugly consolation way down on the bottom rung of Canadian society: lightkeepers had their assistants' fingers underfoot. The Perdues' debacle at Entrance Island in 1914—when the couple were treated like slaves, and had their wages withheld, then garnisheed—was all too typical an experience for people locked away at the mercy of an employer who was pitifully underpaid himself. Even fifty years later, when assistants were hired and paid by the department, the temptations inherent in an unequal relationship often proved too much, even for fair-minded "senior" keepers. Menial chores often fell by default to the "juniors." "I've done my time in hell as an assistant," one keeper told his in 1979, "so you can do the clean-ups every week." As newcomers to the lights, assistants live and work under the ominous cloud of probation for six months or more, and have no recourse to a grievance committee if they do not work out. In 1955, after a keeper at Active Pass had hired and fired five assistants in two years, H.V. Anderson, director of Marine Services in Ottawa, wrote Victoria insisting that this practice be stopped. "I can envisage the possibility of a lightkeeper being dismissed as being unsuitable if he cannot retain assistants to the mutual advantage of both himself and the Department,'' he said.[3]

Unfortunately Anderson's veiled threat never congealed into policy. No keepers have ever been dismissed for mistreating assistants, not even those who have an appalling record for chewing them up and saddling the department with prodigious expenses for moving them on and off stations as a result. One keeper at Cape St. James achieved infamy by sacking assistants within their first two weeks there, then offering to purchase their provisions at a cut rate to save them the bother of packing up.

Naturally the relationship cut both ways. In the summer of 1942 Robert Lally finally fired a man at Estevan Point who refused to work, even though ''Mrs. Lally and Doreen did his washing for him and massaged his feet.'' He was ''too fond of bed—but there. . .[was] one thing he could do: EAT.'' It was a momentous, agonizing decision for the aging keeper. Eliza Lally had left the station for hospital treatment, taking the children with her. Exhausted from manning the light and horns on his own, Lally glumly predicted, ''As I cannot go on very much Longer Under the above conditions, I shall have to have Medical Treatment. The only thing left For me is to put in my Resignation and Get out of the Service.''[4]

Perhaps some assistants should be forgiven if they lacked the zeal to turn out from between their sheets. In 1947 the department slashed monthly allowances for assistants to a minimum of $52, guaranteeing them an annual salary of only $624—the average lightkeeper's wage in 1918. For making up the balance from his own pocket, an assistant's ''boss'' was entitled to enter and inspect his home at any time (though most still lived under the same roof), assign shifts arbitrarily, control the behaviour of his wife and children, as well as determine the use of all lightstation property and equipment. The ''typical'' relationship between keepers and their assistants, if such a thing existed, probably lay somewhere between rank exploitation and Joe Mikas's affection for George Smith. When Joe died at Nootka while George was away on leave, the RCMP officers who searched his dwelling found his will, which bequeathed everything—including a ''dream home'' he had built on stilts—to his ''boss.''

Little wonder, then, that Wilby told *Times* correspondents that ''the keeper often finds it convenient to select one of his family for the job'' of assistant. ''In these days of women's rights there may be instances where the wife demands that portion of the cheque which the keeper would have to pay an assistant,'' the reporters allowed, ''but in any event the families would join. . .in resisting a change in the present system which is in the main in force as the result of their own representations.'' Some might resist—but only for the reason that they could ill afford to hire someone else. In fact, if the agent had handed them the keys to his files, the journalists could have cut an archeological trench through half a century of letters, sifted through cartloads of paper, and still failed to unearth a single such ''representation.'' Instead the agent passed the press a wide brush sopping with whitewash. He had only to reach behind him and pluck out any station file at random to produce reams of desperate letters pleading for an end to such "convenience."

The same week that Michael O'Brien's wife drowned rowing home to Entrance Island, Wilby made the ludicrous claim that most keepers had telephones, and that "in most cases schools are available for the children, although in some cases they have to go a longer distance than children are accustomed to." Telephones? If only the reporters had asked for some phone numbers! A year later, Sophie Moran lay marinating in Lysol-soaked sheets, shrieking in pain up at Triple Island, but no one heard her. Fifty-five years later only nine of forty-three lightstations had telephones; only five offered access to both elementary and secondary school. The rest were wired into the outside world by the department's VHF radio circuit, hardly a personal or private means of communication. As late as 1978 a keeper strictly forbade his assistant and his wife to use the radio, and had it removed from their dwelling after they answered a call from Seal Cove base about an error he had made in their grocery order.

Wilby conceded one issue "on which lighthouse keepers...[had] just cause for complaint": holidays, the very antidote which Robertson, Halkett, and Wilby constantly prescribed to relieve the affliction of isolation. All other civil servants, himself included, enjoyed three weeks paid holiday a year, but Wilby agreed, "[The lightkeeper] appears to have been discriminated against....He receives no yearly holiday with pay and it is often true that the man he employs to relieve him will demand more for the occasional work than the lighthouse-keeper receives for the time that he takes off for a holiday." So one would hope, unless a relief keeper performed his services as a charity.

However tempting it may be to pillory Wilby and others in Victoria for their keepers' tribulations, the agents and their underlings were mere instruments of a calculated policy. In fact, they often took up their keepers' cause, demonstrating time and again—with little success—that abysmal wages robbed them of dignity and health, though Robertson and Wilby each crawled cravenly out on limbs to salvage what they could of the department's image, besmirched by the Sadler and Maynard revelations. When Wilby died, legend on the lights (unfounded, of course) held that no one from the department attended his funeral.

For all his fastidiousness, Gordon Halkett won a special place in the hearts of his wards. Only when Halkett came was there any hint of camaraderie, however fragile. Even George Watson had pronounced him a "good samaritan" compared to all those Pharisees and "stool pigons" in Ottawa and Victoria. "Mrs. Davies sends her Best regards to you," James Davies wrote Halkett, with the Triangle Island house shaking around him on New Year's Eve 1912. "She is getting along fine but she is a little short winded yet, the children want too know when you are cuming too Triangle."

Perhaps Halkett's own harrowing experience earned him the keepers' esteem. He had been horribly disfigured after leaning into the hatch of an acetylene buoy to inspect it at the yard in Victoria. He struck a match for a better look and the resulting belch of flame seared off his eyelids. Gordon Halkett went through the rest of his days with tinted goggles strapped around his head. Once they overcame their initial fright, lighthouse children found him a very amiable gargoyle indeed. When shore parties came to summon him back to the tender, they usually found Halkett in the keeper's parlour with toddlers straddling his lap, fishing in his tweed suit for candy while he regaled them with tall tales.[5]

The real culprits were the politicians. Their marine agents, the missionaries, the Red Cross nurses—all knew there were slat-sided children and fretful, barefoot parents out there, but no premier or prime minister ever came calling, though the Governor General once sailed by. The question of blame may be a moot one (though the government of Canada has seldom done worse things to more people over a longer time), but the credit for banishing hunger and indentured servitude of assistants, and for wresting sick pay and paid holidays out of Ottawa, can easily be shared among four unsung champions: lightkeepers Harold Okell, Jack Hunting, Ernie Dawe, and a Vancouver postal clerk named Jack Waddell.

The situation of West Coast lighthouse keepers virtually guaranteed that the fledgling union amounted to much more than a faceless institution for them. With mail coming ashore three or four times a year, *The Organizer* assumed a revered significance on the lights, which might well have puzzled its editors, accustomed as they were to militant fervour. P.G. Cox sent his Christmas mail off from Cape Beale on 11 December 1929, and in the bag went personal ''Season's Greetings'' to every officer and member of the Amalgamated's Victoria branch. ''In the short time since the Lightkeepers were taken into the association, the work that has been done on their behalf is, in my opinion, little short of marvelous,'' Cox exclaimed. In this first *signed* letter from a keeper published in *The Organizer*, he hailed the landmark victory of paid sick leave: ''I cannot say how very much I appreciate the most kind and friendly letters I have received from our National President and our National Secretary, but I would say that those letters have made me feel that they are both my personal friends, although I have never had the pleasure of meeting them up to the present.'' Joe Pettingell, wrestling hard with his ''temptations'' over at Cape Mudge, also thanked the executives of the ACS of C for the attention they had given his letters and the interest they had shown ''at all times.''

This sort of imagined intimacy breathed life into the jargon of solidarity and fraternity, and consoled the keepers in the face of their heavy setbacks. And setbacks there were. In May 1930 the department asserted it was ''definitely against consideration of increased salaries for full-time lightkeepers at the present time.'' Two years later keepers opened their cheques to discover wages had arbitrarily been slashed by 10 percent. Incredibly, after Sophie Moran was dragged into the winch up at Triple Island, the commissioner of lights balked at installing radio-telephones, pleading lack of funds even though towing companies had put them in the wheelhouses of all their tugs. In April 1935 Ottawa reclassified all the lights at an even lower pay scale, effective as soon as new positions were filled upon retirement or resignation, thus dashing the keepers' traditional means of bettering their abysmal conditions by transferring to more isolated and higher paying stations. That May, Addenbroke's keeper wrote Hanson, the agent in Prince Rupert, complaining that, after three years' service, there had "been many changes and new men put in over" him. He made a poignant appeal for fairness "in regard to promotion," saying, "[It] is my only means of getting an increase in salary, which I badly need as my salary here is only $849.00 per annum, which is very little to feed and clothe a family of eight on."[6]

Harold Okell entered the fray that May. Okell was at Albert Head, which put him in closest touch with the Amalgamated's Victoria branch. Its secretary asked him to outline his views on the lighthouse service for the upcoming edition of *The Organizer*, and the keeper gladly raked over all the long-simmering issues: rotten wages, no holidays, no paid assistants, round-the-clock shifts, no compensation for assistants. "Another serious handicap which is very often lost sight of is the education of our children," Okell added, "which, with very few exceptions, necessitates sending the children away from home and paying board, which in British Columbia costs approximately $30 per month."

That August he and Ada invited the Victoria Branch out to the lighthouse for their monthly meeting. "The night was wet and dreary but our hosts had things bright and warm inside," the secretary reported. Okell reported on other grievances as well as his own, and for the first time in history, outside workers were ushered into the lightkeepers' world. "The maze of machinery was a revelation to the members, who realized that a Lightkeeper needs to be a versatile man in order to safeguard those at sea," *The Organizer* glowingly reported. "Hats off to lightkeepers and those who assist them." Okell had them all back again in June 1936.

In February 1937 Jack Hunting exhorted his fellow keepers from Pachena to line up behind Okell and their union. "It takes a lightkeeper to explain matters clearly where our service is concerned," Hunting affirmed. After all, Harold Okell spoke from thirty years' experience. Hunting praised his dedication to clarifying issues and prosecuting grievances through the Victoria Branch. Slackers and scabs should take note and "not let the other fellow carry . . . [their] load as well as his own," Hunting urged. "Let us come under one organization, and above all let us have one mouthpiece. The natural thing is to turn a deaf ear to a babble of voices. We have a remedy to that in our own hands; let's use it. Join the A.C.S. of C. and pull your weight." George Ericson, an assistant at Estevan Point, took heart from Hunting's appeal, and urged the Association to accept lowly assistants into its ranks too. "Join the A.C.S. of C. and put up a fight for decent standards of living, running water, modern sanitary conveniences, good equipment to work with . . . and . . . a good living wage," Ericson pleaded.

As the union spread like an anti-government plague up the coast, C.D. Howe tried to innoculate the public against *The Organizer*'s effective propaganda. In an open letter to the Amalgamated's national secretary, the millionaire minister of Marine curtly dismissed lightkeepers' desperate pleas for paid holidays. While he was

Harold Okell, the lightkeepers' shop steward and agitator.

"assured" that each application for leave received "careful and sympathetic consideration," Howe likened a lightkeeper's lot "to that of a farmer or small merchant" who had no use for vacations. After all, their work was one long holiday, "a family affair," he claimed, ignoring a recent crushing financial blow he had dealt those same "privileged" families by ruling against wives' serving as paid assistants. Besides, Howe argued, lightkeepers' hours were unregulated—unlike other civil servants'—and many were located within settlements or close to a town.[7]

When Howe's letter was read aloud at the next Victoria branch meeting in Okell's livingroom, "some very caustic remarks were made, especially by two . . . Lightkeeper members." John Moran, recently retired from Green Island light, snorted, "This statement is simply priceless." How could anyone be so stupid as to compare a civil servant's lot with that of a farmer and merchant, "that of an owner and proprietor"? "Has the Minister been informed how long it takes for a lightkeeper to obtain this permission [for leave]?" Moran demanded. "If the Minister has been persuaded that lack of statutory leave works no hardships on the Lightkeeper or his family, I wish he might hear the opinions of Lightkeepers and their wives." True, there was no need to regulate lightkeepers' hours of work, Moran conceded—"the Department demands their full time."

Before he retired, Harold Okell wrote a farewell feature article for the July 1939 issue of *The Organizer*. Under the banner "Canada's Keepers," he reiterated:

Many conditions as they exist at present in the Lightkeeping Service
   1. Are not consistent with the Civil Service Act;
   2. Are not in the best interests of efficiency in the service;
   3. Do not enhance the prestige of the service;
   4. Do not compare favourable with other branches of the Federal service or other similar branches of the service of other countries;
   5. Are injurious to the physical and mental well-being of the Lightkeepers.

In December the Victoria branch voted unanimously to confer an honourary life membership on "Bro. Okell," who had seldom missed a meeting despite a forty-mile drive over "none too good roads" in the dark, with a peg-leg on the clutch, and who had "fought long and strenuously for improvements in the light service."

Okell's exit brought the curtain down on the first act of the struggle as the war submerged the keepers' plight. Little had been gained aside from sick leave, but Okell and Hunting had carefully cultivated the deeply rooted discontent on the lights. Like a common umbilical cord, *The Organizer* vented despair, once confined to humiliating letters to agents and ministers, and nourished hopes. For the first time lightkeepers were not alone. They had a common "friend" only a short walk from Parliament Hill, and they felt part of something big and good and growing.

Unlike most of the Association's officers, and their corner crew in the Victoria branch, who either enlisted or pulled any punches aimed at the wartime government, lightkeepers desperately tried to keep up the good fight. Their adversary was much more tangible than the Axis; until the mysterious shelling of Estevan lighthouse, the war was much farther away than Ottawa. The Victoria branch met in April 1941 for a meeting which "became very stormy when the matter of Lighthouse Keepers' grievances came up." When the secretary read conciliatory letters from the national office on the subject, "great indignation was expressed when it was realized that, apparently, this vital matter. . .[was] not making any headway at Ottawa." While the secretary hammered hard for order, the unruly members introduced a "very strong resolution" castigating their national president, but later elected to table it until he appeared before them later that month. "So great was the feeling" that a twelve-year veteran of the Amalgamated, past president of the local, resigned "then and there. . .in protest," feeling, as many did, "that something should have long ago been done for the lighthouse keepers. . .and that the whole case. . .[had] not been strongly enough pressed at Ottawa."[8]

That August C.D. Howe once again brushed aside their longstanding agitation for annual leave, complaining that "the duties of Lightkeeper in general are not onerous." *The Organizer* set the tone of the Amalgamated's wartime stance by featuring a message from the mayor of Saskatoon. Emphasizing the need for common "sacrifice," he urged union members "to accept many inconveniences and do without many, if not all, of the luxuries" to which they had been accustomed. Meanwhile C.D. ("What's a million?") Howe was turning the levers of government and the keys to the Treasury over to his "dollar a year men," who laid sound foundations for the postwar branch plant economy. In September the Victoria local referred in passing to "the age-old Lighthouse Keepers' question," and lamely explained, "We, as a local, have done all possible for them."

For two years *The Organizer* published no more letters from the lights. By late July 1943, however, one issue could no longer be ignored: rationing. Most lightkeepers had no access to stores, yet were bound by the same ration restrictions as everyone ashore, so they were desperate when construction crews or shipwrecked seafarers were "thrust upon the keeper's generosity." There had always been precious little to go around; now there was even less. "The inevitable result," *The Organizer* predicted, "will be that these lightkeepers will refuse to starve and will leave for better paid jobs in war work closer to civilization (so called)"—a prediction borne out by Jack Hunting's assistant at Pachena, who left "to better himself in War Industry" in October 1943. "It is understandable his wanting to leave with all the stairs we have here," Hunting wrote Stamford. "It is a wonder he stayed so long for he is nearly 80 now."

By December 1944, with the Germans and Japanese in full retreat, the militant Victoria branch switched back to the offensive against Ottawa. In their "whole history. . .no other body of Civil Servants has been put aside, in the seeking of much-needed adjustment of conditions of work and living and equipment, as have the Pacific Coast Lightkeepers," they admitted. Lionel Chevrier, the new minister of Transport, received yet another list of grievances, rehashing all the same prewar issues. He pledged his "sympathetic consideration" in return for "the manner in which they assumed added responsibilities as part of the war effort." Their reward came in April 1947—a wage cut of nearly 1 percent. Keepers were granted "$35 per month for each assistant actually employed," an allowance which "[should] not in any case exceed 40% of the total compensation paid to the assistant(s)." At Estevan Point, the highest paid station, the maximum pay for an assistant was therefore $1046—less even than Walter Erwin's pay at Point Atkinson in 1912—which left the keeper $2074.[9] For twelve hour days it worked out to a rate of forty-seven cents an hour, two-thirds the going rate for unskilled labour. Like the rest of Canada's public servants who had sacrificed so much, their only "consideration" was the artfully penned lists of casualties under glass cases in government offices.

A "lightkeeper's wife" pointed out that she and her husband bore the same "expenses of a city dweller, rent, fuel, food, clothing and insurances," in these postwar years, to be carved somehow out of $175.10 a month take-home pay. "The present day cost of living has forced practically all keepers of stations calling for assistants to carry on alone, working 24 hrs. a day, 7 days a week and all holidays, with his wife helping," she revealed. And wives were now ineligible as paid assistants. On three-man stations requiring two assistants, most keepers "made do" with one. "On this coast try and find a reliable, clean, decent man for $87.50 per month," she challenged. "Common labour commands $1.00 an hour."

Women still filled in, though the department would no longer pay them. "I don't care who he is, he has to sleep sometime," Hunting pointed out after his octogenarian assistant quit. Pachena and many more lights up and down the coast would have been out of service long ago were it not for their "womenfolk." In November 1945 Mrs. Hunting was hospitalized, suffering from exhaustion. Her doctor ordered her "under no circumstances to do again as she . . . [had] been doing through the last fog season, irregular hours, put off meals, and the exertion of climbing a lot of stairs." Her husband told the agent, "This rules her out of ever again participating in any of the work on the station."[10] Three months later she had no choice. Jack was certified as medically unfit for a month due to "lumbago" contracted from "walking in rain."

Nothing had changed since George Watson's day, except lightkeepers no longer had to limp forward to seek charity when they were sick or hurt. "I have always maintained," Jack Hunting wrote, "the needs of Lightkeepers are supplied in the following ratio, 10% by the Department and 90% by the grace of God."[11]

Jack Waddell took leave of absence from the Vancouver post office and went out to organize for the Amalgamated and alter the ratio in 1952. He soon discovered that lightkeepers ranked lowest in a public service that was chronically underpaid and still subject to political intimidation, constituting Canada's very own "third world" on her western fringe. No organizer ever faced a tougher challenge than Waddell, working a shop floor five hundred miles long, appallingly remote, accessible only to management, with a body of workers who rarely, if ever, met or talked with one another over the course of their whole working lives. Half his members worked for the other half. Many sought solace in attitudes which would baffle any union activist. Elsewhere they might have been sneered at as management toadies and raw material for scabs, but not on the lights. Owen Evans from Trial Island probably spoke for a majority of his peers in a letter to Colonel Keith Dixon, the marine agent, in March 1955. Evans was one of the few who still *favoured* hiring his own assistants, though he admitted, ''In doing so, maybe I am a little selfish.'' Here at last lies the solution to the riddle of why they put up with it all:

1. I am very happy at this type of work and though I work long hours with little time off, I have a deep sense of security and accomplishment.
2. I am able to appreciate my wife and family as I am at home with them all the time.
3. I have also learned to live very close to God and Nature for which I am truly thankful.[12]

However wealthy in spirit they were (and still are), their material condition cried out for reform. So Jack Waddell discovered, as A.W. Niell had done thirty years before, when he followed Minnie Patterson's footsteps down from Bamfield to Cape Beale, or came ashore on the island outposts after some ''pretty hectic'' boat trips. It was not unusual, for example, for the organizer to answer his phone in 1960 to hear a distraught keeper, on the verge of tears, calling from the Salvation Army hostel downtown, stranded with his wife and children because all their money ran out on holiday and the agent refused to take them home until their contract with the relief keeper expired.[13] Then there were assistants, injured or crippled on the job, who had to pay their own medical expenses, right down to the rubber tips on their crutches. There were constant complaints about drinking water turned milky-white by seagull droppings. And the wages—wages far below the legal minimum calculated over twelve-hour days and seven-day weeks. Transfers and promotions remained a matter of the agent's fiat. Seniority counted for nothing, not if a man dared cross Keith Dixon. ''These people were desperate,'' Jack Waddell remembered.

Dixon and Beketov, his Prince Rupert counterpart, ruled their fiefs with the same schizoid combination of paternalism and coercion that James Gaudin had exercised seventy years before. Quite different in temperament, both were ex-military men (''Why do we have to see some *Colonel* to get some aids?'' mariners asked the assistant deputy minister in the 1950s). Beketov, a former Czarist admiral, had won the undying gratitude of the Canadian government when he absconded to Halifax with three new cruisers after the Bolsheviks seized power in 1917. Both agents could be engaging or intransigent in turn, when the mood suited them. Lightkeepers on leave in Prince Rupert often joined the Beketovs for supper. No keeper ever had a bad word for the ''Admiral.'' Not so for Dixon. Waddell once suggested that

Above: Prince Rupert depot looking east, 1918. Below: Agent's residence, Prince Rupert depot.

Left: *Col. Dixon on bridge of C.G.S.* Alberni. Right: *Marine Agent N. Becketov, 1950.*

refrigerators should be provided when stations were electrified, as a cure-all for malnutrition and food poisoning. "My wife has no faith in deep freezes," Dixon icily replied. "She believes, and I support her, that the best way is for these people to preserve their stuff in jars." With iron conviction, both agents believed they knew what was best for *their* keepers. Ottawa backed them up. "We're proud of our keepers," H.V. Anderson proclaimed to the press in October 1950. "We have a loyal group of men." The director of Marine Services' acting agent, Tom Morrison, added, "The last thing they complain about is loneliness."[14]

To refute management's blinkered view of its employees, Jack Waddell found a tireless ally in Ernie Dawe out at Point Atkinson, "a key person for organization at that time." Dawe had helped nurse his stricken father-in-law from Nootka, and had climbed four million stairs by his own count. Now he had it made. The man the *Vancouver Province* dubbed "a modern Barnacle Bill" had a lease on the cosiest in-station of them all. "I know of a dozen lightkeepers, friends of mine, just waiting for me to die off," he chuckled.

Yet Ernie and Marjorie Dawe were far from content. They had arrived there the hard way, and their son had just gone on the lights. However much Vancouverites might envy him, Dawe was acutely aware that Point Atkinson was just a street light compared to a typical West Coast light station, to say nothing of what went on up north. Ernie Dawe and Jack Waddell converted Point Atkinson into a secret cell of union activity. Lightkeepers on leave from anywhere up the coast brought their grievances down to Dawe. Ernie got on the phone and the ''union man'' drove out to Lighthouse Park to share more shocking revelations at Ernie's kitchen table. The agents never suspected and were always caught off guard when the upstart peppered them with embarrassing facts and figures garnered from as far afield as Green Island. ''I think you can understand the resentment that would be created when I went to see the Marine Agent in Victoria or. . .Prince Rupert,'' Waddell recalled. It was almost as if he was into the files! Never again could a marine agent proclaim lightkeepers' good fortune to a gullible public, nor claim anything as stupid and wounding as the disappearance of isolation, like Wilby did in the autumn of 1928. The incident of the Wellards at Carmanah in November 1953 brought the truth to the front pages.

The West Coast was in a shambles that fall, pounded week after week by winds and waves, the like of which had not been seen since the early years of the century. On 8 November Gerry Wellard's wife collapsed with severe abdominal cramps. There could only be one diagnosis up there, way beyond reach of the ''flu bug,'' where people ate out of cans: food poisoning. Wellard radioed for help but no vessel could land in the heavy swells, rolling in like glass mountains that shattered on the deserted beach. There was only one way out.

They packed some food and hiked painfully along the trail to Clo-ose. Clo-ose had no doctor, and the keepers watched in dismay as the Union steamship wallowed out to sea after snapping all her lines in a foiled attempt to tie up at the wave-washed government wharf. Port Renfrew, the nearest settlement, lay nineteen miles away as the crow flies, through the world's densest rain forest. It was a grim choice—to die there or on the way. ''My sickness was nearly driving me mad,'' Mrs. Wellard lived to tell reporters, ''so we decided to try and hike to Port Renfrew.''

Minnie Patterson's race to Bamfield forty years before was a leisurely stroll by comparison. The Wellards followed what was barely a slash of track, with cables strung across the deepest canyons, used only in emergencies by machete-swinging linesmen. ''My husband had to tie a rope to me when he pulled me over the canyon cables on the trail. We must have been dangling about 300 feet in the air at times,'' she said. Racing against time, Gerry hacked through the bush until nightfall, half dragging her behind by her tether. He hooked his arm around her neck and swam the flood-swollen creeks that were clotted with stumps and deadfalls. At night while she lay doubled over, exhausted and shivering under the trees, he fried up pancakes and corned beef. ''It doesn't sound very inviting now,'' she admitted afterward, ''but it gave us the strength to follow the trail the next day . . .'' and the next. Three days later the Wellards, their clothing in shreds, staggered up Port Renfrew's main street, two sodden and battered tramps offering striking proof to the world that isolation had yet to disappear from lighthouse life.[15]

Jack Waddell knew how to use the power of the press in less dramatic situations as

David Milne, Percy Pike, Col. Dixon, Esther Milne, Mary Pike at party.

well. He invited the local reporters to the Amalgamated's district convention in the packed ballroom of Victoria's Douglas Hotel on 27 September 1957. The press sat up front, pencils poised, when he strode to the podium. "Operators of the 45 lighthouses in British Columbia are working under grim last-century conditions that the government would not tolerate in private industry," he began. Muttering in disgust, his hushed audience heard all about the "deplorable and incredible" plight of their brothers and sisters on the lights. Assistants, Waddell explained, toiled as long as eighty-four hours a week. "Until recently, they have been making just $180 to $200 a month (sixty cents an hour)," he revealed, "and they get no statutory holidays, sick leave, and no leave credits." As their "employers," lightkeepers had to pay premiums for compensation and unemployment insurance. "Many haven't radios and some have no communication with the outside world."

Once they had recovered from their shock, the embittered members leaped to their feet and voted a resolution that "further action be taken to make these conditions subject to investigation by a parliamentary committee."[16] Parliament ignored their appeal, but Jack Waddell had set a match to some very dry tinder. When Dixon stormed into his office Monday morning, he decided to fight fire with fire. He dialed the *Colonist* and suggested they send some reporters out to Albert Head to have a chat with Percy and Mary Pike. They could see for themselves if there was any substance to Waddell's slanders or if he was not just a hothead letting off steam.

The atmosphere in the Pikes' parlour (once the scene of stormy meetings of the Victoria branch of ACSC) certainly refuted the notion of "last century" living conditions. Percy had no complaints—he had been *forty-two years* on the lights and "wouldn't swap jobs with anyone." Forty years ago his teenaged bride had lost their second child following the agent's orders, another had suffered from rickets, but Pine Island in 1915 was light-years away from Albert Head in 1957. Yet even the Pikes agreed with Waddell that the department should hire assistants and grant them all the "advantages" of full-time civil servants.[17]

A week later Keith Douglas and his wife wrote the *Colonist* to "applaud" the ACSC protest. After serving a bleak year and a half as assistants at Carmanah, they could confirm the story of an eighty-four-hour work week without holidays, and also agreed that "food deliveries at the more remote sites sometimes were as infrequent as once every six months."[18] Dixon himself had written Anderson in Ottawa two years before, bemoaning the flood of applications the department received "from office workers, pensioners, disabled persons and amputees, alcoholics, John Howard Society proteges, etc"—the only people willing to accept the work and pay conditions offered by the department.[19]

The raucous Amalgamated convention of 1957 was a turning point. The Department of Transport backed away from its shameful position on assistants, isolation, and wages, then went into full retreat. Assistant keepers became full-fledged civil servants in 1958. In 1962, with a policy right-wing businessmen have railed against ever since, Lester Pearson (himself a lifelong civil servant) at long last conceded union rights to all government workers. It made for a revolution in lightkeepers' lives, increasing their personal income and providing paid assistants at a single stroke. In terms of real wages and benefits they had nearly caught up—to the colony's keepers at Fisgard and Race Rocks in the 1860s.

Endangered Species

The union virtually wrote the last chapter in the horrifying history of a forgotten people. Collective bargaining exorcised the spectre of malnutrition. Lightkeepers still ranked among the lowest paid Canadian workers, though their employer never tired of pointing out that they enjoyed free rent, even if few people might wish to rent an estate on Green Island or Sisters Rocks in January. Paid holidays and paid assistants provided a welcome release from the cycle of depression described so eloquently by A.W. Niell forty years before. Electrification came gradually in the sixties, and lightkeepers slung refrigerators ashore. The harsh regime of coal, kerosene, winding-up weights, and maggoty meat became a thing of the past. Radio provided a tether to the world over the horizon, only a helicopter ride away. Never again must families get out the shovels and build ''some sort of box,'' or keep that grotesque watch for a ship to come fetch their dead, nor endure long nights caring for their sick and injured alone. Correspondence programs and regional libraries placed lighthouse children on a par with their peers. Canada built its last three manned lights to cater to traffic bound for the new Alcan smelter at Kitimat: Chatham Point and Cape Scott (where Anderson should have built instead of Triangle Island in 1910) went up in 1959; Bonilla Island light in the early sixties. Whether they knew it or not, once the crew had cleaned up and left the Bonilla site, a hundred years of construction came to an end.

Radar, a jealously guarded defense monopoly in wartime, quickly found its way into wheelhouses on fishboats and freighters, relegating navigation by sound and lead to a lost art. Ship traffic came to depend upon radio beacons rather than the lights alone, yet lighthouses and fog horns, driven by machinery closely monitored by their keepers, remained the cornerstone of safe navigation. As the masters of the BC Ferries' northern vessels insisted in an open letter to fellow users of aids to navigation in May 1986, ''On no account should the manning of West Coast lighthouses be reduced or curtailed: quite the contrary, some of the larger ones should be augmented.''

The sharp edges had been planed off their isolation, but the twelve-hour day remained, seven days a week, all year long. Summers and nights were always hardest. In summer, all winter's wounds had to be dressed—siding and shingles replaced, railings and boardwalks rebuilt, concrete poured, boats repaired, winches inspected and overhauled, gardens and lawns tended. A keeper might spend all the daylight hours with a paint pail and brush, arches aching from the ladder's rungs, dizzy from glare and fumes, climbing down to ''do the weather'' every three hours. Then all through the night, all year round, someone staved off sleep to make weather reports, alert for the advancing phalanx of fog. But lightkeepers have always treasured being their own bosses, tailoring time and labour to suit the weather and family life, so there have always been consolations. Calendars mean less than tide tables. Any day can be a Saturday, a time for jigging out over the kelp forest, organizing a picnic and fire on the beach, playing improvised team sports with children, or hiking through forests and along the shore. Just when their private reality seemed to be gaining ground on the popular myth, however, the keepers faced their toughest trial in a century of struggle.

"There is little chance modernization will ever replace the lighthouse keeper himself since mechanical equipment can fail," Colonel Keith Dixon predicted publicly in 1954, declaring, "There is no substitute for personal attention." He was, as it turned out, only half right. The equipment could, and would, fail, but even so the keepers were soon living on borrowed time. By 1962 engineers in Ottawa were hard at work on their "substitute." John Ballinger, director of Maritime Services on the West Coast, revealed that electronics had already replaced manpower on 161 of 211 East Coast lights. He predicted that "electronic advances" would give the "[West Coast] region total automation in five to ten years." Dixon still disagreed, pointing to the remoteness of West Coast stations, and to their radically different topography and traffic patterns, which "could very well place B.C.'s coastline outside the electric trend." The keepers were trapped in a vice between the aims of Victoria and Ottawa; between the need for fail-safe aids and fiscal restraint. Their union would unwittingly tighten the screws by asking for overtime pay.

The Amalgamated's successor, the Public Service Alliance of Canada, was an altogether different union by the 1970s. Bargaining units and committees seated along tables in plush Ottawa boardrooms took the place of conspiratorial coffee klatches at Albert Head and Point Atkinson. Treasury Board bureaucrats who would never land at a light took the agents' place across from union negotiators. Jack Waddell had rolled up his sleeves to do battle with his adversaries on a postal clerk's wage when most ACSC staff were volunteers. A pensioner in 1986, struggling on behalf of his fellow senior citizens for decent pensions, he lamented the fact that his successors in the "old outfit," with their Commerce degrees and three-piece suits, earned so much more than the men and women they represented. The lights were far beyond their ken. One PSAC representative advised the author in 1982 to ignore the radio if it buzzed after 5 P.M. "You're not getting paid overtime," he pointed out, "so why do the work?" Clearly, a vocation which still cements family ties and draws people closer to God and Nature, as it did Owen Evans, has no place in a world which reduces work to a mechanical exchange of time for money. Under this regime, mariners had better schedule their distress within working hours.

When Alliance negotiators trooped into an Ottawa boardroom that fall of 1971 and passed their demand for an eight-hour day plus overtime across the table, it all seemed reasonable enough. With an average annual salary of $6500 for an eighty-four hour work week, lightkeepers were still Canada's lowest paid public servants. The annual straight time payroll for 703 lightkeepers on both coasts stood at slightly more than $4 million. At the conventional rate of time-and-a-half, the increase would have amounted to $5 million, for an annual total of $9 million.

For its part, Transport Canada's management might have pointed to the unique situation on the West Coast, where lightkeepers lived rent-free in isolated locations. After all, they hardly had anywhere to go "after work." Living in their workplace, they were obliged merely to stand watch—no one had to toil through the night. In the give-and-take of collective bargaining, some synthesis between the two positions was well within reach.

Unfortunately, the Alliance had no inkling that Transport Canada had already elected to turn the lightkeepers' fate over to its engineers, whose interests flew in the face of bettering living and working conditions on the lights.

In their next submission to the Treasury Board, these analysts pounced upon the demand for overtime and waved it before their cost-conscious audience. In order to avoid paying overtime, they calculated future costs as straight time, which would mean *doubling* the number of keepers to work the 168-hour work week, and putting up new dwellings to house them. For the next decade this swollen four-man-station concept became the central performer in a complex mathematical gymnastics successfully labelled the "status quo," although half the workers existed only on paper.

This was a preposterous fiction which, in retrospect, serves only as a reliable measure of the vast chasm of geography and experience between Ottawa and the West Coast. Keepers on tiny islands like Pointer, Green, Chrome, Race Rocks, and the Sisters (not to mention Sand Heads and Triple) could have told them there was no room for the additional dwellings that were built on paper, but the analysts never sought their opinions, and arrived at a bloated estimate of $298 million required to maintain the "status quo" over the next fifteen years.[1]

By contrast, Ottawa's engineers claimed that the approach they favoured, automation, would "only" cost $160 million over fifteen years. However, if one subtracts the inflated four-man figure and overtime (which continues to elude keepers, fifteen years later), automation would save taxpayers $2 million over fifteen years.

In place of actual comparative costs, the analysts baldly calculated a "cost effectiveness ratio" of 2.59 over that same period. If actual projected costs based upon the *genuine* status quo are calculated, the cost benefit quickly evaporates. At the rate of $2712 an hour, $2 million amounted to a month's worth of technician and helicopter time to maintain deserted lightstations. The estimates were flimsy, but figures often carry the day just because so few people enjoy checking them.

Armed with their flawed submission and binders bulging with technical studies, Transport Canada quickly converted Treasury Board to their staunch faith that "automation of these stations will allow the Department to eliminate lightkeepers as such," supplanting them with a "monitor group" of 258 technicians to maintain the equipment. They sketched out a program in two phases. A semi-automatic phase, beginning immediately, would "permit the employer to assign hours of work to a reduced work force," with no union interference. Phase Two—full automation—would accomplish the extinction of manned lights, "with monitoring

Lonely Cape St. James Lightstation was established atop Cape St. James Island in 1914.

of the systems the only function,'' undertaken by 258 technicians based at forty-three monitor stations, who would ''gather, record and take the necessary action on all data acquired.'' In the event of a failure, a notice to shipping would be issued and technicians would be dispatched by helicopter to deal with the fault, weather permitting. As for the keepers, their fate was foretold in arid bureaucratese, drained of all human juices:

> As lightkeepers become redundant to the service, it is proposed to (a) retrain, where possible, for the monitoring function; (b) retrain, where possible, for maintenance; (c) offer alternative employment in the service, if available. It is expected resignations, retirements, deaths, etc., will account for the balance of lightkeepers who are not accounted for under (a), (b) and (c).[2]

The U.S. Coast Guard, embarking upon its own automation program in the seventies, at least paid lip service to humane benefits. Their primary project goal was ''to eliminate isolated and hazardous duty . . . that can be expected at many . . . light stations, thereby improving morale and personnel retention rates.'' But morale and retaining personnel held no place in Transport Canada's scheme. No need for polite fiction when wages were at issue.

Simple arithmetic also gave the lie to the prospects for ''redundant'' lightkeepers. How, for example, could 703 of them be divided into 258 ''monitors''? Other positions within a highly specialized government department would entail considerable retraining, to say nothing of the culture shock and depression affecting unwilling refugees from isolation. Even assuming that 200 positions could be conjured up (no mean feat in a time of cutbacks), there remained 250 keepers to resign or die. Besides, for the sake of accuracy these additional straight-time costs should have been thrown onto the scale as an added cost of automation over fifteen years.

There was a raft of technical troubles, too. For example, there was the Lister diesel, the basis of the new unmanned engine room design. Two or more generators, driven by Lister diesels, would supply power to new electric horns which proved far less effective than the time-tested diaphones. Battery chargers would ensure auxiliary power to an emergency standby light and the horns in the event of a complete shutdown. The advent of the new Mechron SR3 diesel system at Scarlett Point in 1977 provided some insight into how effectively engineers replaced lightkeepers. ''When I first arrived at Scarlett Point, we were using the last of the non-automated power, a Lister HR3 coupled to a Stamford 15 KW alternator,'' the keeper recalled. ''We changed the oil every 10 days, and the fuel filters every 10th oil change. That's *all*.''

Then came the modified Lister with a ''dry sump'' system to eliminate frequent oil changes. Lister's field representative cancelled the company's warranty on all the converted SR3s when he saw the modification. In essence, the system intended to replace lightkeepers with a twelve-volt battery that powered all the remote monitoring devices as well as the fuel system—an Achilles heel that could (and often did) bring the whole operation to a halt for want of a 25-cent fuse.

After their station shut down a week after the new system came ashore (their old unit had 36,000 hours on its clock), Scarlett's keepers radioed for help. Two helicopter trips later, a fuse was replaced. The keepers' analysis of automation was heresy to faith in unmanned lightstations:

> We start with a simple, time proven machine like a Lister diesel which rarely fails, and we design a sophisticated, complex system to monitor it. We now have a much higher chance of failure in the monitoring system than in the machine it's supposed to look after. So. . .failures occur, and the engineers call it the ''bugs'' that have to be ironed out. Ironing them out involves adding devices that monitor the sophisticated complex system that monitors the machine. We now have a whole engine room full of engineering challenges and toys, any of which can fail, so let's throw in a few devices to make it all ''fail safe.''

MacInnes Island Light, built 1921, marks a landfall for ships inbound through Queen Charlotte Sound.

One of the toys in this Rube Goldberg gallery was the Videograph, an electric-eye fog detector, manufactured by a Canadian branch plant of Sperry-Rand. The videograph emitted a pulsating beam of light. When the beam was broken within a range of two miles, it would trigger a sensor that would switch on the fog horns. Light, of course, travels in a straight line. Even assuming flawless performance, a videograph would only detect fog in one direction, and as any lightkeeper knows, fog is fickle. It seldom moves in from the wings to centre stage on cue to perform before a blinking electric eye, but might blanket the sea in one direction, leaving unlimited range in another.

The Americans never made the leap of faith which rated their invention superior to the watchful human eye. Instead, their program envisaged horns blowing twenty-four hours a day. In their Automation Technical Guidelines, the U.S. Coast

Guard emphasized that ''a fog detector should be used only when nuisance [noise] abatement is a necessity.'' Videographs should only control the coding of the signal, the USCG warned, ''*not* the power to the signal.''[3] Moreover, the very assumption that fog detection was the cornerstone of the program was shallow at best. Gordon Odlum looked out his bathroom window one morning and saw a freighter making straight for Race Rocks in clear weather. Luckily, his compressor held enough pressure for two short blasts, followed by a long one—signalling ''You are standing into danger.'' The vessel altered course. In spite of all the warnings and drawbacks, Transport Canada laid out over $1.5 million by 1975, installing 246 videographs on both coasts.

Another ''toy,'' the Event Data Recorder, was designed to keep a continuous log of plant operation as it regurgitated a roll of paper with five digits, each for a separate function. By June 1979—eight years and $230 thousand later—the department abandoned the recorders and recommended against installing any more ''due to continuing problems with the Sperry event recorder and the increased cost of repair and maintenance.''[4]

Leaving aside the problems of mechanical failure, the advantages of keeping men on the lights were ignored by the proponents of the new system. In September 1971, when the Western regional headquarters took the first hesitant step and eliminated the third keeper on three-man stations, managers from the Prince Rupert and Victoria districts raised a flurry of objections to automation. After all, lightkeepers made up 80 percent of all surface weather observers on the coast, and had provided assistance to tens of thousands of mariners since records were kept.

None of the Treasury Board submissions made more than passing reference to these two fundamental areas of service. Who would suspect that lightkeepers were the pioneer meteorological observers on the coast, that each manned light had

Dryad Point Light, built in 1899, was kept for many years by a Bella Bella Indian named Captain Carpenter.

provided surface weather observations, some every three hours, for nearly sixty years? Paul Leblond, a UBC oceanographer appointed to a one-man commission to investigate loss of life in a horrendous West Coast gale in October 1984, discovered that lightkeepers were "the only monitors of sea states and weather conditions on the West Coast of Vancouver Island. . . . It's fine to talk of automation," he allowed, "but there should be some method of reporting on weather conditions. The lightkeepers are the only source of information on local weather conditions available to mariners. Their contribution is invaluable."[5]

What Paul Leblond could not know, however, was that Transport Canada had attempted to obscure their "contribution" by rewriting the description of lightkeepers' duties. "Care will be taken. . . to avoid listing synoptic weather observations and water sampling," it was decided, "and any questions raised in this area will receive a standard reply that these duties are performed outside the regular duties of the lightkeeper."[6]

Managers on the West Coast may have been kept in the dark about the true motives and extent of the automation program, since the district aids superintendents from Victoria and Prince Rupert wasted much of an afternoon debating the dilemma of paying overtime to the two keepers remaining on three-man stations once the third position was terminated, and pondered the reaction they might expect from existing two-man stations if conditions at the former three-man stations were improved. Captain William Exley, superintendent in Victoria, had risen from cabin-boy to captain on the tenders; Ed Harris, his Prince Rupert counterpart, was a former fisherman. Both men knew what a welcome sight a light was from a wheelhouse at night. They knew that the names in their files were real people, even friends. Exley had seen something of the old conditions on the lights and had witnessed the desperate struggle for improvements. In his deckhand days he had bunked with the keepers when they moved, mixed concrete shoulder to shoulder with them in the rain, and shared meals at their tables. At the Victoria base, his door always stood open to lightkeepers on leave. Whatever they said about him in private, they always hastened to add, "He's all for the keepers." Now both men faced the indignity of undoing their keepers' lives, or fighting a rearguard action to save them.

With the onslaught of automation, Exley and Harris speculated that lightkeepers would soon be reduced to virtual caretakers, probably working an eight-hour day. Under such a regime, they questioned the policy of higher pay for isolated stations. Isolation wasn't what it used to be, what with helicopters, road access, and electricity. They could easily recruit lightkeepers from the ranks of young people eager "to get away from the city environment," and were installing a new breed, "better educated, much younger and happier," on the lights. They elected to draft a letter to the keepers, "primarily a public relations exercise," to lay to rest fears of lay-offs and wage cuts. They agreed there was no immediate likelihood of laying-off full-time employees, but allowed that one or two "term" keepers might be "terminated."

Barret Rock Light near Prince Rupert was built in 1919 and discontinued in 1963.

The evolution of the term employee, a hybrid between part-time and casual worker, would be the most dismal feature of the program. Historically, everyone from acrobats to ex-convicts had the lights available as an escape. For all that toil and trouble, there was always a promise of full-time employment in a pristine and private environment. No more. With the machines on the way, new keepers would only be hired for fixed terms as short as three months, on a ''contract''—a terse declaration of management's power, the easier to ''terminate'' when the time came.

''Nothing in this letter should be construed as an Offer of Indeterminate appointment,'' the contract began, ''nor should you in any way plan or anticipate continuing employment in the Public Service. . . .'' So the security of making long-term plans, even for vacations, was gone. People who had coped, for five years or more, with the rigours of isolation and still given their best never knew for certain whether they would have a job the next month, or if a new contract would arrive in the mail before their existing one lapsed.

All through the 1970s technicians descended upon the lights with their videographs, prefabricated buildings, diesels and generators, event data logs, and battery chargers. Unaware of their ultimate fate, most lightkeepers welcomed the innovations. The videograph allowed a few hours' ''shut-eye'' between weather reports in the night. Larger generators meant more home appliances. Lightkeepers had standing orders to keep ''hands off'' equipment to allow some reckoning of the man-hours that would be involved once they were gone. From 1976 to 1980 the cost amounted to *nine man-years* on the West Coast alone, much of that time (ironically) in overtime when technicians were stranded by weather. It would have risen much higher, too, if most keepers had not instinctively flouted the instructions when they encountered a fault they could easily treat themselves.

Meanwhile, back in Ottawa, the rickety framework of the original cost benefit study had collapsed, leaving the department with the forbidding challenge of explaining how $9.6 million, 60 percent of the original $14 million budgeted to achieve full automation by 1978 (an amount equal to more than two years' overtime for keepers), had been squandered in three short years, with Phase I still far from complete. Worse than lame, the department's excuse was a cripple. Citing delays in contracts and deliveries, and vague references to "social and economic" conditions, the cracks were papered over by simply redefining the program. Phase I was rechristened: "that condition in which each lightstation is automated and monitored by on-site staff"—in simpler words, all that hardware and lightkeepers too.

The department blithely maintained it had met "an unqualified guarantee to reduce present lightkeeper positions by 86 persons prior to April 1, 1972": the third man on three-man stations. They even added insult to the injury of unemployment, earmarking $125,000 (a year's pay for nineteen keepers) to make a film, "necessary from a historical point of view," to capture lightkeeping "in its traditional form," an added advantage "for public relations dealing with the automation program."[7]

Phase II underwent a similar, if hazier, metamorphosis. By now someone had conceived "a more expandable, more versatile and more sophisticated remote monitoring system." The forty-three monitor stations, with their staff of 258, were now pronounced "redundant" too—which says something about the initial guarantee of work in those stations for displaced lightkeepers. Breakthroughs in satellite communication would one day bind the entire Pacific system to a single Marine Services Information Centre on the West Coast. This would be even more "cost effective," they argued, since it would involve fewer staff (as if the former lightkeepers had already been at work). Without providing any details, the department solicited another $2 million to implement a pilot project in one region in 1979-80. The original monitoring network, with its forty-three centres and staff, had been priced at $3,809,000.

All term lightkeepers would be laid off in three years. Though 187 would still be required out on the stations, they would be *redefined* as maintenance staff. In the final analysis the Automated Lightstation Alarm Network aimed to displace 516 lightkeepers at virtually the same price it would cost to keep them on as an integral part of an aids-to-navigation network, on both coasts, which they have kept fail-safe for two centuries—since the first lighthouse was built at Louisburg in 1740.

If it was not likely to save money on automation, why was the department so determined to replace the lightkeepers? However popular, the notion that government greed is boundless in its lust for tax dollars is naive. There are finite limits—*some* revenues must be devoted to non-profit public service, if only to assure re-election. In the case of the automation program, the contest was *within* a department which relied increasingly upon an administrative and technical upper crust that could only justify itself by formulating new programs and searching out new applications of technology. Otherwise, like any assistant keeper James Gaudin dispatched to Ivory Island at the turn of the century, they would be paid "only to keep each other company."

The most damaging blow fell in December 1983 when the Auditor General, Parliament's "watchdog," reported that savings in the order of $20 million could be accomplished by full automation of lighthouses. "A breakdown of direct and indirect costs for manned lighthouses is not available," he conceded. "Despite the fact that the unmanning program has been under way for 13 years we had difficulty obtaining satisfactory cost information."[8] In fact the cost benefit calculations had existed since 1972: the bogus status quo based upon twice the number of keepers.

The Auditor General is something of a folk hero to the media and public, and the press had a field day. Headlines like "Coast Guard Drifting" and "Automatic Lighthouses would be Cheaper to Keep," made taxpayers groan at yet another example of government inefficiency and waste. It was a crucial breakthrough for the proponents of automation, as lightkeepers finally became redundant in the public mind. Thereafter they could, and often did, claim their "initiative...[stemmed] from a number of reports done by the Auditor General suggesting that CCG [Canada Coast Guard] was not getting good value of money the way...[it was] currently operating...lightstations."

In the autumn of 1985 the title of assistant was abolished. This move may have appealed to the status conscious, who could now call themselves keepers, but they never suspected it portended the actual abolition of assistants—the hardest fought reform of all—as stations would be downgraded to "one man lights." When the Mulroney government froze the public service and insisted upon 700 lay-offs for 1986, lightkeepers out on the West Coast were easy targets as expendables. Like a scared octopus devouring its tentacles, Transport Canada began eating away at an essential service to nourish engineering, management, planning, purchasing, and public relations at the head. In March 1986 word came from the minister: Trial Island, Porlier Pass, Chrome Island, Pointer Island, Boat Bluff, and Lawyer Island would be downgraded to unwatched aids. Keepers at East Point, Point Atkinson, Cape Mudge, and Pulteney Point would be deprived of their assistants, leaving these accessible stations easy prey to vandals sixteen hours a day, and drastically curtailing weather reports—unless lightkeepers reverted to the dark ages on the lights, when women and children "filled in" as assistants, and families lived in twenty-four hour confinement on their stations.

When even these final humans are brought in from the lights, will the machines work? With satellites overhead which can tell a man from a woman on a Moscow street, there can be no doubt that the *technology* is available. But can it fail, if only for as long as it took Gordon Odlum to dash from the bathroom to the engine room, or for a Korean airliner to wander five hundred miles off course?

Lawyer Island Light was built at the northern entrance to Chatham Sound in 1901.

It can and it will. By 1982 Captain Exley had carefully monitored the system's failures and resulting ''downtime,'' and sent off figures which should have convinced even the most partisan proponent of automation of its hazard to navigation. In five years, videographs, fog horns, and main lights, from Race Rocks to Cape Scott, had failed 2091 times for a total ''downtime'' of 211 days.[9] The system was less effective and more costly than the trained dogs of a century ago that barked when they heard a ship's horn, yet Transport Canada boasted, ''Based on fault reports submitted thus far, the present automatic operation of light stations is giving an adequate level of service to the mariner.'' So they were, but only because the keepers were still out there, and still performing another function as old as the service—one which would fall first casualty to automation.

When Albert Argyle braved the rip-tide and rowed out after two hysterical ''seamen deserters'' drifting by Race Rocks on a deadhead in the fall of 1874, he established a tradition. Virtually every keeper of every light ever since has performed the equivalent of tossing ropes to drowning men, hauling them over the transom, mending bruised, burned, or broken bodies. By 1906, in the sensational aftermath of Minnie Patterson's rescue of the *Coloma*'s crew, the lights were fixed in the public mind as something more than beacons and horns. They became cornerstones of search and rescue. If they were always aloof from heartbreak and hunger on the lights, ministers, their deputies, and marine agents eagerly trumpeted their keepers' heroics, and always found time and a suitable forum to commemorate their work.

The keepers' life-saving function posed the stiffest challenge ever to automation, since eliminating them meant pricing mariners' lives. No Treasury Board document ever evaluated the role; a comprehensive private sector study explicitly disavowed any detailed consideration of search and rescue; and since the advent of automation the department has actively *discouraged* keepers from going after people in trouble. The tactic translates into a policy of ignoring requests from keepers, fishermen, yachtsmen, and many more, that Transport Canada provide ship-to-shore radios for its keepers. They purchase their own, of course, and many fit out private boats at considerable cost to take out in emergencies. They always act ''on their own,'' however, freelance or as members of volunteer search and rescue bodies. Transport Canada disavows any responsibility, as if lightkeepers are on the scene by some quirk or coincidence.

But who, after all, can stand idly by when a seiner goes over, or ignore screams coming up from the surf in the night, knowing better than anyone that it can take an hour or more for a helicopter or cutter to come out? The policy of pretending lightkeepers can and should ignore distress is crucial to unmanning the lights. The public will hardly protest their passing if lightkeepers can be portrayed as costly anachronisms—bumpkins like Captain Highliner, paid only to paint houses and change bulbs in the age of the microchip.

If manned lights survive on the Pacific, their keepers will have saved them by heeding Captain Exley's stricture about keeping accurate logs of their assistance to mariners—a concise reckoning of lives and property to be sacrificed. Such tallies fell

Wave-swept Holland Rock Light was built in 1913. The wooden structure was destroyed by fire in 1946.

into the hands of longstanding Users Committees on Aids to Navigation in Vancouver and Prince Rupert in April 1986, and enabled them to forestall automation for a time. The logs described 4770 incidents in six years, from Green Island to Race Rocks, ranging from ''mere'' special weather reports, given any time on request, to providing first aid to a child carried off by a cougar near Carmanah, to say nothing of keepers who pulled men out of the water and off overturned hulls.[10]

Once this rough nugget of truth surfaced, automation assumed a new, moral significance. Opposition became something of a crusade. ''The Lightstation keepers are the eyes and ears of Search and Rescue,'' Dr. Robert Somerville, head of the Campbell River Power Squadron, wrote the minister of Transport. ''The false economies of reducing manpower and salaries by Ottawa over the years . . . make me feel embarrassed to call myself a Canadian.'' Somerville's sentiments were echoed by virtually the entire cross-section of maritime users: fishermen, ferry masters and workers, RCMP, power squadrons, the B.C. Maritime Council, yachtsmen, and marina operators.

Even from the crass perspective of cost it was obvious that it would require massive outlays to beef up existing search and rescue efforts to achieve the same level of service, thus absorbing the precarious ''savings'' from automation. In a petition that was widely circulated and quickly signed, users called for a full public inquiry into the safety implications of taking men off the lights. ''They're *all* strategic,'' Bert Ogden, safety director of the United Fishermen, told the CBC when asked if there were too many lights.

Conflict between ideals and self-interest, cost and casualties, may never be resolved. The temptation to array the vast majority of taxpaying landlubbers against a few seafarers has always been there, since before the *Valencia* went down, and will always remain. For the keepers it may soon all be over. There may be no escaping across the bridge now; no waiting out the gale deliberately conceived in committee rooms and at drawing boards in Ottawa. And what of this elusive legion of planners and mandarins? Out on the lights, watching the Aurora run wild across another winter sky, or the big Greys shepherding their calves back up from Baja, we wonder: what makes them tick? What stake have they in the world they are building, with its Social Insurance Numbers, malls, fast foods, and condos, infinitely more stultifying than the magic monotony of lighthouse life. Surely in the angst of their most private moments they must feel that timeless, desperate craving to see the light, to seek, somewhere, an island of sanity in a sea of madness, to draw closer to God and Nature. Yet next morning they are back at work in their fluorescent world, championing the destruction of the last and the best opportunity for a hardy few, and with it the very foundation of safety on the sea.

Appendix

LIGHTHOUSES OF THE BRITISH COLUMBIA COAST

Fisgard	16 November 1860 – 1928	Estevan Point	15 April 1910
Race Rocks	26 December 1860	Triangle Island	1 November 1910 – 1920
South Sand Heads	4 January 1866 – 1879	Nootka	15 March 1911
Cape Beale	1 July 1874	Sheringham Point	30 September 1912
Point Atkinson	1 May 1875	Holland Rock	25 January 1913 – 1941
Berens Island	5 March 1876 – 1925	Sand Heads No 16	15 April 1913 – 1957
Entrance Island	8 June 1876	Capilano	27 May 1913 – 1946
North Sand Heads	May 1884 – 1905	Langara Point	1 October 1913
Active Pass	10 June 1885	Cape St. James	15 February 1914 – 1945
Discovery Island	10 April 1886	Addenbroke Island	15 April 1914
East Point	1 January 1888	Amphitrite Point	23 March 1915
Chrome Island	1 January 1891	Barret Rock	1919 – 1963
Carmanah	15 September 1891	Triple Island	1 January 1921
Portlock Point	1 November 1895 – 1964	McInnes Island	1921
Bare Point	1897 – 1926	Gallows Point	1923 – 1986
Cape Mudge	16 September 1898	Albert Head	1930 – 1985
Ivory Island	1 October 1898	Sand Heads	1957
Prospect Point	1 October 1898 – 1926	Cape Scott	1959
Egg Island	7 October 1898	Chatham Point	1959
Fiddle Reef	2 December 1898 – 1959	Bonilla Island	1960
Sisters Rocks	December 1898		
Pointer Island	5 November 1899		
Dryad Point	7 November 1899		
Ballenas Island	1 December 1900		
Lawyer Island	28 November 1901		
Porlier Pass	15 November 1902		
Brockton Point	1902 – 1926		
Merry Island	6 November 1903		
Lennard Island	1 November 1904		
Scarlett Point	12 April 1905		
Pulteney Point	12 September 1905		
Sand Heads	18 October 1905 – 1913		
Green Island	1 April 1906		
Trial Island	1906		
Lucy Island	1 January 1907		
Pine Island	1 April 1907		
Boat Bluff	1907		
Pachena Point	1 July 1908		
Quatsino (Kains Island)	1 October 1909		

MARINE AGENTS OF THE VICTORIA DISTRICT

1872 – 1879	Captain James Cooper
1879 – 1885	Captain F. Revely
1885 – 1892	Herbert George Lewis
1892 – 1911	Captain James Gaudin
1911 – 1919	Captain George Edward Livingstone Robertson
1919 – 1942	Colonel A.W.R. Wilby
1942 – 1948	W.L. Stamford
1948 – 1954	Thomas E. Morrison
1954 – 1964	Col. K. Dixon
1965 –	L.E. Slaght

MINISTERS RESPONSIBLE FOR THE FEDERAL DEPARTMENT OF MARINE AND FISHERIES (to 1960)

Sir Albert Smith	1873 – 1878
J.C. Pope	1878 – 1882
A.W. McLelan	1882 – 1885
G.E. Foster	1885 – 1888
Sir Charles H. Tupper	1888 – 1894
J. Costigan	1894 – 1896
Sir Louis H. Davies	1896 – 1901
J. Sutherland	1902
J.F. R. Prefontaine	1902 – 1905
L.P. Brodeur	1906 – 1911
R. Lemieux	1911
J.D. Hazen	1911 – 1917
C.C. Ballantyne	1917 – 1921
Ernest Lapointe	1921 – 1924
P.J.A. Cardin	1924 – 1930
A. Duranleau	1930 – 1935
C.D. Howe	1935 – 1936

MINISTERS RESPONSIBLE FOR THE FEDERAL DEPARTMENT OF TRANSPORT (to 1960)

C.D. Howe	1936 – 1940
P.J.A. Cardin	1940 – 1942
J.E. Michaud	1942 – 1945
Lionel Chevrier	1945 – 1954
George C. Marler	1954 – 1957
George Hees	1957 – 1960

SOURCE: Thomas E. Appleton, *Usque ad Mare: A History of the Canadian Coast Guard and Marine Services* (Ottawa: Department of Transport, 1968), p. 274.

Notes

THE INSIDE PASSAGE

1. Captain Charles Robson, Public Archives of BC (hereafter cited as PABC), Aural History Division, 2102 – 2, p. 1.

ACTIVE PASS

1. Captain James Gaudin, marine agent, to H. Georgeson, 3 November 1893, Victoria, Transport Canada (hereafter cited as TC Victoria).
2. Archie Georgeson, "Early Days in the Gulf Islands." PABC, Aural History Division, 793 – 2, p. 3.
3. Colonel A.W.R. Wilby, marine agent, to A.B. Gurney, 18 November 1938, TC Victoria.
4. R.W. Mayhew, MP, to W.L. Stamford, marine agent, 26 April 1944, TC Victoria.
5. George Smith to Thomas Morrison, marine agent, 14 April 1944, TC Victoria.

DISCOVERY ISLAND

1. Royal Commission Report, cited by Thomas E. Appleton, *Usque ad Mare: A History of the Canadian Coast Guard and Marine Services* (Ottawa: Department of Transport, 1968), pp 235 – 236.
2. Gaudin to Colonel W.P. Anderson, chief engineer, Department of Marine and Fisheries, 28 January 1895, TC Victoria.
3. J. McPhail, commissioner of lights, to Edward Robertson, marine agent, 9 June 1914, TC Victoria.
4. Mary Ann Croft to D.B. Plunkett, MP, 25 February 1932.

EAST POINT

1. Gaudin to Ralph Smith, MP, 21 May 1907, TC Victoria.
2. E. Hawken, deputy minister of Marine and Fisheries, to Wilby, 23 January 1920.

CHROME ISLAND

1. Gaudin to Francois Frederick Gourdeau, deputy minister of Marine and Fisheries, 13 August 1901, TC Victoria.
2. Robertson to McPhail, 22 February 1913, TC Victoria.
3. G.A. Couldery to Wilby, 31 July 1927, TC Victoria.
4. Mrs. Couldery to Wilby, 28 June 1929, TC Victoria.
5. Couldery to Wilby, 22 August 1933, TC Victoria.
6. Couldery to Wilby, 28 August 1933, TC Victoria.

7. E.A. Moden to Colonel Keith Dixon, marine agent, 13 January 1951, TC Victoria.

PORTLOCK POINT

1. George Watson to Hon. J.D. Hazen, minister of Marine and Fisheries, 4 July 1914, TC Victoria.
2. Gordon Halkett to Robertson, 31 October 1913, TC Victoria.
3. Watson to Hazen, 4 July 1914, TC Victoria.
4. Robertson to Watson, 24 July 1914, TC Victoria.
5. Robertson to McPhail, 18 August 1914, TC Victoria.
6. Watson to Robertson, 19 March 1916, TC Victoria.
7. F. Cullison to Robertson, 20 June 1917, TC Victoria.
8. John Georgeson to Robertson, June 1917, TC Victoria.
9. Halkett to Robertson, 28 June 1917, TC Victoria.
10. T. Mayne to Robertson, 5 July 1917, TC Victoria.
11. Robertson to Mayne, 7 July 1917, TC Victoria.
12. S. Percival to Robertson, 5 July 1917, TC Victoria.
13. Watson to Robertson, 17 July 1917, TC Victoria.
14. Watson to Robertson, 8 October 1918.
15. Watson, letter to the editor (copy), *Family Herald and Weekly Star*, 25 October 1919, TC Victoria.
16. A.J. Dallain, acting marine agent, to Alexander Johnston, deputy minister of Marine and Fisheries, 23 December 1919, TC Victoria.
17. Halkett to Wilby, 14 June 1920, TC Victoria.
18. Watson to Wilby, 3 September 1920, TC Victoria.
19. Wilby to Messrs. Crease and Crease, 4 October 1920, TC Victoria.
20. Wilby to Ethel M. Bruce, asst. secretary treasurer, Canadian Red Cross Society, 21 October 1920, TC Victoria.
21. Canadian Red Cross Society, *Annual Report, 1920*, p. 11.
22. Watson to Wilby, 9 September 1924, TC Victoria.
23. Johnston to Watson, 14 November 1924.
24. J.N. Waugh to Wilby, 20 December 1933, TC Victoria.

262

25. A.H. Perry, district engineer, Department of Pensions and National Health, to Wilby, 19 July 1941.

THE SISTERS
1. Gaudin to Gourdeau, 15 April 1904, TC Victoria.
2. Gaudin to Gourdeau, 24 November 1904, TC Victoria.
3. Gaudin to Gourdeau, 8 March 1907, TC Victoria.
4. Walter Buss to Robertson, 30 October 1912, TC Victoria.
5. McPhail to Robertson, 25 March 1912, TC Victoria.
6. C. Clark to Robertson, 2 August 1924, TC Victoria
7. C. Lundgren to Wilby, 31 January 1948, TC Victoria.

CAPE MUDGE
1. Gaudin to Gourdeau, 7 September 1909; Gourdeau to Gaudin, 8 September 1909, TC Victoria.
2. John Davidson to Gaudin, 2 February 1911, TC Victoria.
3. Davidson to Robertson, 11 June 1912, TC Victoria.
4. Davidson to Robertson, 7 August 1914, TC Victoria.
5. Davidson to Robertson, 5 August 1911.
6. Doris Anderson, *Evergreen Islands: The Islands of the Inside Passage: Quadra to Malcolm* (Sidney, B.C.: Gray's Publishing Limited), pp 35 – 36.
7. Davidson to Robertson, 18 September 1917, TC Victoria.
8. Davidson to Robertson, 15 April 1918, TC Victoria.
9. H.W. Smith to Wilby, 28 April 1927, TC Victoria.
10. J.E. Pettingell to Stamford, 30 November 1942, TC Victoria.

BALLENAS
1. Halkett to Anderson, 9 June 1906, TC Victoria.
2. Gaudin to Gourdeau, 2 May 1905, TC Victoria.
3. Gaudin to Gourdeau, 21 April 1906, TC Victoria.
4. John J. Vickers to Department of Marine and Fisheries, 5 March 1917, TC Victoria.
5. Robertson to Arthur Broughton Gurney, 26 August 1914, TC Victoria.
6. Vickers to Department of Marine and Fisheries, 5 March 1917, TC Victoria.
7. Robertson to Johnston, 20 February 1918, TC Victoria.

PORLIER PASS
1. Gaudin to Smith, 7 November 1902; Gaudin to Frank Allison, 7 November 1902, TC Victoria.
2. Devina (Allison) Baines to Captain L.H. Cadieux (n.d.); Porlier Pass Lighthouse, 1902 – 1941, PABC, Aural History Division, 795:1, copy 2.
3. Allison to Smith, 12 March 1904, TC Victoria.
4. Allison to Robertson, 10 April 1915, TC Victoria.
5. Baines, "Porlier Pass Lighthouse, 1902 – 1941," PABC, Aural History Division.
6. Allison to Robertson, 8 February 1919, TC Victoria.
7. Allison to Robertson, 10 January 1919; Robertson to Thomas McLeod, 7 March 1919, TC Victoria.
8. Allison to Hon. C.C. Ballantyne, minister of Marine and Fisheries, n.d., TC Victoria.
9. Allison to Halkett, 20 August 1920, TC Victoria.
10. Allison to Wilby, 3 December 1921, TC Victoria.
11. Fred Rogers, *Shipwrecks of British Columbia* (Vancouver: Douglas and McIntyre, 1980), pp 40 – 41.
12. Allison to Wilby, 5 December 1927, TC Victoria.
13. Elizabeth Allison to Wilby, 15 January 1930, TC Victoria.
14. George F. Askew to Wilby, 12 February 1930, TC Victoria.
15. British Columbia Provincial Police Crime Report, 25 August 1930, TC Victoria.
16. Allison to McPhail, 2 February 1942, TC Victoria.
17. Allison to William Lyon Mackenzie King, prime minister of Canada, 25 March 1942, TC Victoria.

MERRY ISLAND
1. Johnston to Robertson, 20 April 1915, TC Victoria.
2. Will Franklin to H.S. Clements, MP, 5 January 1918, TC Victoria.
3. Franklin to Clements, 10 August 1918, TC Victoria.
4. Franklin to Halkett, 10 January 1919.
5. Franklin to Robertson, 27 March 1919, TC Victoria. There is no record of other keepers pursuing the issue of back pay owing to them, and, needless to say, it is highly unlikely that the department would have made them aware of

Franklin's settlement.

6. British Columbia Provincial Police Crime Report, 26 March 1927, TC Victoria.

7. Mary Franklin to Wilby, 1 June 1929, TC Victoria.

8. Arley Franklin to Morrison, 17 February 1954, TC Victoria.

9. E.J. Leclerc to Wilby, 17 December 1939, TC Victoria.

10. Olive A. Hill to Wilby, 25 July 1940, TC Victoria.

11. G.H. Potts to Dixon, 1 February 1953, TC Victoria. Potts headed all his monthly reports: "Merry Island News," and concluded this issue: "However it is a grand place for the kids and we like it."

12. Potts to Dixon, 6 May 1953, TC Victoria.

13. Department of Transport, "News on the D.O.T.," May 1957.

14. Department of National Health and Welfare, Physician's Certificate of Disability for Duty, 22 December 1958, TC Victoria.

15. Potts to George Hees, minister of Transport, 9 June 1960, TC Victoria.

16. Dixon to H.V. Anderson, director of marine services, 5 October 1961, TC Victoria.

SCARLETT POINT

1. Gaudin to Gourdeau, 20 July 1908, TC Victoria.

2. Ibid.

3. William Hunt to Wilby, 24 February 1930, TC Victoria.

4. Hunt to Wilby, 19 July 1930, TC Victoria.

5. Hunt to Wilby, 17 February 1932, TC Victoria.

6. Hunt to Wilby, 7 October 1933, TC Victoria.

7. Hunt to Wilby, 22 January 1935, TC Victoria.

8. Hunt to Wilby, 3 September 1935, TC Victoria.

9. G.L. Smith to Wilby, 25 January 1941, TC Victoria.

10. Smith to Wilby, 8 October 1941, TC Victoria.

PULTENEY POINT

1. Halkett to Austin McKela, 11 October 1910, TC Victoria.

2. McPhail to Robertson, 16 November 1917, TC Victoria.

3. Toivo Aro to Halkett, 9 October 1920, TC Victoria.

4. Wilby to Johnston, 17 September 1925, TC Victoria.

5. Aro to Wilby, 30 January 1930, TC Victoria.

6. Oliver Maisonville to Nicholson, engineer, 27 February 1937, TC Victoria. By postscript Shorty asked, "Please do not let the 'Freedom of the Press' see this."

7. Maisonville to Wilby, 29 March 1937, TC Victoria.

8. Maisonville to Morrison, 6 May 1946, TC Victoria.

PINE ISLAND

1. G.L. Smith to Wilby, 21 December 1930, TC Victoria.

2. S. Montgomery to B.H. Frazer, asst. chief engineer, Department of Marine and Fisheries, 15 June 1907; Gaudin to Gurney, 11 September 1907, TC Victoria.

3. Gurney to William Sloan, MP, 1 January 1908, Ottawa, Public Archives of Canada (hereafter cited as PAC), RG 42, vol. 522.

4. Anderson to Sloan, 6 January 1908, PAC, RG 42, vol. 522.

5. Gaudin to Gourdeau, 20 October 1908, PAC, RG 42, vol. 522.

6. Gaudin to Gourdeau, 7 October, 2 November 1908, PAC RG 42, vol. 522.

7. Frazer to Gourdeau, 13 November 1908, PAC, RG 42, vol. 522.

8. Gurney to MacDonald, MP, 17 February 1909, PAC, RG 42, vol. 522.

9. G.S. Pearson to Smith, 20 February 1911, TC Victoria.

10. Gurney to Robertson, 23 September 1911, TC Victoria.

11. Gurney to Robertson, 11 March 1912, TC Victoria.

12. Robertson to Gurney, 6 August 1912, TC Victoria.

13. Percival Pike to Wilby, 17 March 1920, TC Victoria.

14. Pike to Halkett, 18 July 1921, TC Victoria.

THE NORTHERN LIGHTS

1. Captain Norman McKay, interview, 20 June 1981.

EGG ISLAND

1. Gaudin to Anderson, 5 January 1900, TC Victoria.

2. Gaudin to Anderson, 30 September 1900, TC Victoria.

3. R. Scarlett to Gaudin, 23 November 1904, TC Victoria.

4. Gaudin to Anderson, 6 February 1905, TC Victoria. Anderson scrawled his recommendation across the top of Gaudin's letter.

5. Arnold Moran to Hon. A. Duranleau, minister of Marine and Fisheries, 2 January 1932, PAC, RG 42, vol. 529.

6. "Navigating the Coast: A History of the Union Steamship Company," *Sound Heritage* vol. vi, no. 2 (Victoria: Provincial Archives of British Columbia, 1977), p. 39.

7. J.W. Brown to Johnston, 23 January 1935, PAC, RG 42, vol. 529.

POINTER ISLAND

1. Captain J.T. Walbran to Gaudin, 28 June 1900, PAC, RG 42, vol. 528.

2. Violet Seaman, "46 Years at a BC Lighthouse," *Vancouver Sun*, 17 April 1948; Lyle Bigelow, "Story of Pointer Island," unpublished monograph loaned to the author.

3. Lyle Bigelow, interview, 8 October 1981.

IVORY ISLAND

1. Gaudin to Gourdeau, 24 March 1899, PAC, RG 42, vol. 528.

2. Gourdeau to Gaudin, 17 April 1899, PAC, RG 42, vol. 528.

3. Anderson to Gaudin, 22 August 1899, PAC, RG 42, vol. 528.

4. Hon. J.F.R. Prefontaine, minister of Marine and Fisheries to R.G. McPherson, MP, 9 May 1904, PAC, RG 42, vol. 528.

5. Robertson to Johnston, 25 February 1916, PAC, RG 42, vol. 528.

LUCY ISLAND

1. Tharsyle Ouellette-Celinas, "Les Phares dans La Nuit . . . et dans La Vie" (Laval: n.d.), p. 24.

2. Octave Ouellette to Rev. George Henry Raley, n.d. Collected in "Correspondence re: Lighthouses," PABC H/D/R13/R13.13.

ADDENBROKE ISLAND

1. Hannah's cryptic note was in a BC Provincial Police case file loaned to the author by Cecil Clark.

TRIPLE ISLAND

1. Gordon and Jean Odlum kindly loaned the author letters and diaries relating to their stint at Triple.

2. Tom Moran, interview, 22 June 1981.

3. Johnston to Stamford, 24 December 1929, PAC, RG 42, vol. 530.

4. *Vancouver Sun*, 11 March 1960.

CATCHING UP

1. *Victoria Daily Times*, 30 October 1928 (hereafter cited as *Times*).

2. M.C. Urquhart and K.A.H. Buckley, eds., *Historical Statistics of Canada* (Toronto: The Macmillan Company of Canada Ltd., 1965), p. 87. Series D 40 – 59: "Hourly wage rates in selected building trades by city, 1901 to 1960."

3. H.V. Anderson to Dixon, 28 March 1955, TC Victoria.

4. Robert Lally to Stamford, 20 July 1942, TC Victoria.

5. Evelyn (Forsyth) Mackenzie, interview, June 1984.

6. Wallace to Hanson, marine agent, 22 May 1935, PAC, RG 42, vol. 537.

7. *The Organizer*, June 1937.

8. *Civil Servants Digest-Organizer*, April 1941.

9. Ibid., June 1947.

10. Jack Hunting to Stamford, 1 November 1946, TC Victoria.

11. Ibid.

12. O.H. Evans to Dixon, 28 March 1955, TC Victoria.

13. Jack Waddell, interview, 16 April 1983.

14. *Times*, 5 October 1950.

15. *Vancouver Province*, 24 November 1953.

16. *Victoria Colonist*, 28 September 1957.

17. Ibid., 4 October 1957.

18. Ibid., 29 September 1957.

19. Dixon to Anderson, 28 March 1955, TC Victoria.

ENDANGERED SPECIES

1. Department of Transport, *Treasury Board Submission*, 6 February 1970. All figures are drawn from this and succeeding Treasury Board submissions; the calculations are mine.

2. Ibid., p. 2.

3. United States Coast Guard, Ocean Engineering Report No. 41: *Automation Technical Guidelines* (Washington, D.C.: 1973), pp 2 – 18.

4. G.L. Smith, chief of Marine Aids Division, circulating memorandum, 7 June 1979.

5. *Globe and Mail*, 26 December 1984.

6. Minutes of meeting, 9 September 1971.

7. Transport Canada, Automation of Lightstations, update, December 1974, p. 14.

8. Report of the Auditor General to the House of Commons, Fiscal Year Ended 31 March 1983, p. 412.

9. Summary of *Lightstation Fault and Status Reports, 1978 – 82.*

10. *Participation of Lightkeepers in S.A.R. Incidents, 1979 – 82.*

INDEX

Photograph credits: Page 113b, 116, 117, 120, Vic Aro. Page 149, 151(b), 175, N. Beketov. Page 133(b), 135, Pen Brown. Page 75, 76, G. Butler. Page 28, 35, 38, 42, 45, 53, 59, 60, 62, 69, 73, 74, 108, 125, 189, Cadieux Collection. Page 176(b), 185, 194(l), 203, 211(l, br), 226, 239, 240(l), 247, 249, 250, 252, 255, 257, Canada Coast Guard. Page 193, Cecil Clark. Page 240(r), R. Crawford. Page 18, Ellen Georgeson courtesy M. Harding. Page 64, Agnes Lamb. Page 147, 159, 183, Captain Norman MacKay. Page 142, 199, 200, 201, 208, Evelyn (Forsyth) McKenzie. Page 106, 151(t), 242, Esther Milne. Page 211(t), Museum of Northern BC. Page 79, 211(tr), 213, 216, 219, 221, Gordon Odlum. Page 156, 167, 194(r), Public Archives Canada. Page 22, 29, 37, 62, 69, 78, 89, 97, 104, 110, 136, 162, 170, 176(t), 187, Jim Ryan. Page 57, 130, 163, Transport Canada. Page 154, Jamie Tuohy. Page 210, 157, World Ship Society. All other photos are from the collection of the author.

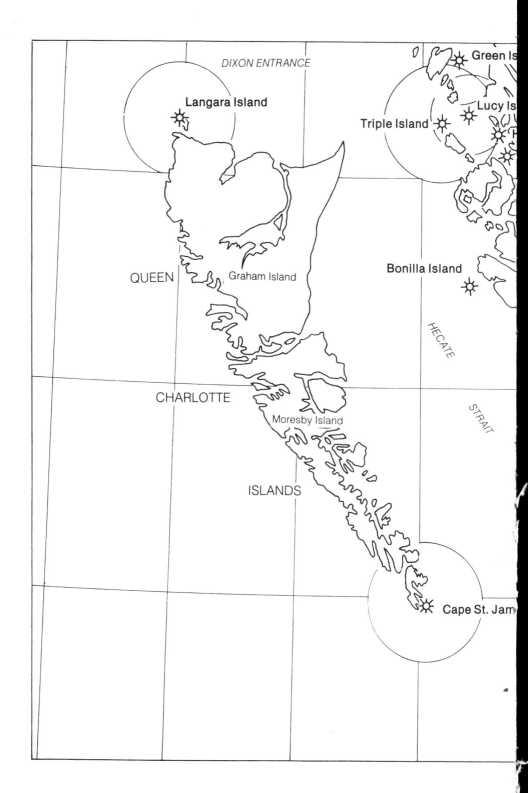